T0338205

THE PRACTITIONER'S GUIDE TO GOVERNANCE AS LEADERSHIP

THE PRACTITIONER'S GUIDE TO GOVERNANCE AS LEADERSHIP

Building High-Performing Nonprofit Boards

CATHY A. TROWER

JOSSEY-BASS™

A Wiley Brand

Published by Jossey-Bass
A Wiley Imprint
One Montgomery Street, Suite 1200, San Francisco, CA 94104-4594—www.josseybass.com

Jossey-Bass books and products are available through most bookstores. To contact Jossey-Bass directly call our Customer Care Department within the U.S. at 800-956-7739, outside the U.S. at 317-572-3986, or fax 317-572-4002.

Wiley publishes in a variety of print and electronic formats and by print-on-demand. Some material included with standard print versions of this book may not be included in e-books or in print-on-demand. If this book refers to media such as a CD or DVD that is not included in the version you purchased, you may download this material at http://booksupport.wiley.com. For more information about Wiley products, visit www.wiley.com.

Library of Congress Cataloging-in-Publication Data

Trower, Cathy A. (Cathy Ann)
    The practitioner's guide to governance as leadership : building high-performing nonprofit boards / Cathy A. Trower. — 1st ed.
        p.   cm.
    Includes bibliographical references and index.
    ISBN 978-1-118-10987-8 (cloth); ISBN 978-1-118-22423-6 (ebk);
    ISBN 978-1-118-23736-6 (ebk); ISBN 978-1-118-26237-5 (ebk)
        1. Nonprofit organizations—Management.   2. Corporate governance.   3. Directors of corporations.   I. Title.
    HD2769.15.T76   2013
    658.4'22—dc23

                                                                            2012033556

Printed in the United States of America
FIRST EDITION

HB Printing   SKY10076802_060524

To my husband, Bill, for his steadfast love and support.

To Richard Chait, William Ryan, and Barbara Taylor, for their wisdom.

To Alison Hankey, for planting the seed and encouraging this project.

CONTENTS

LIST OF EXHIBITS, FIGURES, AND TABLES

FOREWORD

This Foreword starts with a look backward. Readers of *Governance as Leadership* will not be surprised by this orientation, as William Ryan, Barbara Taylor, and I (hereafter, we) accentuated the importance of retrospective sensemaking, of drawing meaning from experience.

Within the relatively small but growing niche of books on trusteeship, *Governance as Leadership,* published seven years ago, became a best seller. Fiduciary, strategic, and generative modes of governance, the fundamental framework of the book, entered the vocabulary and repertoire of many boards. We were gratified and even a little surprised by the book's success.

What explains the generally positive reception? We suspect that *Governance as Leadership* responded to frustrations prevalent among trustees and, to some extent, nonprofit executives too. The exasperations included mundane agendas, ritualized meetings, sterile discussions, passive roles, predetermined decisions, and wasted time—ingredients that summed to a disengaged, underutilized board. In a word, trustees were asked to attend and affirm, not to think.

In contrast, *Governance as Leadership* encouraged trustees to think, and more specifically to think in three different but closely related ways: as fiduciaries, strategists, and sensemakers—or, as we now like to say, trustees should provide oversight, foresight, and insight. This approach, effectively enacted, yields an outcome that in hindsight might have been a better title for the book: *Consequential Governance*. We are hard-pressed to offer a crisper definition of the primary aim of *Governance as Leadership*.

The book emphasized that elevated purposes produce elevated performance. Boards need to do better work, not simply work better. Boards need to be a source of leadership as well as stewardship. Toward that end, we stressed mind-set over mechanics, construct over structure. We emphasized modes of governance rather than tasks of trustees.

More than we anticipated, boards focused on one mode more than the others, probably because the generative mode seemed most different, least practiced, and potentially powerful. In the process, some boards started to think of generative work as a separate activity, decoupled from the other modes, that was variously an existential review of mission; a "pie in the sky" planning exercise, or a "bet the ranch" deliberation. On reflection, we should have conveyed more emphatically that the scope, scale, and sequence of generative work will and should differ. Even more significantly, we should have highlighted that generative work serves to *generate* the understanding, meaning, and insight that create a shared perception of the problems and opportunities at hand and on the horizon. Generative work means think first and think hard about what's at issue and what's at stake. In shorthand, we urged boards to Find, Frame, and then Focus on matters of paramount importance to the organization's current and future welfare.

As consultants and coaches to nonprofit boards and as speakers and panelists over the past seven years, we have had many opportunities to learn about the challenges (and payoffs) that governance as leadership presents. The most crucial impediments concern often invisible, almost always influential, organizational subsystems akin to the software that underpins and enables computer applications. Governance as leadership requires that boards cultivate the art and skills of retrospective sensemaking, nuanced discernment, and robust discourse, plus the mental dexterity to think self-critically in three modes, all as a group. With those proficiencies as preconditions, four subsystems become pivotal:

1. Cognition: How trustees think individually and collectively.
2. Culture: The values, assumptions, and norms that shape board behavior and practice.
3. Group Dynamics: The interplay among trustees and the capacity for team play.
4. Leadership: The ability of trustee and organizational leaders to galvanize the board.

Had we been more attentive to these phenomena, we might have had a better book. We surely would have had a longer book. Even more germane, we could not have linked these support systems to the experiences of boards that have now actually embraced governance as leadership as a template. In short, we would have been unable to connect theory to practice. This book by Dr. Cathy Trower does just that.

After a smart synopsis of the central tenets of governance as leadership, Trower synthesizes plainly a wide swath of relevant research, some classic, some contemporary, that ranges from neuroscience to political science, from behavioral economics to organizational behavior. Trustees need not be experts in meta-cognition or social psychology, for example, but boards and CEOs will benefit appreciably from the implications research in these realms carry for the practice of consequential governance. Each chapter marries ideas to actions within the context and framework of governance as leadership. The book combines sophisticated thinking with instructive vignettes, illustrative documents, and practical recommendations to optimize the value added and the value derived by the board.

Trustees and executives favorably disposed to governance as leadership in theory are sometimes uncertain about what to do in practice. We are often asked questions such as: "How can be we more generative yet remain responsible fiduciaries?" "Should we have a different committee structure?" "How should we modify our agendas and meetings to engender lively discussions?" "How does the role of leaders change?" "What could go wrong?" In different ways, we were almost always asked the same question, "Now what?" And while we have been able to answer that question, albeit at some length, we now have a shorter, better response: "Read Cathy's book."

I cannot imagine someone better qualified than Cathy to write a "field guide" to governance as leadership. For more than a decade, she has been a well-regarded consultant to dozens of boards across the nonprofit sector from education to health care, the arts, and social services. She has also been a popular speaker and workshop leader at countless conferences and seminars. Since the book was published, Cathy, as much or more than the authors, has worked directly with boards to adopt and adapt the precepts of governance as leadership. Along the way, she has developed useful language, exercises, questionnaires, and other tools and techniques to convey critical concepts and facilitate critical changes. Somewhat like a trustee, Cathy has substantial knowledge about the enterprise—here a particular approach to governance—and, at the same time, just enough detachment to offer new insights, a fresh perspective, and a pragmatic viewpoint.

On a personal note, I am especially gratified to write this Foreword. I have known Cathy for over fifteen years, first as a doctoral student, then as a protégé, now as a colleague. No one has worked harder to learn more about governance or to master the craft of consultant to nonprofit boards. And while I am tempted to proclaim this book as the culmination of Cathy's efforts, I know her well enough to realize that she will barely pause at this plateau before resuming her ascent.

Richard Chait
Professor Emeritus
Harvard Graduate School of Education

PREFACE

The primary principles and themes of the book *Governance as Leadership* (Chait, Ryan, and Taylor 2005) are summarized in Chapter One. That book was motivated by four questions (p. xvi):

1. Why is there so much rhetoric about the centrality of nonprofit boards, *but* so much empirical and anecdotal evidence that boards of trustees are only marginally relevant or intermittently consequential?

2. Why are there so many "how-to-govern" handbooks and seminars, *but* such widespread disappointment with board performance and efforts to enhance it?

3. Why do nonprofit organizations go to such great lengths to recruit the best and brightest as trustees, *but* then permit them to languish collectively in an environment more intellectually inert than alive, with board members more disengaged than engrossed?

4. Why has there been such a continuous flow of new ideas that have changed prevailing views about organizations and leadership, *but* no substantial reconceptualization of nonprofit governance, only more guidance and exhortation to do better the work that boards are traditionally expected to do?

As they grappled with those questions, and wrote *Governance as Leadership*, the authors revealed how different this approach is from others. First, it is about modes (a way of doing) rather than tasks (what is done) and mind-sets (mental attitudes) not mechanics (technical aspects). Second, it views board performance on a spectrum from least effective to most effective. The least effective boards are "rubber stamps" for management's propositions; what is presented to the board are "no-brainers" so that trustees do not need to think very hard; they simply provide basic oversight to ensure compliance with legal requirements. Mid-level boards do *some* thinking, typically about proposed solutions to prepackaged problems presented by management. The boards that perform at the highest level are those that have incorporated the principles of governance as leadership; they raise and discuss crucial questions that require critical thinking.

The concepts and approach described in *Governance as Leadership* were well received for at least three reasons; the material was: (1) responsive to trustees' frustrations, underutilization, and boredom; (2) consistent with the national climate for stronger governance and more engagement (in the social and private sectors); and (3) a way to think, not simply a way to do.

Many nonprofit boards have embraced the concepts and theories introduced in *Governance as Leadership* and have made strides to implement the framework in their organizations; yet, many CEOs and trustees report that their boards still underperform. Two primary reasons are that most nonprofits have not yet fully embraced the generative mode—introduced in *Governance as Leadership* as "the most neglected, yet most consequential type of work a board can do" (inside front flap, book jacket)—or they have been unable to create and sustain a culture where they govern seamlessly in all three modes. Using the actual experiences of numerous nonprofit boards, learned through my consulting practice, this book will showcase some common stumbling blocks and pitfalls, but also breakthroughs and successes as boards put into practice *Governance as Leadership*.

This book was motivated by my experience working with nonprofit boards that were passionate for excellence, eager to improve, and hungry for "how-to" steps. Many chief executives and board members had read *Governance as Leadership*, or had heard one of the authors speak about it, but wanted help applying the principles *with* their boards and working *collectively* to implement the ideas. They wanted to ensure a shared understanding of purpose to thereby drive higher performance. They wanted assistance translating governance as leadership into practice. Because the majority of my governance consulting work has been with colleges and universities, health care organizations, and independent schools, the examples throughout the book reflect those types of nonprofits. But the message and the application of the *Governance as Leadership* framework works regardless of organizational type; although the issues vary by sector, and more or less capital and human resources may be at stake, the challenges for boards composed of volunteers, representing various stakeholder interests and sometimes personal agendas, remain the same. In fact, many members serve on numerous boards that cross sector lines, and yet all boards involve relationships, group dynamics, and leadership and all nonprofits face competition, issues of mission and markets, and require transparency and accountability.

WHO SHOULD READ THIS BOOK

Like the authors of *Governance as Leadership*, the author of this book is a student of governance, a consultant to boards, and a nonprofit trustee who has also served as a full-time administrator in nonprofit institutions. And like those authors, I believe that scholars, students, and other board consultants will enjoy this book; but my primary audiences are nonprofit board members, chief executives, and senior staff members who want to reflect on governance, discern how to govern better, and achieve higher performance in the process. Another primary audience includes graduate and undergraduate students taking courses in nonprofit management.

This book was *not* written for honorific or ceremonial "boards" or "councils" whose primary purpose is philanthropic or completely fiduciary, or for those boards whose leaders feel that board performance is "fine as is" and governance cannot be improved, or for those organizations who firmly believe in the attractiveness of the status quo.

As for readers of *Governance as Leadership*, "the greatest value will accrue to boards of trustees that read this book in tandem with their organization's CEO and then consider together what changes would improve the quality and centrality of institutional governance" (Chait et al. 2005, p. xxi). This book and its predecessor are grounded in the beliefs that:

- CEOs and boards are not inextricably interdependent—the relationship is a partnership, but it is not equal. CEOs have less formal authority and more risk, both personally and professionally, than do boards.

- Governance is not a zero-sum game. A strong CEO does not require a weak board or vice versa; instead, the more deep engagement on substantively important issues by the board, the more opportunity for influence and leadership for all.

- The best way for the CEO to improve the board is to ensure that the board is doing better work, not just working better. Higher stakes drive higher performance when the board knows what it is doing.

- Good governance has a reciprocal quality—when trustees understand how to add value, they also derive more meaning from the experience; they will be less likely to "micromanage" when they have more opportunities to "macro-govern" (Independent 2011, remarks by Richard Chait at the Council of Independent Colleges President's Institute).

This book is for organizations that subscribe to these beliefs and to the tenets of governance as leadership.

STRUCTURE OF THE BOOK

This book is informed by research and enlightened by practice. Each chapter, therefore, summarizes the most relevant literature on the central topic and applies it to boards and governance in the context of governance as leadership in principle and in practice with actual boards. The practice-based material presented in this book is drawn from my consulting practice, in-depth interviews with the CEOs and board chairs of sixteen nonprofits organizations (six colleges and universities; four independent schools; four health care organizations; and two community service organizations), reflective practice conversations with Richard Chait and William Ryan to discuss our board consulting and coaching work, and on polls of CEOs and trustees at conferences, workshops, and board meetings over the past several years.

Chapter One provides an overview of *Governance as Leadership*; to get the full benefit, readers of this volume may wish to read or reread that book rather than rely completely on this chapter's descriptive highlights. Chapter Two is about the challenges in implementing governance as leadership and offers thoughts about getting started and overcoming barriers to progress. Moving beyond the barriers requires that boards understand the "invisible systems" that may impede better board performance through the lens of governance as leadership—the subjects of the next three chapters. Chapter Three addresses the cognitive piece—the critical thinking that governance as leadership demands. Chapter Four is about working together—building a high-performing board team to govern more consequentially, and includes three types of assessments: a 360 in which each board member evaluates all other board members; one where each individual board member assesses his or her own performance; and one where the board assesses its performance as a team. Chapter Five considers creating a climate conducive to putting governance as leadership into practice; this chapter includes two additional types of assessment: for board meetings and retreats, and for committees. Chapters Three, Four, and Five move from the relevant research to what boards need to know and do in the context of governance as leadership. Chapter Six is about the centrality of leadership by addressing what the governance-as-leadership model means specifically for the CEO and board chair. Chapter Seven concludes by helping boards think about what might be next for them as they transition to more meaningful engagement and higher performance; it includes additional forms of board assessment including interviews, observations, a self-assessment based on governance as leadership, and one in which the board assesses how informed it is and should be about a variety of topics. This chapter concludes with a look at how to sustain governance excellence through constant vigilance—by leaders within the organization (typically the CEO, the board chair, and a governance committee) or with a consultant or a coach.

THE PRACTITIONER'S GUIDE TO GOVERNANCE AS LEADERSHIP

CHAPTER

1

THE GOVERNANCE AS LEADERSHIP MODEL

Discovery consists of seeing what everybody else has seen and thinking what nobody else has thought.
—Albert Szent-Györgi, 1937 Nobel Prize for Medicine

The influential work *Governance as Leadership* (Chait, Ryan, and Taylor 2005) broke new ground by linking two concepts that previously had not been joined—governance and leadership—noting that there really was "one river, not two streams." The authors stated that "governance and leadership are closely related, and the more clearly this linkage is seen, the brighter the prospects will be for better nonprofit governance" (xix).

PREMISES

Four basic premises underlie the views advanced in *Governance as Leadership* (Chait, Ryan, and Taylor 2005):

- First, nonprofit managers have become leaders. The days of the naïve nonprofit executive director leading a sleepy organization fueled by a few passionate "do-gooders" are long over, as stakeholders expect greater sophistication and leadership on the part of CEOs and their staff members.

- Second, board members are acting more like managers. Although board members are often admonished not to micromanage, many nonprofit board committee structures essentially invite board members into the senior staff's domains. This occurs because the board structure tends to mirror that of the organization—for example, both will have committees in finance, government relations, development, and marketing—and nonprofits populate their boards and committees with professional experts in those same fields. "Constructed and organized in this way, boards are predisposed, if not predestined, to attend to the routine, technical work that managers-turned-leaders [premise one] have attempted to shed or limit" (4).

- Third, there are three modes of governance, all created equal. The authors recast governance from a "fixed and unidimensional practice to a contingent, multidimensional practice" (5) that includes fiduciary, strategic, and generative work (described in more detail later in this chapter) whereby the board provides oversight, foresight, and insight. Although each mode "emphasizes different aspects of governance and rests on different assumptions about the nature of leadership," all three are equally important.

- Fourth, three modes are better than one or two. Boards that are adept at operating in all three modes will add the most value to the organizations they govern.

UNDERLYING ASSUMPTIONS

The authors acknowledged at the outset that many board members express frustration with service on nonprofit boards, asking themselves, "Why are we here?" and "What difference do we really make?" No wonder they feel this way, given that many nonprofits have asked very little of board members beyond philanthropy and basic legal and fiduciary oversight. Much of what has been written about the problems facing nonprofit governance has focused on poor performance—either group dysfunction manifested in disorderly discourse, disengagement evidenced by poor attendance and bobble-headed board members who pay more attention to the clock than to what's on the table, or lack of understanding of board roles and responsibilities because there were no clear job descriptions or lines demarking management and board territory.

Chait, Ryan, and Taylor (2005) noted that a reframing of these issues moves us from problems of *performance* to problems of *purpose*; board members are not just confused about their roles, but dissatisfied with them. Why?

- Some official work is highly episodic. Boards meet regularly at prescribed intervals whether or not there is important work to be done; therefore, in order to fill air time, committees and staff members make reports and board members listen dutifully (or snooze). If board members are awake, in an effort to show diligence and attentiveness, they sometimes chime in with a question or two, but those questions are often operational in nature because the material on the table invites little else.

- Some official work is intrinsically unsatisfying. Some governance work is not episodic—that which involves overseeing and monitoring management must be done regularly and is critically important. Boards must, by law, meet duty of loyalty and care requirements to ensure that the organization is operating lawfully and its leaders are meeting standards of minimally acceptable behavior. But board members do not typically join nonprofit boards to "hold the organization to account" (Chait et al. 2005, 19) but instead because they identify with the mission and values of the organization. This disconnect can cause disappointment and disengagement.

- Some important unofficial work is undemanding. Just by meeting, boards create legitimacy for organizations. Further, because boards meet, management must prepare data and reports, which keeps management alert. But such passive roles are hardly motivating for board members.

- Some unofficial work is rewarding but discouraged. Because the rules about what is permissible board work (for example, fundraising, advocacy, and community relations) and what is not (for example, human resource management and program development) are often unstated or unclear, board members sometimes dive in only to be told to back off—that they are in management's territory.

In summary, "Boards may know what to do, and do it reasonably well, but in the end they are derailed by the meaninglessness of what they do" (Chait et al. 2005, 23).

GOVERNANCE REFORM

Given what has been said thus far, a natural response might be to simply assign a more attractive set of tasks to boards that could inspire new board structures to accomplish those tasks. But this would be risky for three reasons: (1) a revised set of appealing tasks might lead to a happier board but not necessarily to a better-governed organization (the ultimate goal); (2) focusing on tasks, or technical work, tends to encourage microgoverning; and (3) task clarification does not always promote effectiveness (Chait et al. 2005, 24).

We must resist the urge to assume that task and structure are the sum total of governance. We can more easily do this if we shift our thinking from "What is governing?"

to "Toward what ends are we governing?" By thinking about the type of organization—for example, how large it is, how established, its complexity, and how varied its stakeholders—we begin to think of different requirements for governance, focus, board membership, and structure. Relating this to the governance modes briefly introduced earlier, "boards set goals in the strategic mode and ensure the organization meets them in the fiduciary mode" (Chait et al. 2005, 30). In the generative mode, we begin to think about the organization as more than simply productive or logical but also expressive by considering values, judgments, and insights. "Before they use various forms of managerial expertise to solve problems, organizations need to figure out which problems need solving. Before they figure out the best strategy for getting from the present to a preferred future, organizations need to figure out what that preferred future is. Before they can dedicate resources to the things they consider important, they have to figure out what things are important" (30).

Governing by mode as opposed to task may seem complicated, but once practiced it begins to make sense. And the benefits are profound. As Mihaly Csikszentmihalyi (2003) noted, good work balances opportunity and capacity. The basic idea is for board members to achieve "flow"—the mental state where a person in an activity is fully immersed in a feeling of energized focus, full involvement, and success in the process. There are three conditions that are necessary to achieve flow: (1) The activity must have clear goals; (2) there needs to be balance between the perceived challenges of the task at hand and one's skills (too little challenge leads to boredom, whereas too much challenge produces anxiety); and (3) the task at hand must have clear and immediate feedback. Although this makes sense intuitively, achieving "flow" in the boardroom is no small feat. One person's high challenge level and skill set are not another's. However, the model is helpful for understanding the issue of higher purpose leading to better governance.

THE THREE MODES OR MENTAL MAPS

The governance-as-leadership model can be depicted as an equilateral triangle (Figure 1.1) because all three modes, or types, are equally important. Despite this, Types I and II are the dominant modes of nonprofit governance and Type III is the least practiced (Chait et al. 2005, 7). It is helpful to think of the types or modes of governance in terms of mental maps; a street map shows actual street names, landmarks, and places of interest whereas a mental map is how we organize what we see while we walk around those streets, such as an economy, a culture or subculture, or a demographic strata. A walk along Broadway in New York City elicits different mental maps as you start at Battery Park, pass between Chinatown and Tribeca, through the Garment and Theater districts, and beyond.

Type I, fiduciary work, is intended to ensure that nonprofits are faithful to mission, accountable for performance, and compliant with laws and regulations (7–8); Type II concerns the strategic work that enables boards and management to set the organization's priorities and course, and to employ resources accordingly (8); Type III, the generative mode, involves the board as thoughtful leaders bringing wisdom and insight

FIGURE 1.1 *The Governance Triangle*

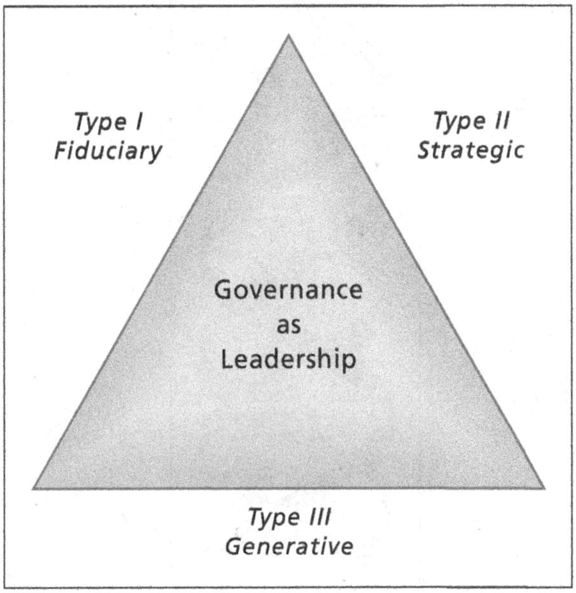

Type I
Fiduciary

Type II
Strategic

Governance
as
Leadership

Type III
Generative

Source: Chait et al. 2005, 7. Reprinted with permission of John Wiley and Sons, Inc.

to critical issues facing the organization before or while policies, strategies, plans, and tactics are formed and discussed.

Another way to visually grasp the three modes is to picture a "triple helix" (see Figure 1.2)—a term that evolutionary biologist Richard Lewontin (2000) used to take the DNA double-helix model a step further by recognizing that we will never understand living things if we continue to think of genes, organisms, and environments as separate entities. Instead, all organisms are the product of intricate interactions between their genes and the environment; organisms are influenced in their development by their circumstances and, in turn, create, modify, and choose the environment in which they live. In this diagram, one strand represents fiduciary work, another the strategic, and the third generative.

In addition to the simple triangle and the triple helix, a third way to picture the Governance as Leadership framework is as a curve (or stream) that starts high and flows down over the course of time (see Figure 1.3). In the fiduciary mode, opportunities for boards to move "upstream" (from oversight to inquiry) and provide greater leadership are numerous. *Oversight* means watchful and responsible care, whereas *inquiry* requires an additional step of a systematic investigation of the facts or more thorough description of the issue. Within the strategy band, lower-stream board activity might focus on *planning* and further upstream on *thinking*. Finally, far upstream—prior to strategy and stewardship—is generative, or framing, work.

Each of the three modes—fiduciary, strategic, and generative—is described more fully in the next sections.

FIGURE 1.2 *Depiction of a Triple Helix*

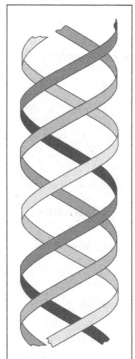

Source: William Trower, graphic artist.

FIGURE 1.3 *Governance Modes or Mental Maps*

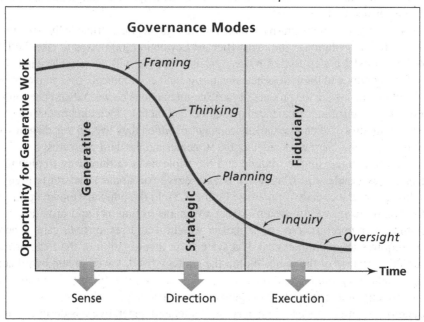

Source: Printed with permission from Richard Chait.

Type I: Fiduciary

The board's role in fiduciary mode is to think and act like stewards of tangible assets—like night watchmen on the lookout for any breach of security. By law, this mode represents the duties of loyalty and care. Problems within the organization are to be spotted. Board members in fiduciary mode ask a set of very important questions: Are we acting in accordance with our mission? Is something amiss or out of order? Is anything contrary to established policies, procedures, and precedents? Is the organization compliant with certifications, accreditations, state and federal rules and regulations?

In order to ensure proper fiduciary oversight, boards construct committees around organizational charts—not organizational priorities—a design that makes perfectly logical sense for fiduciary work. What better way to oversee management than to have committees mirror and monitor management functions? Boards doing their fiduciary work rely on relatively formal and standardized procedures to ensure and document due diligence.

The organization is viewed primarily as a bureaucracy and leadership is typically hierarchical and sometimes heroic. Board members meet to oversee operations and ensure accountability. With a fiduciary mental map, it's common to hear board members say that their primary responsibility is to select, assess, and, if necessary, fire the CEO. In addition, they ratify policies presented by management. The board-CEO relationship may be best described as "hub and spoke." Board members are typically socially prominent and many are affluent and financially sophisticated; they attain power by and through their relationship with the CEO.

Meetings tend to be dominated by staff and follow parliamentary procedure. The information provided to board members for meetings tends to be voluminous and partial to a point of view, typically that of management. Normative behavior of the group is one of deference—mostly to whomever is speaking—oftentimes a staff member or committee or board chair. The group dynamic is "great minds think alike"; the board learns by listening to the CEO, and the board decides by following protocol and reaching resolution. Communication with constituents is limited, ritualized, and done primarily to legitimize the work of the board. There is little or no board education.

Note the different forms of questions a board might consider as it moves slightly upstream from oversight to inquiry (Table 1.1).

According to the authors, although Type 1 work is effective for certain tasks, relying on it completely runs the risks of institutionalizing four flawed assumptions, including:

1. *Nonprofits are bureaucracies.* Nonprofits may have bureaucratic features, but they are not bureaucracies (Chait et al. 2005). Most nonprofits have bureaucratic features such as organizational charts, job descriptions, and bylaws, as well as standardized processes for payroll, purchasing, and accounting, but a weakness of the Type I mental map is that it sees *only* these features and not all the "uncharted" organizational dimensions such as "constituent views, political dynamics, human

TABLE 1.1 *Fiduciary Oversight to Fiduciary Inquiry.*

Fiduciary Oversight Questions	Fiduciary Inquiry Questions
Can we afford it?	What's the opportunity cost?
Did we get a clean audit?	What can we learn from the audit?
Is the budget balanced?	Does the budget reflect our priorities?
Should we increase departmental budgets by 2%—or 3%?	Should we move resources from one program to another?
Will the proposed program attract enough clients?	How will the program advance our mission?
Does a merger make financial sense?	Does a merger make mission sense?
It is legal?	Is it ethical?
How much money do we need to raise?	What's the case for raising the money?
Can we secure the gift?	How will the gift advance our mission? Does the donor expect too much control?
Is staff turnover reasonable?	Are we treating staff fairly and respectfully?

Source: Chait et al. 2005, 38. Reprinted with permission of John Wiley and Sons, Inc.

relations, and social interactions" (42) that may be sources of conflict or serve as disruptions to the chain of command.

2. *CEOs are merely agents of the board.* "The Type I board imagines the board and CEO in a principal-agent relationship" (42), but most CEOs of nonprofits truly function as leaders, not merely as agents of their boards.

3. *Boards are principals, directing their CEO agent.* As CEOs lead, and assume more power, fiduciary boards too often resign themselves to advisory and policy-making roles and find themselves "watching, not directing, the CEO" (44).

4. *Organizations are closed systems.* When boards act primarily in mode I, they tend to undervalue or ignore almost entirely the external influences on the organization.

In short, "Type I governing does not pose problems. Type I boards do" (45). Type I governing is essential but operating solely in fiduciary mode, or only using a fiduciary mental map, can limit board member leadership and participation, and more seriously, cause a board to be so focused on routines that they overlook promising opportunities or potential problems outside of their role as stewards.

Type II: Strategic

For many reasons, nonprofits need strategies; therefore, boards need another mental map that allows them to understand the organization as a complex, open system susceptible to outside forces. "In Type II governance, an organization seeks to align internal strengths and weaknesses with external opportunities and threats" (Chait et al. 2005, 52). Unfortunately, many nonprofit boards attempt to do Type II work within their Type I mindset; as a result, they treat fiduciary responsibilities in the same way they do planning, where the board has oversight of the strategic plan, without playing a leadership role in its creation or evolution.

Typical questions for boards to ask are technical in nature, such as: Do we have the money, space, and personnel necessary to execute the plan? Is the timeline feasible? Are the market projections reasonable? Have we included benchmarks and milestones? Strategic plans were handed down to the board as a fait accompli to be rubber-stamped. The result has been strategic plans that are neither strategic nor a plan but instead a (too often unfunded) utopian construct rather than a solid, realistic plan of action. Chait et al. (2005) highlighted several reasons for this and for why board members become disillusioned with their relegated strategist role.

1. *Plans without traction.* Too many strategic plans do not have the traction needed to succeed because they focus too much on a "blue-sky" future without paying attention to what must change about the present.

2. *Plans without patterns.* Those planning have not discussed the pattern of decisions and actions related to organizational, structural, and procedural (let alone cultural) changes that must occur to ensure the strategy's success.

3. *Plans without strategies.* The plans have tight, well-defined goals but only a vague, overarching strategy.

4. *Ideas without input.* Oftentimes, CEOs determine plans with staff members, without board member involvement, which are then presented to the board for approval; as a result, board members are disengaged and unattached to the outcomes.

5. *The pace of change and unforeseen outcomes.* Because many unanticipated events can occur over the course of a plan's period, and some quite quickly, strategic plans may become irrelevant, or success can be found outside of the strategic plan. In either case, board members begin to question the need for a plan and become disinclined to participate.

Rather than following a Type I, formulaic, ritualistic approach to strategic planning, then, nonprofits are well served to arrive at strategy through thinking, asking critical questions, and applying intuition. By doing so, the board partners with management to provide brains, not just brawn. "In Type II governance, 'What do you think?,' when asked of board members, does not mean 'What do you think of management's plans?' It really means, 'What is *your* thinking about the organization's future?'" (65).

As within the fiduciary mode, board members working as effective strategists can move upstream from traditional planning to "big picture" thinking, by asking different kinds of questions (Table 1.2).

"Unless and until ideas, rather than plans, are the drive motors of strategy, the full range of board members' talents will be vastly underutilized" (Chait et al. 2005, 68). As the board shifts its role focus from that of steward providing oversight to that of strategist providing foresight, important changes must occur in the areas of structure, meetings, and communication.

- First, *board structure must change.* Because flexibility is so important for Type II governance, and creative, strategic thinking is required, nonprofits are well served to rethink their committee structures and break free of the traditional Type I model where structure mirrored the organizational chart. Becoming more strategic and nimble oftentimes requires boards to consolidate or merge some committees, and to form task forces or ad hoc groups to work on strategic imperatives that cut across traditional committee boundaries.

- Second, *board and committee meetings must change.* Just as form follows function in architecture, so should it for meetings. Figure out what needs to get done and then construct agendas to accomplish that work. This will mean fewer reports and more future-oriented, strategic discussions of important issues facing the organization. Meeting agendas are fluid and strategy-driven, and time is built in for participative discussion.

TABLE 1.2 *Strategic Planning to Strategic Thinking.*

Strategic Planning Questions	Strategic Thinking Questions
Do we have the money, space, and personnel?	Is the business model viable?
Does this plan build on our strengths?	Are we a victim of our virtues?
What is the size of the market?	Are there new, unexplored markets?
What is?	What could be?
Are the assumptions valid?	Should we consider making new rules?
Can we predict the future?	Do we understand the past?
What are our internal preferences?	What is the customer's value proposition?
What work does management have for committees to do?	What is the most important work the board must organize to do?

Source: Printed with permission from Richard Chait.

- Third, *communication and information changes*. Type I work is insular, supported by "show-and-tell" reports from management and committees, which does nothing to advance Type II work. In order to partner with management strategically, board members need to understand not just the internal factors affecting the organization but also the external ones including how key stakeholders think. Two-way communication with various constituents, including experts, is a good way for board members to get information that is needed for a fuller understanding of the big picture. The idea is for board members to ask "intelligent questions" rather than have "brilliant answers" (73).

The focus of Type II governance is on performance rather than compliance (as with Type I), so boards need comparative data—across institutional peers and over time—on meaningful indicators. In strategic mode, problems are to be solved and the group norm is one of consensus. The group dynamic is that reasonable people can reasonably disagree about what the data mean and what to do about it. Table 1.3 provides a comparison of Type I and Type II governance.

Because nonprofits are more than rational strategies and plans and encompass cultures, political systems, and symbolic contexts, the sense people make of events often matters more than the events themselves. In addition, the drivers of strategy are ongoing, may fluctuate over time, and quite often strategies are emergent rather than part of a formal planning process. Board member engagement is also fluid, and board meetings are periodic. Therefore, the authors argue that a third, "largely unrecognized, yet equally critical mode of board membership: generative governance" (Chait et al. 2005, 78) is necessary.

TABLE 1.3 *Comparing Type I and Type II Governance.*

Type I Governance	Type II Governance
Management defines problems and opportunities; develops formal plans. Board listens and learns, approves and monitors.	Board and management think together to discover strategic priorities and drivers.
Board structure parallels administrative functions. Premium on permanency.	Board structure mirrors organization's strategic priorities. Premium on flexibility.
Board meetings are process-driven. Function follows form. Protocol rarely varies.	Board meetings are content-driven. Form follows function. Protocol often varies.
Staff transmits to board large quantities of technical data from few sources.	Board and staff discuss strategic data from multiple sources.

Source: Chait et al. 2005, 75. Reprinted with permission of John Wiley and Sons, Inc.

Type III: Generative

Although generative governance may seem novel for boards, board members most likely engage in similar activities every day. Generative thinking is something we do so naturally and automatically as individuals that we do not have to name it; this is the thought process prior to acting—that is, the "genesis" of work that is later translated, further downstream, into policies, plans, strategies and tactics.

Type III governance means that the board generates: (1) insight and understanding about a question, problem, challenge, opportunity, or the environment; and (2) a sense of the organization's identity in order to most effectively respond to the problem or environment, or to seize the opportunity that best reflects what the organization is, how it sees itself, and what it values. It is about deciding how the organization, or board, wishes to frame—consider, examine—an issue.

Charles Kettering, an inventor and head of research for GM from 1920 to 1947, once said, "A problem well-stated is a problem half-solved." And Jeffrey Pfeffer, an organizational theorist, said, "The framework within which issues will be viewed and decided is often tantamount to determining the result" (1992, 203). If these statements are true, it is essential that boards spend time framing issues prior to trying to solve them; in other words, they need to make sense before they make decisions.

To engage in generative thinking requires that we become aware of how we think and how we have come to understand what we take for granted; "generative thinking produces a sense of what knowledge, information, and data *mean*" (Chait et al. 2005, 84). Everyone has experienced times when their perspective shifts, they see things differently, and suddenly they are able to solve a problem or understand a set of circumstances—"When you put it that way, it does make sense" (84). But not everyone has thought about what brings about those epiphanies. The authors suggest three steps:

1. *Notice cues and clues.* Two people can look at the same data and derive completely different interpretations. Why? Because, in part, they each notice and focus on different cues and filter out others; therefore, each constructs different meanings.

2. *Choose and use frames.* Because the world is messy, people have a natural tendency to use frames to help them make sense of the stimuli that bombard them constantly. Frames may be used unconsciously or reflexively, for example, lawyers hardly notice using a legal frame; frames may be values-based, for example, those committed to equity will note how decisions might marginalize some and favor others; or frames may be based on temperament, for example, an optimist may see an opportunity and a pessimist may see a problem. "People notice what they are predisposed to see based on the frames they use" (Chait et al. 2005, 86). Although frames shape our thinking—from taking in cues to proposing solutions—we are not prisoners of our frames. We can deliberately choose to view the situation or data through a variety of perspectives.

3. *Think retrospectively.* Thinking about the past is important to collective sense-making. Organizations are well served to have board members examine some

sentinel event of the past, or to discuss what worked well and less well in terms of strategy or programs, in order to set a "dominant narrative" (88) of the nonprofit. A successful narrative provides a "coherent story line that appeals to people's sensibilities, values, and traditions" (89).

Generative governance demands that the board is brought into deliberations early enough to make a difference—when the situation is still ambiguous and subject to multiple interpretations—because "the opportunity to influence generative work declines over time" (Chait et al. 2005, 101), as depicted in Figure 1.3. Once an issue has been framed one way, it is difficult to see it any other way. People, especially committee or staff members to whom the issue has been delegated, become vested in not only the frame but also data used and the possible solutions that frame allows them to see. Questioning the original frame, once the issue is downstream, will cause eye-rolling, frustration, consternation, and possibly conflict; fresh ideas and solutions will be difficult to generate and unlikely to be accepted. The mentality at this stage tends to be, "Too bad; you're too late. You should have thought of that earlier." As theologian Dietrich Bonhoeffer said, "If you board the wrong train, it is no use running along the corridor in the other direction."

Looking through a lens of generative thinking, the authors offered four "governance scenarios" (Chait et al. 2005, 98) (see Figure 1.4)—two that are dysfunctional (quadrants I and III), one that is prevalent but problematic (quadrant IV), and one that is uncommon but preferred (quadrant II) (98).

FIGURE 1.4 *Generative Thinking: Four Scenarios*

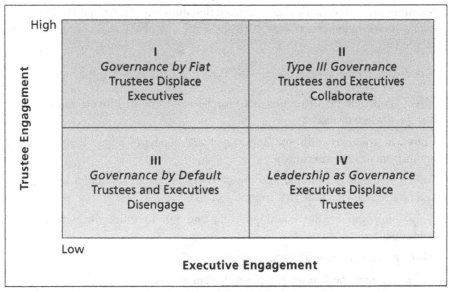

Source: Chait et al. 2005, 98. Reprinted with permission of John Wiley and Sons, Inc.

When the engagement of both trustees and executives in generative work is high (Quadrant II), the result is optimal: Type III governance. The other quadrants in Figure 1.4 depict unbalanced engagements that lead to problematic situations. In Quadrant I, trustees commandeer most of the generative work and impose the results on executives. This might be described as governance by fiat. In Quadrant III, neither executives nor trustees attend to generative work. This produces governance by default, wherein the generative work of other actors inside and outside the organization (for example, staff, funders, regulators, and industry groups) exerts greater influence than that of trustees and executives over strategy, mission, and problem solving. In Quadrant IV, executives dominate generative work, which renders leadership as governance. (Problems of purpose are likely to be acute here.)

WHY THREE MODES?

If boards operate only in Type I mode:

- That which is deemed to be urgent drives out that which is important.
- The stress placed on efficiency displaces the quest for effectiveness.
- The board adds primarily technical value but does not get to the core purposes of the organization, or to adaptive work.
- The board's work becomes predictable, tedious, monotonous, and perfunctory, which may lead to board member disengagement, missed opportunities for effective leadership, failure to see the big picture, or a tendency to see all issues as fiduciary ones.
- Meetings are so mechanical and scripted that thinking is not required and does not occur. Board members, if they even show up, can check their brains along with their coats.

If boards embrace Type II along with Type I, but not Type III, they may:

- Miss significant opportunities because issues were ill-framed initially or not reframed when needed.
- Embrace strategies with the largest perceived payoff rather than the greatest enthusiasm or best mission-fit.
- Fail to understand and take account of how various stakeholders view the issue and proceed down a path that cannot succeed.
- Only think about what could go right and fail to think through unintended consequences.
- Allow process to triumph over substance.
- Fail to tap into the full array of board member insights that generative thinking may elicit.

TABLE 1.4 *Comparing Types I and II to Type III Rules.*

Type I & II Rules Help Boards:	Type III Rules Help Boards:
Choose among alternatives	Generate alternatives
Make decisions	Decide what to decide
Solve problems	Discern and frame problems
Preserve congeniality	Promote collegiality
Pursue consensus	Pursue perspectives
Meet efficiently	Discuss robustly
Consider realities	Consider hypotheses
Pose pragmatic questions	Pose catalytic questions

Source: Printed with permission from Richard Chait.

Note the important differences between utilizing the Type I and II rules and the Type III rules shown in Table 1.4.

The authors noted that lower curve work is important: "What good is a cleverly framed problem without a solution, an attractive mission without a strategy, or a great plan without execution?" (Chait et al. 2005, 101). They advised that boards not spend all their time high on the curve, but to engage in generative governing at least some of the time.

Why Boards Need a Type III Mental Map

There are three features of nonrational, generative organizations (Chait et al. 2005, 105) which make generative thinking (Type III) especially important:

1. *Goals are often ambiguous, if not contested.* In a completely rational, closed system, a crisply articulated mission can inspire a coherent strategy which in turn guides operations. However, numerous nonprofits have missions that can be met in many ways, ambiguous goals, and complex purposes with fluid participation by multiple stakeholders. One stakeholder's top priority is another's lowest interest. What matters one year matters less the next.

2. *The future is uncertain.* Strategic plans must be revisited frequently and leaders cannot allow a plan to dictate every move. Organizations must be ever vigilant and prepared to seize opportunities as they emerge.

3. *Meaning matters.* The way CEOs and board members make sense of facts matters as much as the facts themselves as it is "meaning that enables understanding and action in ambiguous environments" (106).

Essentially, as it has been said in the context of war in the late 1990s, we live in a "VUCA" world—marked by volatility, uncertainty, complexity, and ambiguity. The nature, speed, and catalysts of change are different from those of the past. The prospects for surprise are greater as the world is less predictable. Confounding issues are numerous and reality is hazy. There are mixed meanings to be derived and there is a large potential for misreads; in many contexts cause and effect is difficult if not impossible to determine. Because all of this is true, boards facile enough to think and work in three modes—as necessary—will be better partners in leadership with management. But not every issue needs to be "triple-helixed." So how do you know?

Spotting Generative Opportunities

There are five primary markers (Chait et al. 2005, 107) of a generative opportunity, including:

1. *Ambiguity.* There are, or could be, multiple interpretations of what is really going on and what requires attention and resolution.

2. *Saliency.* The issue, however defined, means a great deal to a great many, especially influential people or important constituencies.

3. *High stakes.* The stakes are high because the discussion does or could invoke questions of core values and organizational identity.

4. *Strife.* The prospects for confusion and conflict and the desire for consensus are high.

5. *Irreversibility.* The decision or action cannot be easily revised or reversed, due as much or more to psychological than financial commitments.

The Three Types of Governance Summarized

The following table, adapted from Exhibit 6.9 (Chait et al. 2005, 132) and presentations made by Richard Chait, highlights the distinctive characteristics of the three modes, mental maps, or types of governance.

CHAPTER ONE HIGHLIGHTS

The benefits and challenges of putting the principles of governance as leadership into practice will be explored more fully in the next chapter. To conclude this chapter, as nonprofit CEOs and board members consider governing trimodally, there are several cautionary advisements to keep in mind:

- Do not overuse any one mode; be a three-type board, not a typecast board.

- Do not be formulaic about working in three modes, for example, setting aside one meeting a year for generative work; or apportioning a set amount of time at each meeting for strategic work.

TABLE 1.5 *Comparing the Three Types of Governance.*

	Type I Fiduciary	Type II Strategic	Type III Generative
Nature of organizations	Bureaucratic	Open system	Nonrational
Nature of leadership	Hierarchical	Analytical; visionary	Reflective learners
Board's primary role	Sentinel	Strategist	Sensemaker
Board's central purpose	Stewardship of assets	Partnership with management	Source of leadership for the organization
Board provides	Oversight	Foresight	Insight
Board's core work	Technical; oversee operations; ensure accountability; select and assess CEO; ratify policy	Analytical; shape strategy; review performance	Reconcile value propositions; manage accountability; discern and frame adaptive issues; think collectively; make sense of circumstances
Organization of the board's work	Fixed structure of standing committees focused on operations	Fluid arrangements focused on an understanding of strategy	Community of learners focused on strategy of understanding
Board's source of power	Formal authority; relationship with CEO	Expertise	Ideas
CEO-Board relationship	Hub & spoke	Strategic alliance	Think-tank peers
Key question	What's wrong?	What's the plan?	What's the key question?
Problems are to be . . .	Spotted	Solved	Framed
Strategy	Set by CEO; ratified by board	Board and CEO plan strategically together	Board and CEO think strategically together

TABLE 1.5 (Continued)

Performance metrics	Facts, figures, finances, reports	Strategic indicators; benchmarks; comparative data	Signs of learning and discerning
Agendas and meetings	Standardized; staff-dominated; passive	Variable formats; strategy-driven; participative	Collective mind of board doing generative work
Deliberative style	Parliamentary and orderly	Empirical and logical	Robust and sometimes playful
Information	Voluminous, partial to a point of view	Selective; analytical; diagnostic	Forensic clues; alternative explanations
Group norm	Deference	Consensus	Robust discourse
Group dynamic	Great minds think alike	Reasonable people disagree agreeably	Great minds think differently
Way of knowing	It stands to reason; listen to the CEO	The pieces all fit; consult the data	It makes sense; gather the clues
Way of deciding	Reaching resolution; protocol and exception	Reaching consensus; group process	Perceiving, grasping, and grappling
Board members	Socially prominent; financially sophisticated; preferably affluent	Type I plus experts in various fields	Create comparative advantage re: intellectual, reputational, and political capital
Communication with constituents	Limited and ritualized, mostly to legitimate	Bilateral and episodic, mostly to advocate	Multilateral and ongoing, mostly to learn
Board education	Little or none	Episodic, strategic	Continuous; inside/outside boardroom, academic and experiential

- Do not "find" generative work everywhere—some issues are obviously and completely fiduciary and do not require strategic or generative thinking.
- Do not use governance as leadership as a pretext for "hobby horses" or "reforms." Do not force the model on the board or on management; if the board and management feel that governance is not broken, or cannot be improved, attempts to govern differently will be futile.
- Do not underestimate the durability and attractiveness of the status quo.
- Do not mount the generative curve *after* the staff or committee work has been done.
- It is crucial that boards also understand what generative thinking is *not*. It is not:
  - Synonymous with bold ideas, radical departures, pie-in-the-sky planning
  - About wholesale changes in core mission, or bet-the-organization decisions
  - Clever solutions to operational problems
  - To be used in lieu of fiduciary and strategic thinking
  - The answer to every question or crisis

The benefits of trimodal governance include:

- Less micromanagement in exchange for more macrogovernance
- Higher level of board member engagement; board in "flow"; enhanced board performance
- Board members better prepared for meetings and thinking at a high level means more value-added
- More value-added and intellectual brainpower tapped means more meaning derived from board membership
- Engaging the collective mind of everyone around the board table should lead to better deliberations and better decisions

CHAPTER

2

GETTING STARTED AND GAINING TRACTION WITH GOVERNANCE AS LEADERSHIP

A little bit of governance as leadership is worse than none at all.

—Chait, Ryan, and Taylor, 2005

In an ideal world, all boards of nonprofits would be capable and effective, and would govern consequentially. In reality, by their own admission, most boards underperform to some degree and see large portions of their board meetings as a waste of precious time. When I have asked CEOs, board members, and staff members to estimate the percentage of time at board meetings, on average, that is *not* put to good use, answers range from as low as zero to as high as 90 percent. Although those extremes are rare, the average is 33 percent; one third of the time at regular board meetings is perceived to be wasted. When you consider the value of busy board member volunteers' time, that's too much. If we put this into dollars, and thought of our boards as pro bono experts donating their brilliance to our nonprofit organizations, we can do the math. Let's say there are twenty-five board members who meet four times a year for six hours and their time is valued at $500 per hour. That's $300,000, of which we're wasting $99,000; no nonprofit should tolerate such waste.

The authors of *Governance as Leadership* pointed out a primary reason for board underperformance—mundane purposes—and provided ideas to raise the stakes for boards to better discern, deliberate, and decide issues of consequence. Though the concepts presented in that book are compelling, boards face real challenges in getting started and gaining traction—the subjects of this chapter. First, what do most boards optimize?

WHAT IS OPTIMIZED AT BOARD MEETINGS?

Part of the issue of less than stellar governance is that boards are not really designed to provide consequential governance. Observations over the years have revealed that the prevalent practices of many nonprofit boards optimize the following: task efficiency rather than process efficiency or effectiveness; congeniality, conflict avoidance, and harmony, rather than collegiality and rigorous debate; convergent thinking rather than divergent thinking; and fiduciary oversight more than strategic or generative insight. In addition, many nonprofit boards were constructed to allow board members to provide philanthropic support and advocacy, while at the same time building social and business connections, and status. Board meetings are designed to allow for executive discretion and feelings of control for the CEO. Board members bring technical expertise and provide legitimacy for the organization as they help build the nonprofit's reputation by their presence. Governance helps nonprofits preserve values, culture, traditions, and the status quo; risks are managed or mitigated.

All these factors are important but they stop short of the highest performance in the governance-as-leadership context where boards optimize still more, including: flow (high skill and high purpose), discernment, meaningfulness, engagement, deliberation, prudence, divergent thinking, insight, consequence to the organization, and integrity.

WHAT IS DIFFERENT ABOUT GENERATIVE GOVERNANCE?

On its face, governance as leadership is deceptively simple—it's easy to grasp the concept of three modes or mindsets—but most boards find that putting the third mode in practice is anything *but* simple. With generative governance, just about everything that has been familiar is different. The hallmark characteristics of the generative mode are:

- *A different view of organizations.* Organizations do not travel a straight line and rational course from vision to mission to goals to strategy to execution.
- *A different definition of leadership.* Leaders enable organizations to confront and move forward on complex, value-laden problems that defy a "right" answer or "perfect" solution.
- *A different mindset.* Beyond fiduciary stewardship and strategic partnership, governance is tantamount to leadership.

- *A different role.* The board becomes an asset that creates added value and comparative advantage for the organization.
- *A different way of thinking.* Boards are intellectually playful and inventive as well as logical and linear.
- *A different notion of work.* The board frames higher-order problems as well as assesses technical solutions, and asks questions that are more catalytic than operational.
- *A different way to do business.* The board relies more on retreat-like meetings, teamwork, robust discourse, work at the organization's boundaries, and performance metrics linked to organizational learning. (Chait, Ryan, and Taylor 2005, 134)

Because so much is different in generative governance, boards may resist changing the way they have been governing.

MOVING TO HIGHER PURPOSE AND OPTIMIZING PERFORMANCE: BEGINNING THE CONVERSATION

Changing from a Type I, or a Type I and II board, to one that truly practices governance as leadership by thinking and working in three modes is complex and requires organizations to overcome any number of obstacles, fears, or apprehensions in beginning the conversation and attempting to break free of the status quo.

Reluctance to Change

Changing time-honored board traditions and culture can be daunting because the status quo bias (Tagg 2012; Kahneman, Knetsch, and Thaler 1991; Samuelson and Zeckhauser 1988)—a tendency to prefer to leave things as they are—is pervasive. Individuals tend to see change in terms of loss, of giving up the existing conditions, so the disadvantages of leaving the status quo loom larger than the advantages. Because the status quo bias is typically very strong, board members are reluctant to raise the issue of its cost; if the cost of the status quo is not questioned, many board members will simply think "leave well enough alone." Most self-assessments, after all, show that boards see themselves as above average. If that is true, isn't that good enough? Why go through all the hassle of governing differently? Why raise governance as an issue at all? Thus, for some boards, "we've always *done* it this way" means "we'll always *do* it this way."

Fear of Change

Actual fear of change takes reluctance to change one step farther. Edgar Schein (1993) makes the case that one reason people are so reluctant to change is because so many of their past experiences with change have been negative. His basic premises are: (1) organization or group cultures can be thought of as the accumulation of prior learning based on prior success (the way we do things around here); (2) organizational culture change requires learning; (3) learning requires knowledge acquisition and insight (therefore, learning is not easy); and (4) without learning, there can be no culture change.

Although having boards provide wisdom through thinking generatively is a seductive proposition, eliciting such collective insight is often elusive. When people cannot solve a problem because it seems too complex, they become frustrated and anxious. If frustration and anxiety are high enough, people become unable or unwilling to learn (or change their practices) because it seems too difficult or disruptive, which Schein (1993) calls Anxiety 1 (Anxiety 2 will be introduced later in the chapter). To avoid Anxiety 1, people deny the problem, simplify it (even if that means distorting it), or project the problem onto someone else. If any of these happen, the group fails to learn and the status quo is maintained. This happens with boards when they will not even entertain the idea that they could govern better; when they see governance in only the simplest, Type I terms; or when they deflect governance issues onto management.

Vulnerability and Fear of the Unknown

The fear of the unknown is strong in part because board members and CEOs alike may feel vulnerable in this alien governance-as-leadership world. Many board members feel they are on safer ground discussing fiduciary issues and occasionally strategic ones; that is, after all, the turf they know best if their experience is primarily corporate.

CEOs and chairs interviewed for this book acknowledged some uncertainty about engaging the board in generative thinking, especially: "The generative discussions are difficult because the answers are unclear . . . it's about what our approach is at this high level. You can get to the answers of the operational and tactical but the generative questions do not have ready-made answers and that fogginess is uncomfortable for many people," said a CEO. Another CEO noted that the board has the fiduciary and strategic areas figured out, "but struggles a bit with the third piece—the big, hairy, upstream questions."

"The generative parts are the most difficult for board members to think about. Part of it is history, and part is just getting people to speak up on what feels like less solid ground for them. Fiduciary work is much more natural and easy for most board members," commented one CEO. Said another, "A lot of board members are just more comfortable with the fiduciary work and want to stay operationally focused—that's where they see their expertise. When you're used to the fiduciary oversight stuff, it's a big leap; generative thinking is more of a challenge for some people."

Furthermore, it can seem like a high-wire act for the CEO to upset the status quo—does the upside potential outweigh the existing situation on the attractiveness scale, or as Chait, Ryan, and Taylor (2005) put it in their final chapter, "Is the game worth the candle?" (163). CEOs can be especially lukewarm or even unreceptive to disrupting business as usual in the boardroom. One reason, expressed by Schein (1993) is that there are strong cultural norms and expectations for leaders to "appear to be in control and to have solutions for all our problems" (85). It is common for CEOs to wonder about the risks of presenting questions rather than solutions to the board; after all, trial balloons can be readily shot down. "The challenges that governance as leadership pose for executives are more about sharing, not assuming, greater responsibility. Whether in response to the board's signals, personal preference, or socialization by peers, executives are often cast as lonely heroes who have nearly all the answers nearly all the time" (Chait et al. 2005, 180). It is no wonder, then, that many executives express ambivalence about changing the way she or he engages the board, when, and how.

CEO and Board Ambivalence

Because CEOs are typically hired by their boards as the centrally responsible leader of the nonprofit organization, and not merely as the board's agent (a point made in Chapter One), transitioning to a different way of governing and truly partnering in leadership requires not only a shift in the CEO's mindset but also that of the board. The board will need to adjust to the fact that board members will not be the only ones asking questions in the boardroom, and indeed, will need to change how it views the CEO who brings questions and not just answers to the table. CEOs will be evaluated, in part, on the centrality and criticality of the questions she or he brings to the board (this will be covered in more detail in Chapter Six).

Depending on how the CEO views his or her board, it may seem a lot easier to "handle" than to "engage" board members (discussed in Chapter Six). In several forums, Richard Chait has noted that there are a variety of ways CEOs perceive their boards, which explain the ambivalence some executives feel about boards and why the status quo is maintained. The board is seen as: (1) a nuisance or a threat, requiring a tight hand on the reins; (2) an ATM, where board members with the most wealth garner the most favor, wield the most power, hold the most sway, and have the ear of the CEO; (3) as fiduciaries or stewards where oversight is tolerated; (4) as consultants where board members are treated as experts providing pro bono advice; or most rarely, (5) as thought leaders and fonts of wisdom where board members are true partners in leadership (Carlson 2011).

Some CEOs worry that boards as thought leaders might wield too much power or could require too much "hard work" and thinking on the part of the management team. After all, it seems easier, and is far more customary, to present data and information to board members at board meetings in the form of reports and PowerPoint presentations than it is to engage them in a meaningful dialogue about what the data means or to attempt to clarify and reconcile issues of mission and values.

Another apprehension commonly expressed by CEOs is that the values-based, mission-critical, generative conversations will reveal schisms between board members or between the board and management. The thinking seems to be to let sleeping dogs lie; however, if differences of opinion are not openly expressed, values are not clarified collectively, or issues of mission and markets not addressed, small issues can become big problems.

Some CEOs may be tempted to go halfway with governance as leadership by keeping the board at bay. They achieve this by occasionally allowing some generative discussion about how management frames issues, but no robust exchange or reframing; or by providing glimpses into the organization's culture and core competencies but few opportunities for board members to engage with organizational constituents (Chait et al. 2005).

Navel-Gazing

A primary concern that board members express about being more generative is that it seems like navel-gazing; they think, "Aren't there more important things for us to do?" The propensity to "cut to the chase" is pronounced; after all, these are busy people voluntarily giving their time, treasure, and talent to the organization. Many board members come from the private sector and expect a nonprofit board to function like a corporate one. They expect to gather periodically to make decisions, not clarify values or reconcile mission and markets. Generative conversations seem like diversions from what really matters—finances and strategy.

As with most good things, moderation is advised. Boards need to be careful not to practice governance as leadership "lite" whereby board members share their "generative genius with the CEO and staff for a few hours every time the board meets" which can, without fiduciary and strategic work, "lapse all too quickly into self-absorbed navel-gazing" (Chait et al., 181). Boards should work in all three modes, as appropriate, to ensure that generative work is grounded in organizational realities.

MOVING TO HIGHER PURPOSE AND OPTIMIZING PERFORMANCE: GETTING STARTED

In many organizational activities, getting started is the most difficult part of the process; elevating board purpose and implementing new practices is no different. The next sections offer ideas to help your board take the initial steps.

Survey Members About Board Service and Board Effectiveness

A great way to get started, and establish baseline data, is to survey board members about how they experience serving on the board and how they think the board is performing. When asked what they find most rewarding about board service, members often say that they enjoy the opportunities: (1) to give (or give back) to an organization whose mission they believe in, and (2) to work with very smart fellow board members and staff members. But when asked about what they least enjoy, board members often say: unproductive board meetings; limited board influence and impact; board member disengagement; and uneven board member involvement in the actual work.

When I have surveyed boards and asked members to assign a letter grade from A to F to the board's performance, most boards average a B; when asked what would make it an A, or one action that would improve governance, the most common responses have to do with practicing governance as leadership, including: (1) spend more time framing and deliberating issues of strategic importance; (2) have fewer reports and engender more vigorous debate; (3) increase board member engagement; (4) draw out, and upon, the full range of diverse board member opinions; (5) develop a better understanding of constituents; and (6) foster better committee focus and performance.

Beyond these and other open-ended questions, board self-assessments (discussed more fully in Chapter Seven) allow board members to see areas of strength and weakness without exposing any individual board member's view. Item by item average ratings may be compared to see where the board scores well and less well, and the range of item scores showcase the disparity of board member views. The scores provide a springboard to a conversation about the current state of board performance, a desired future state, and what steps the board can take to close the gap between the two. Board assessments help board members and staff members build support for more work on governance—the next step.

Build Support

No single board member or CEO should attempt to force-fit governance as leadership on everyone else. It helps to create an influential coalition of colleagues who are open to thinking differently about governance while they are governing. Often smart board members wonder, albeit mostly silently, whether the board is making any difference and whether they really add any value to the organization, especially if a large percentage of time at meetings is spent listening passively rather than discussing challenges and opportunities. Staff members frequently feel similarly, seeing board meetings as requiring a lot of preparation before and follow-up after, but without much impact. Following are some ways to position an examination of governance, in order to build support.

An Opportunity for Engagement, Not a Contest for Control. The most successful launches of new governance practices include the CEO, senior staff, and board members working together. If either management or the board operating separately advocate forcefully for change, it will feel one-sided and almost certainly be viewed with skepticism, or worse, as an attempt at control. Instead, putting governance as leadership into practice should be positioned as a way to raise the governance stakes to get the best from the board.

An Opportunity for Fitness, Not a Response to Illness. Governance as leadership is not "the answer" for all the problems boards face and if framed as a response to some diagnosed "illness" of the board, it may be soundly rejected as board members become defensive. Most board members, however, respond well to thinking about moving from "good to great" and making continuous improvement.

An Embodiment of the Organization's Core Values. All nonprofits espouse noble values. Among the stated values at the Southwestern Vermont Medical Center are quality, empathy, teamwork, and stewardship. The core principles at Greenhill School are honor, respect, and compassion. The University of New Haven's mission promises an experiential, collaborative, and discovery-based education. Other common values found on nonprofit websites are diversity and inclusiveness, respect, curiosity, desire for excellence, innovation, and many more. Whatever the values of the organization, they should be evident in the boardroom. Governance as leadership requires that boards practice what the nonprofits they govern say they most value, thus showcasing the board as an exemplar can be a great strategy to get started.

A Reflection of Sector Best Practices.   Situate the principles of governance as leadership within the context of your own sector. Best practices in hospital settings are to listen carefully, diagnose deliberatively, seek second opinions, assess outcomes and adjust protocols, and conduct postmortems. It might make great sense to board members, then, to put those same practices into effect in the boardroom. Should not the boardroom at a school reflect the best classrooms where curious students learn to think critically, how to ask thoughtful questions, and to value multiple perspectives? College and universities prepare students to deal with complexity, diversity, and change as they take courses spanning the sciences and the humanities. Just as college students develop skills for leadership and team building, dialogue and debate, problem framing and problem solving, so should their boards.

An Incremental Experiment.   For reasons cited earlier, most people do not care for wholesale changes to customary practices. Fortunately, putting governance as leadership into practice does not require making drastic changes quickly. Boards can take small steps, evaluate results, discuss what happened, tweak things a bit, and celebrate incremental results. Boards find they get traction by a process of trial and adjustment; making sense of what is happening is, after all, at the heart of generative governance.

An Example of the Organization's Ability to Change and Improve.   Many nonprofits have found the need to bring about changes to organizational culture in order to spur growth, foster innovation, take advantage of opportunities, or reinvigorate fundraising. It helps staff members to change if they can see that the board is willing to try new practices to improve governance.

Calculate the Cost of the Status Quo

In order to get beyond Anxiety 1 (defensiveness and resistance due to the pain of having to unlearn what had been previously accepted), Schein (1993) argued that we need to create a new anxiety, Anxiety 2, and it must be greater than Anxiety 1. Anxiety 2 can be produced through the use of disconfirming data that show that the current methods are no longer working well, or that there is a gap between current and desired performance; as previously discussed, boards can survey board members to get these data. Shifting the focus to actual data can help move people beyond the defensiveness produced by Anxiety 1. But if the data are not enough to produce a high enough Anxiety 2, another strategy is to produce guilt. How? For boards, guilt can be aroused by asking them to calculate the cost of the status quo. As boards ask themselves,

What is the greatest risk to the organization if the board continues business as usual?, they often come to see that changes to board routines and mind-sets might help propel the organization forward.

Just as corporate boards have learned (in some cases the hard way) that, as the world has become increasingly complex and volatile, more focused attention is demanded to govern well, so have nonprofit boards realized the need to optimize the board's performance. An excellent case in point in the nonprofit sector occurred when Harvard University undertook a governance review after 360 years. The public report on governance (Harvard Corporation 2010) stated several reasons for the review:

- Good practice demands that a fiduciary board "step back from time to time and reexamine its responsibilities and workings . . . with an eye to improvement" (1).

- The recent financial crisis led "virtually every part of the University to take a hard look at its roles and operations and the Corporation thought it should not be an exception . . . it should set an example of willingness to contemplate and pursue new and better ways of achieving its aims" (1).

- "The past decade has been a time of unusual challenge, growing complexity, and consequential change both for Harvard and for higher education at large," leading the Corporation to ask, "what such change implies for a governing body created in the 17th century and now facing the opportunities and demands of the 21st" (1).

The corporation realized that there were several potential costs to preserving the status quo including that its collective capacity might not be "commensurate with the University's scale, scope, and complexity" (2010, 2); it could no longer assume that its old structure was well suited to today's demands. If the governing body continued with its long-standing traditions, it might not be able to:

- Ensure the proper balance between serving immediate needs and assuring the institution's long-term health.

- Assure ample time on its agendas to weigh the major strategic challenges and opportunities facing the institution. It must "take special care to see the big picture and take the long view . . . and avoid an over-allocation of time and attention to matters transactional, transient, or tactical" (2).

- Best "consider how governance can monitor, guide, and enable sound management, without conflating the two" (3).

- Fully consider opportunities and risks. "Ambition and innovation must go hand in hand with carefully calibrating and managing risk, especially as the University navigates a more constrained and volatile economic environment and faces rising outside scrutiny of higher education" (3).

- Provide the necessary transparency desired by the Harvard community, while at the same time hearing and learning from them.

At two other universities, when asked to name the greatest risk to the institution if the board continued business as usual, board members noted numerous serious issues. Among them were: erosion of institutional competitive position, institutional direction, and strategic focus; complacency; and disengaged board resulting in less philanthropic support and loss of interest. No nonprofit should risk such possible losses to simply maintain equilibrium, comfort, and the status quo.

Consider Whether to Apply the Three Modes Sequentially or Simultaneously

Boards often get sidetracked and spin their wheels because they are unsure about how to approach a trimodal issue—sequentially (trifocals or three-way mirror) or simultaneously (triple-helix). Although not meant to be scientific, the following examples are instructive.

Working Trimodally Sequentially.   A good rule of thumb is to begin with the generative mode when the board is not quite sure it has the right question and when the issue involves fundamental, broad, pervasive principles and overarching questions about mission, markets, and values which need to be deliberated first, and settled by the board, before moving on to thinking about the strategic and fiduciary issues.

Scenario 1. Suppose the CEO of a hospital comes to the board asking for a decision about adding concierge services. The board would most likely jump in at the fiduciary level, seeing the array of possibilities such as providing dedicated floors, valet parking, high-speed Internet, gourmet meals, overnight guests, and HDTV. They would then think about the cost, space, financing, and construction time line. But unless someone asks whether the board is grappling with the right question, they might never get to the overarching values and mission-based questions about what led to the proposal of adding concierge services in the first place. If the board decides to back up and think generatively first, it might ask: What precipitates the amenities arms race in health care? And then ask, do we have options to pass or play? What principles should guide our response? What would we not do that others might to win the amenities battle? Why? How do concierge services square with values about indigent care, nonprofit status? Then it might think strategically, asking, If we add concierge services, what would be the effect on our competitive position? Image? Reputation? How will peers respond? Are there other ways to compete on convenience, service, quality, or cost?

Scenario 2. The head of school reports to the board that teacher turnover is a problem and asks the board for clearance to modify the pay plan. The board might be tempted to consider the downstream issues about pay scales, pay plans, retention bonuses, recruitment bonuses, work hours, flex hours, and benefits packages. Some might also think strategically about midstream issues such as aligning pay with priorities, or linking teacher compensation to student and parent satisfaction surveys, acquired skills, or productivity. But what if staff turnover is not about pay? What if the real issue is that school is not a very collegial (innovative, supportive, nurturing) place for teachers to work? If the board is working on the wrong question, or statement of the problem, the answer or solution will not be right. The school would be better served by someone asking, "Have we got the right question?" Thinking generatively first, then, the board can get a better "fix" on the real issue. The questions then become: What constitutes a great school from the teachers' perspectives? What are the values and assumptions of the new generation of teachers? How far should we go to accommodate those views?

Additional Scenarios for Thinking Sequentially

- A public university considering taking steps to achieve greater self-determination through emancipation from the state. Nearly all states have reduced their financial support for higher education, leading institutions to consider additional or new sources of revenue from increased tuition, commercialization of intellectual property, more grants, new programs, or greater philanthropy. The board needed to, essentially, "think like a private college." What would be different at the university if we had greater self-control? Where would we set our tuition if it were up to us? Would the freedom enhance or detract from the mission? How will we navigate the complex political process to achieve self-determination? Will the end game truly be more attractive?

- A hospital deliberating about whether to remain independent in a competitive environment where nearly every other free-standing hospital was affiliating with a system. Before talking about the strategic and financial aspects, the board needed to grapple with several critical generative questions: What are the consequences of losing local ownership? How might our mission change if we lose independence? Does our mission *require* local ownership and control? How does the community perceive the value of the free-standing hospital?

- A hospital's decision to focus on population health needed to decide first: What does it mean to take responsibility for a healthy population? How do we create health, not just treat disease? How do we think about the current culture? What will we have to change about the culture to support this change in mission? How do we bring about changes to the culture that are most important and least disruptive?

- An independent boarding school for girls deliberating whether to stay single-sex and whether to increase the number of day students. Although there were numerous financial and strategic considerations, the board first had to decide what it most values—and would never change—and why, discuss how the culture would change if it went coed or changed the mix of boarding and day students, and what "meaning" alumnae, parents, donors, the faculty, and students would attach to such changes.

Working Trimodally Simultaneously.   A board may think in three modes simultaneously when certain that it has the right question and the decision implicates, rather than hinges on, settling first principles. Such decisions should be considered in light of, and align with, first principles, core values, and the central mission; therefore, generative questions may be considered along with strategic and fiduciary ones. By thinking in the three modes simultaneously, the board actually clarifies what its core values mean even as the decision tests the organization's fidelity to them in the face of market realities. In these situations, the board must also consider operational considerations like cost, personnel, and facilities as well as strategic aspects such as competitive responses, effect on brand, and alternative means to achieve the same end.

An example ripe for thinking sequentially is where the Buildings and Grounds Committee of a college brought the following question to the board for deliberations: Should we use union or nonunion labor to build the new science center? There was no dispute that a new building would be built; the board was well past the stage of deciding on science versus the arts. Therefore, the question was clear, but the question implicated the three modes. From a fiduciary standpoint, the board knew that using union labor would cost 5 percent more than using nonunion labor. From a strategic standpoint, the board thought about the college's image and whether there might be negative media attention and perhaps picketing. At a generative level, the board asked whether it wanted to take a stand on fair labor practices. How would the community (faculty and students) view the decision, either way?

Another example, from *Governance as Leadership* (Chait et al. 2005), shows when a simultaneous approach made sense:

- Should the Boston Museum of Fine Arts lend twenty-one Monet masterpieces to the Bellagio Casino in Las Vegas?
  - Type I (fiduciary) questions: Are the paintings travel-worthy? What are the security and risk requirements? How long a loan period?
  - Type II (strategic) questions: Will the absence of the Monet paintings affect MFA patronage? How will the association with Bellagio and Las Vegas affect the MFA's image and reputation?
  - Type III (generative) questions: What will we do (or not do) if the price is right? Should we loan art to the highest bidder? Should we display art where the masses already are?

Examples 1, 2, and 3 (later in this chapter) provide additional examples of "triple-helixing" issues (working simultaneously).

What If You Do Not Know Where to Start?   Whether a result of a problem or an opportunity, it is not at all uncommon that an issue requiring a decision is presented to the board about which it has not deliberated, trimodally or otherwise. By thinking about critical questions in three modes simultaneously, the board may realize that they need to resolve mission- and values-based issues before they can effectively solve the problem or take advantage of the opportunity—and thereby, in the process of getting started, get to the bigger question.

For example, a liberal arts college is presented with an opportunity to partner with a university to offer an applied masters program. Both institutions would receive a large grant to offer the courses. At first blush, it might be logical to think, of course, when do we start? This is found money; the program would provide a much-needed new source of revenue by bringing in new students and tuition dollars. The board deliberated in small groups, thinking in the three modes, to generate questions.

As fiduciaries, the board thought about: How many students will this attract? What tuition can we charge? Will this strengthen our financials? Is the program resource intensive? As strategists, the questions were: Does this contribute to our flexibility (or further entrench us)? Does it build on our strengths? Is it legitimate and sustainable? How new is this program or is everybody else already doing it? Can we experiment first (for example, via a pilot that could be scaled up or down)? Does it fit with our existing strategy?

But it was when the board began to think generatively that it began to ask very different questions: How would the presence of masters students (primarily commuters) change the character and feel of the college? Would a masters program enhance or detract from the mission? What does it mean to be a liberal arts college? What are the implicit messages in the explicit decision? Are we being opportunistic in the best or worst sense of the word? At that point, the board realized that it should "pass" on this particular opportunity and take up the idea of masters programs, in general, by first settling the generative issues.

As the board practices working in the three modes, it will get better at knowing how to approach issues—by thinking simultaneously (in triple-helix fashion) or sequentially (looking through the three lenses separately, beginning with generative and getting a fix on the right question), and by learning from what unfolds. After getting started, the next step is to keep moving up what for some boards is a slippery slope.

MOVING TO HIGHER PURPOSE AND OPTIMIZING PERFORMANCE: GETTING TRACTION

Chait, Ryan, and Taylor (2005) noted three challenges gaining traction with putting governance as leadership into practice, none of which is "inevitable" but each of which "extracts a price" (165). The first of these challenges is the inclination of boards or CEOs to pursue governance too literally by predetermining a set amount of time at each board meeting for each mode, when a better practice is to work in each mode as warranted and to "learn through reflection, deliberation, and experience to move seamlessly from one mode to another" (165–166). Second, boards need to guard against the unproductive overuse of any one mode, particularly the generative one. "Boards would be paralyzed if each and every item on an agenda were deconstructed to locate some elusive generative core" (166). Third, governance as leadership can too easily become a pretext for personal agendas and reforms; boards need to ensure that it is not "used as the solution to every problem encountered by every board member of every board" (166).

To gain traction thinking and working differently while governing, it helps to have a common understanding of each mode, especially the generative one, because it is the least familiar. Then, boards may wish to practice trimodal governance on an actual issue facing the organization.

Discuss and Define Generative Thinking

I often hear that boards have become more strategic, but that they struggle with providing meaningful insight upstream at the level of framing issues. To shed light on this issue, and to allow the CEOs and board chairs interviewed for this book to "make sense" of generative work, we asked them to define it.

A majority of CEOs and board chairs think of generative work *primarily* in one of three ways: (1) as higher-level thinking and drawing those thoughts out of the board; (2) as getting board members to ask and focus on better questions that get to the heart of the mission and values of the organization; or (3) as thinking further into the future about possibilities rather than shorter-term strategic and fiduciary work. In addition, although representing a minority, others expressed a view that generative work has to do with framing the issues prior to problem solving, or with exploring "why" before "how."

Two CEOs captured several of these concepts as they reflected on the meaning and value of generative governance. One CEO said, "Generative governance is about focusing on what matters most . . . asking the right, big questions like, 'What's driving the low enrollment in the lower division at our school?' and then figuring out on what to focus. Generative governance is also about asking, 'Do we have the right issue and have we framed the discussion around it?' It's collective sensemaking on a critical issue." Another CEO said, "It is more philosophical than pragmatic or task-oriented; it is for the purpose of producing shared understanding and, in its final form, greater probability of good decisions on the right issues."

Higher-Level Thinking. Several CEOs and board chairs see generative work as being at a higher level than other work—upstream on the generative curve—reflected in the following statements from CEOs: "It's a level above policy setting. It's a more thought-provoking, global level of thinking" and "It is a level of thinking that goes beyond operational, tactical, and strategic and is focused on institutional effectiveness in its broadest sense—what the institution is all about." A board chair said that, "Generative work is being able to think at a higher and more creative level about what we would do differently . . . proposing the bigger questions as opposed to campus plans and fiduciary stuff. A good generative question might be, 'How would we think differently, and what might we do differently, if we didn't have to think about setting our tuition? And why would that be?'"

Another board chair reflected on generative governance as a "temporary suspension of all of the things we *think* we know about how we are *supposed* to think and problem solve . . . to enter the discussion at an earlier phase and have more philosophical, broader conversations before we discuss a course of action or push for a decision. It's a more creative process that is not solution oriented, and having a freer conversation with no expectation other than having that great discussion . . . not seeking to identify how to get from point A to point B but instead stopping to just think and ponder."

Asking and Focusing on Better Questions and Issues. For several other practitioners, what comes to mind about generative work is that it helps the board ask better questions on more important issues at the right time. A board chair commented that, "Learning about generative governance has helped board members ask the right, upstream questions before the situation develops rather than asking micromanagement questions too late in the game"; a CEO noted, "It's asking the questions *before* strategy discussions happen."

Importantly, another CEO stated that a benefit of practicing generative thinking has to do with the board as a whole getting on one page; she said, "This process helps us ask the right questions at the right time so that we all understand how we're looking at the issue in order to move forward effectively, as a collective."

One board chair acknowledged that asking good questions is not always easy for board members who may prefer to discuss solutions rather than how to look at a problem or opportunity; he said, "I'd define generative work as asking the right questions and having the ability to ask the right questions. From my experience, boards tend to want the solution right away. The right questions have to be asked first . . . so that we can build on that as an organization."

Thinking About the Future and Taking a Longer-Term View. A number of CEOs and board chairs talked about generative thinking as helping the board have better conversations about the long term rather than the more typical meeting focusing on the current economic realities on which many boards have spent the most time in recent years. One chair commented, "For us, it has been thinking out 10 or 15, maybe even 20 years down the road about the meaning of the university in the Gulf region." A CEO commented that learning about generative governance has helped the board "ask those bigger, broader, often not answerable questions that get us to think into the future . . . 'What really matters for the next generation of our institution?' and 'What values do we uphold, now and into the future, and how are they reflected in our decisions?'"

Framing Issues. Three leaders talked about generative work in terms of frames. Said one CEO, "Better governance springs from being able to frame priorities in a way that accesses people's thought processes on issues that deal with values . . . not dealing with the immediate symptoms but assessing issues based on the deeper meaning of what the institution stands for. The questions that come before the board are not just dealt with on a financial basis, but the fundamental questions of why we are here and why we exist in the first place. It's more than just existence; a generative question is how are you going to react to the rapidly changing world?"

A board chair said, "It's all about framing and finding meaning . . . it's making sense out of what's going on around you and this is critical to good decision making." "Generative thinking helps you to define the questions . . . to engage in critical thinking way before the stage of discussing alternatives. It helps the board to have a more well-rounded discussion of the issue," said a CEO.

Exploring Why.   And one board chair eloquently expressed her view of generative work as follows: "Exploring why you want to go down a certain path and examining the pluses and minuses of taking certain paths in light of institutional values and underlying assumptions about the organization."

Practice Thinking in Three Modes

Once the board has a handle on the meaning of generative work, board members can "practice" by deliberately and explicitly evoking all three modes and then discussing the experience. The following three examples show how the boards of three organizations practiced triple helix thinking by generating questions about mission-critical issues.

Example 1: Copley Health Systems Board

At a board retreat, the board learned about governance as leadership and practiced thinking in the three modes about the mission-critical question decided in advance by the CEO, board chair, and chair of the governance committee: "What are the most important questions Copley must address to fulfill its mission in the current and changing economic and health care environment?" Board members formed three groups and were instructed that they had an hour to suggest fiduciary, strategic, and generative questions that the mission-critical question spawned.

That process elicited numerous questions, including:

- How do we fulfill our mission in a fiscally sustainable way?

- How do we make Copley the most desirable place for health care?

- How do we incent the community to be responsible for their care?

- What is a sustainable model which meets community needs *and* our mission?

- What is Copley's role in redefining a sustainable health care network and transitioning to/incorporating wellness?

Perhaps even more important than generating questions was the discussion that followed in which the board discussed the process of thinking in the three modes. One board member generated laughter by saying, "That was like a brain colonoscopy!" While not necessarily *that* bad, there was general agreement that the exercise "cleared the brain's cobwebs" and required critical thinking. For some board members, the fiduciary questions sprang forth easiest, but not for all; others most enjoyed the upstream questions about Copley's mission and values. There was also acknowledgment that not all questions fit into one single category, but many span two, or even all three modes. The question, "How do we fulfill our mission in a fiscally sustainable way?" has fiduciary, strategic, and generative dimensions.

(continued)

After the conversation about the triple-helix exercise, the board broke into four groups to "Describe the most practical, valuable change the board could make in the way it does business to ensure that it spots, and attends to, triple-helix work." Board members decided they would like to ensure that the board:

- Has materials in advance of meetings that includes questions for consideration;

- Spends time discussing what to decide, how to decide, and how to frame the issues;

- Engages in robust discourse so that the board can truly "respond" rather than just "react," and,

- Designs agendas that keep the board on task, spending 90 percent of its time discussing the most critical issues facing the hospital.

The Governance Committee was charged with ensuring that these ideas would be put into practice beginning with the next meeting.

Example 2: Southwestern Vermont Medical Center Board

At its retreat, following an examination of governance and a board self-assessment, the Southwestern Vermont Medical Center board focused on two triple-helix questions; one was: "Should the hospital become affiliated or consolidated with a larger system?" The task was to generate the fiduciary, strategic, and generative questions that the big question elicited; the process produced a number of excellent questions, including these:

Fiduciary

- Are we going to grow our services and numbers?

- What will be the political issues/result; how will the state of Vermont view this?

- Will insurance cover out-of-state service (if we partner out of state)?

Strategic

- How will the medical group view this?

- How will this be viewed in the community?

- What about those doctors who do not want to join?

- What is the intention of the larger entity, for example, altruism or regional dominance?

(continued)

Generative

- Do we lose our identity?
- Who decides what we should do?
- Why do we want to do this? Can we afford not to do this?
- Does this fit with our mission statement?
- How do we ensure cultural compatibility (with the other hospital or system)?

The board chair commented:

We discussed alliances, not from a detailed point of view, but whether the community would feel good about such an alliance. Would we be marginalized or disappear? Would we lose our local influence? The board retreat provided an ideal venue for this sort of thinking and discussion. The community cherishes the organization and it was helpful to have a sense of whether or not this would fly. It really helped management to put some meat on that concept. The hospital is now looking to align itself with an academic institution. I think it's the result of the generative discussions we had on the board. Generative topics tend to bring out the board's critical thinking and discussions are quite interesting, in part, because board members feel that they're on comfortable ground where they can add value. It's not all about technical matters, like finances or things only health care professionals effectively comment on . . . where most board members don't have the background. A generative level discussion liberates the board to bring its best ideas forward.

Example 3: Jane Doe, Inc., Board

Jane Doe, Inc., is a complex organization from a governance perspective because its board is composed of other directors of local coalition member programs as well as community members. It also provides an excellent example of an organization and board interested in and willing to work hard to transform governance and yield greater benefits from doing so. The CEO commented, "This board has been transforming for about five years, and it's still a work in progress. Knowing how you help people stay connected, communicating, focused, and feeling like they're making a difference are the building blocks around supporting governance. We've spent time talking about the rich purpose of the organization and why it does what it does."

At its retreat, the board learned about triple-helix issues and trimodal thinking and put those new ideas to work discussing the first stated purpose of JDI—to create social change by addressing the root causes of sexual and domestic violence, and to promote safety, justice, and healing for survivors. In small groups, the board went to work as

(continued)

stewards, strategists, and sensemakers by constructing a set of critical fiduciary, strategic, and generative questions that the board and management needed to consider in order to fulfill that purpose. Some of the questions generated were:

Fiduciary

- Do we know the cost to fully execute this?
- How do we diversify funding sources to support this work?
- Should we have new staff work with the board on this?
- What is the business plan and how do we fund this?
- How do our budget and programmatic priorities reflect this?

Strategic

- Who benefits if we succeed? How do we market to them?
- Are we engaging the right constituents?
- To whom are we accountable? Who are the membership and community stakeholders?
- How do we ensure that voices of survivors help inform our work?
- Who else is doing this work? As a coalition?

Generative

- Are we asking the right questions?
- Should we be focusing on more than survivors?
- Do we think social change is still relevant?
- When will we know we have achieved social change?
- How are "justice," "healing," "safety," and "root causes" defined, and by whom?

Not only did this process produce useful questions to frame ongoing work, but the board learned a new way of thinking and working together. The board chair expressed great appreciation for engaging the board more fully, saying, "A more participatory process has a lot of benefits and ways to really tap into the resources sitting around the table that enhances the work of the board and the mission of the organization. We all see that we have a stake in figuring out where we are going and there's ever-greater commitment and engagement. The board is thinking well beyond the bottom line and focusing on the broader mission and goals." The CEO concurred, saying, "The board now has new tools and a deeper appreciation and understanding of the board-management partnership. Having those tools and concepts is really helpful because people get caught up in stuff. For someone who has a hard time with conversation in the boardroom, working and thinking in the three modes has really helped them to open up in

(*continued*)

critical dialogue knowing that we will move to a decision-making mode at another time after we have a shared understanding of the issue."

The organization has also seen improvements in three key areas: (1) donor cultivation and fundraising; (2) oversight by a finance committee that meets monthly with the executive director and senior finance staff as well as annually with the auditor to preview the audit and 990 prior to the final presentation of the audit to the full board by the auditor; and (3) board member ambassadorship in representing the organization to the communities they serve and those communities back to the board. "We seem to have found a comfortable balance between oversight and leadership where I can let the board do its job and they can trust me to do mine. The board is not afraid to ask hard questions and to demand evidence of good policies and practices, but without micromanaging," remarked the CEO.

The board chair exclaimed, "I keep coming back to seeing the board experience as more rewarding for myself and all the board members, now that we're shifted from primarily fiduciary, oversight work to partnering in leadership on all three levels. You reap the benefits of this process tenfold in terms of engagement and moving the organization forward."

Apply Trimodal Thinking to Committee Work

The Ripon College example shows how one committee was able to recast the work it did not only to reinvigorate its members but also to ensure that the committee was working and thinking in the three modes. The committee also stepped outside of its comfort zone by having its members visit peer institutions to learn what they do and bring ideas back to campus.

Example 4: Ripon College Board

At Ripon College, the Committee on Infrastructure (formerly called the Committee on Operations; the name was changed to more accurately reflect the committee's evolution, vitality, and breadth) formed three "task force" subcommittees on facilities, technology, and maintenance and asked the leader of each subcommittee to pose questions relative to raising money in a capital campaign.

The technology subcommittee generated these questions:

- Where does Ripon College need to be on the technology curve and why?

- How do we plan for technology investment when it is such a moving target?

- What role does technology play in campus life now and what role do we want it to play?

(continued)

- What part does or should technology play in enabling our strategic initiatives?
- Is our technology infrastructure hindering our ability to achieve our strategic initiatives?
- If we were to rank areas for technology investment, what are the criteria we should be using?

The deferred maintenance subcommittee asked:

- What industry processes are available for identifying deferred maintenance projects?
- What elements of those industry processes should we adopt for Ripon College?
- What strategy should we use for deferred maintenance?

The Committee on Infrastructure asked, "How do we get smarter on these issues?" As a result, its members decided to arrange campus visits to a set of peers and aspirant colleges to interview the presidents and peer board members and to see for themselves how other campuses were dealing with aging facilities and the pressures for updated technology.

Ripon's board chair remarked on this process, "We are insular if we don't look outside a bit. If you raise fifty million dollars, what should be on the list? Should you have a science building or a new recreation building? What questions do we need to first ask before we ask what kind of building do we want? The Committee on Infrastructure said, 'We need to ask framing questions. What is the potential of new buildings versus maintenance on old buildings and technology?' They really wanted to take a step back and ask those generative questions that maybe weren't asked before. That thinking is going to help us greatly."

Discuss How the Board Is Doing

Once the board begins its transition to governing more consequentially, it is wise to reflect together, in generative fashion, about what sense board members and executives make of the process. A good question to ask is, "What is the board optimizing?"

Although putting into practice governance as leadership principles is still fairly new at most of the organizations featured in this book, CEOs and chairs were pleased to report that their efforts so far have led their boards to optimize: higher-level thinking; strategic focus; quality of discussion, dialogue, and deliberation; expression of divergent views; board member engagement; and time at meetings.

The following comments from chairs and executives reflect the progress boards have made as they have taken their first steps toward exercising more consequential governance.

- "We are optimizing the board's collective capacity to think at a higher, more conceptual, and strategic level."

- "We're definitely optimizing our fiduciary responsibility, but also the board's input on strategic issues. This has happened more as we've optimized our relationships with each other, the CEO, and management in general."

- "The organization is optimizing questioning and discussion of larger issues. We are getting away from dwelling on the day-to-day management issues that previously took up so much of our meeting time. Board members now do their reading and come to meetings prepared to discuss critical questions; they know that if they don't, they will be left behind. This certainly optimizes the time spent together."

- "We're optimizing a culture of openness, frank speaking and a willingness to disagree, so we can get the best out of the board."

- "We're optimizing involvement in discussion and the commitment of the board to look at issues from all angles; we are finding ways to ensure that disparate views are forthcoming."

- "Good, open dialogue; board member participation, rather than dependence on staff to carry the meeting; an agenda that is full of pretty big ideas; a real desire, and pretty good implementation of that desire, to engage appropriately with constituents."

- "The board is now optimizing discussions about governance and transparency, as well as focusing on its relationship to senior management."

- "Because we have strengthened our muscle around generative thinking, which has in turn challenged us to think about the work and the role of the board in a different way, we are now able to take up big issues in much more meaningful ways."

As board members and senior staff engage in discussions about what the board is optimizing as it learns about putting into practice governance-as-leadership principles, especially compared to the old way, momentum can be gained to help keep the board from backsliding. The next two examples provide illustrations of the progress two organizations have made to optimize board member engagement, critical thinking, and board effectiveness.

Example 5: American University of Beirut Board

Following a board self-assessment and board and committee observations by a consultant, the American University of Beirut held a forty-eight-hour retreat during which the board discussed the president's vision statement, the meaning of preeminence in

(continued)

medicine and of being a great comprehensive university, and the competitive landscape in the Gulf region. In addition, the board grappled with several other weighty issues surrounding diversity and enrollment; institutional values and culture; and repercussions of an expanded medical center on interdisciplinary collaborations and research. These discussions were followed by small groups working on board committee structure; fostering a culture of critical and strategic thinking at board meetings; board composition; board information needs; and board norms, expectations, and accountability.

"Our board retreat really got us moving in the right direction," remarked the president. The board chair agreed, "Pulling together that international group of board members was wonderful. We also now have a more rigorous governance system."

AUB reorganized its board committee structure, jettisoning some, consolidating others, and creating a trusteeship committee that is systematizing the nomination and membership processes. The revised committee structure has led to broader board member participation and allowed a more judicious distribution of board members to committees, and has changed the agendas for full board meetings to reflect far less reporting, which has streamlined and focused the work of the board.

"We are no longer determined to report everything; the committees no longer rehash material. We focus on votes taken to move the board forward and to leave time for strategy and other important discussions," said the president. "The board is more actively engaged, as a collective, in the values of the mission and the purposes of the university."

"There was an important discussion of priorities at the retreat which galvanized the board members around the real purpose of building a new medical complex. It was realized that we had a choice of maintaining the hospital as a good medical care facility or, to go ahead with a combined mission of training, care, and research that could significantly impact the region. In order to follow our mission we had to devote the campaign to building a new medical center. It's the most ambitious campaign in AUB's history."

The board chair noted, "There is no question that the retreat helped to launch our effort to lead a major campaign around the medical center that will extend to the entire campus."

Overall, said the president, "The retreat allowed us to think about the medical center and the university in strategic ways that were extremely useful by getting board members in a secluded environment and learning how these types of discussions can work. The exercise of the retreat itself changed the dialogue which ultimately has to do with board member governance. The retreat got us together to think about what questions to ask, to understand the connection between the discussions and what the university does, and it helped board members see how the university can move forward in ways that we can all embrace."

Example 6: Parish Episcopal School

Parish Episcopal School convened the board for two governance workshops—one in the fall and another the following spring. During the first clinic the board learned about governance as leadership, discussed the board's legacy, and decided together what defines a "remarkable" board and settled on three primary characteristics: engaged, strategic, and accountable. The board now rates itself on those three (as well how it is performing as fiduciaries, strategists, and sensemakers). The board now focuses more board meeting time on strategic and generative questions; following is an example of how that works.

In the fall, board members considered tuition pricing options for the lower school. The head of school remarked, "Board members met as committees—advancement, facilities, and finance—for twenty minutes to consider the question, 'Through your committee's unique lens, what tuition pricing options or programs will allow us to increase our admissions funnel in the lower school?'"

Each group shared ideas during the following plenary session of the board. Finance discussed the pros and cons of various pricing options. Advancement weighted the relative attraction to funders of enhancing physical space versus contributing to innovative new programs such as a "STEM lab" for young learners. The facilities committee considered the merits of investing in an aging original campus versus merging two programs on one campus. In October, the administration will share five to seven of the best ideas generated by the committees and board members, in small groups, will be asked to prioritize and or blend the various initiatives to help determine tuition markers for next year.

"This process allows us to maximize the intellectual capital of board members. We are using breakout groups to ensure the engagement of all members and their feedback is that the activities and dialogue are stimulating. We are also trying to derive some action from these discussions, so everyone can see the benefit," said the head of school.

The board chair commented:

> Our process has evolved into the head and chair developing ideas/questions and confirming them with the Executive Committee prior to setting the final meeting agenda. Every agenda now includes a reminder of the tenets of good governance and then the questions are posed along with instructions. While members receive the questions prior to the meeting, they may or may not know what position they will be asked to advocate. This process has created an environment where everyone has to think and prepare prior to meetings and then actively participate at the meetings. Active engagement of all members is a constant goal and these exercises have gone a long way in that regard; at the same time, the board is providing valuable insight and feedback to the school's leadership team.

CHAPTER TWO HIGHLIGHTS

- **One-third of the time spent in board meetings is wasted.** Meetings optimize task efficiency over process efficiency or effectiveness; congeniality over collegiality; conflict avoidance over debate and dissent and convergent over divergent thinking; and fiduciary oversight over strategic foresight or generative insight. Too little attention is paid to discernment, meaning-making, board member engagement, deliberation, and consequence to the organization.

- **Generative governance is different in many ways.** Organizations are not completely rational bureaucracies; leaders enable the board to confront value-laden propositions and questions without easy answers; governance is tantamount to leadership; the board is a comparative advantage to the organization; board members are intellectually engaged; the board helps frame higher-order problems and spot important opportunities; and the board does business differently.

- **Governing trimodally is not as easy as it seems.** Getting started requires that organizations overcome reluctance to change, resistance, fear, and feelings of vulnerability, cynicism, and ambivalence on the part of chief executives, senior staff, and board members.

- **Use a variety of techniques to get started.** Survey board members about board service and the board's effectiveness; build a coalition of support; and calculate the cost of the status quo.

- **Gaining traction requires work.** Governing differently, especially in generative mode, does not come naturally to some board members or CEOs. It helps to discuss and define generative thinking, being careful to delineate what it is and is not; practice thinking in all three modes and learn to distinguish one from the others; discover ways to apply trimodal thinking beyond the boardroom (for example, on committees and task forces; with key stakeholders); discuss how the board is doing and what the board is learning.

- **Generative work, in particular, takes practice.** A CEO said, "This generative governance is not easy to do. We've had different levels of success. Our board chair has tried to bring us in that direction, but it's a process that's not terribly intuitive. If you don't do it a lot then you lose the skill. It's a continued work in progress." Another noted, "I'm not sure this is a challenge per se, but it does take time; you need to shift agendas to allow the thinking and questioning moments to emerge. Since starting this process, we've also learned that we need to spend even more time playing the devil's advocate and really pushing hard to think through issues from multiple perspectives." Because thinking and working in all three modes is not necessarily intuitive or easy to do, some board members will gravitate to it more naturally than others, but to succeed, persistence is crucial.

- **Even boards with consequential work to do underperform.** The governance-as-leadership model places a premium on four pivotal subsystems that undergird the work of effective boards, including critical thinking, teamwork, culture, and leadership; these are the subjects of the next four chapters.

CHAPTER

3

ENCOURAGING CRITICAL THINKING IN THE BOARDROOM

We live in a society bloated with data but starved for wisdom.
—Elizabeth Lindsey, ethnographer

Tell me what you know, then tell me what you don't know, and only then can you tell me what you think.
—General Colin Powell

I recently asked a large group of CEOs and board members, representing a broad swath of nonprofit organizations, to say what percentage of board member brain power, on average, is left untapped at typical board meetings—and the figure was an astonishing 50 percent! Although it would be difficult to imagine fully tapping 100 percent of the brain power of 25–40 people seated around the boardroom table, utilizing only half is a terrible waste. Though admittedly unscientific, this same straw poll revealed that the board is fairly "passive" 67 percent of the time at typical board meetings. Time was apportioned as follows: 32 percent listening to reports or presentations by the CEO, staff, or committee chairs; 24 percent conducting regular business—for example, the consent agenda, approval of reports and minutes, updates, notice of upcoming events; and 11 percent getting educated—for example, outside expert(s) talking; topical panels; and constituent experience. About a third of the time, CEOs and board members said they are in a more "active" mode: 20 percent spent discussing or debating ideas or courses of action and 13 percent collectively making sense, including framing issues, talking about other ways in which something might be viewed, and thinking from the perspectives of various constituents.

Putting into practice the principles of governance as leadership requires that board members utilize their brains at meetings, rather than switching to "autopilot," as they listen to reports and rubber-stamp management's initiatives. By design, board meetings are typically more efficient than effective; typically, they are not *designed* to elicit critical thinking on the part of board members. But even when agendas are redesigned and more time is allocated for strategic and generative conversations, boards still spin their wheels and report giving up and reverting to the old ways.

Part of the problem is that, during board meetings, invisible systems operate—unconscious group processes (the subject of Chapter Four), individual cognitive biases and propensities, and just plain old human nature (the subjects of this chapter)—that may impede governing consequentially in trimodal fashion. These factors are the "elephants" in the boardroom of which some board members may be blissfully unaware—or of which some board members *are* aware, but no one wants to name. Whether topical, behavioral, or personal, acknowledging the elephants in the room presents special challenges to nonprofit organizations and strikes many board members and CEOs as too great a risk for too scant a reward.

The very markers of generative issues—ambiguity, saliency, high stakes, strife, and irreversibility—demand a lot of board members and may actually compound the problems as the invisible systems and thought processes take hold and bring out the worst of the board. The elephants are no longer benign; instead, they stymie forward momentum completely. Boards are likely to underperform unless board members (1) learn to confront the issues skillfully (highly improbable, but possible with coaching—see Chapter Seven); or (2) institutionalize compensatory measures. Compensatory measures are "workarounds," tactics, tools, and techniques that either minimize or circumvent the often invisible, rarely discussable, ever-present "complications."

This chapter defines critical thinking (essential for high performance in the governance-as-leadership context), highlights the facets of human nature that impede it, contextualizes the implications for boards using the governance-as-leadership framework, and provides ideas to help solve or work around the problems boards face as they work on the "thinking" aspect of board performance.

CRITICAL THINKING AND METACOGNITION

Governance as leadership requires that boards think critically as individuals and as a group. As individuals, critical thinking—the "art of analyzing and evaluating thinking with a view to improving it" (Paul and Elder 2008, 2)—requires metacognition, or thinking about thinking (Lehrer 2009, 249). Metacognition is the experience and knowledge we have about our own cognitive processes (Flavell 1979). The basic idea is that the more an individual engages cognitively with ideas and information, the greater the learning; if engaged this way when deciding, the better the judgment.

Metacognition requires that we self-overhear (Tetlock 2005)—that we study our own brain at work as we listen to the argument inside our head (Lehrer 2009, 250). Good judgment is a "precarious balancing act" that requires "cognitive skills of the highest order"—the capacity to monitor one's own thought processes for telltale signs of excessive closed- or open-mindedness and to strike a reflective equilibrium faithful to one's conceptions of fair intellectual play (Tetlock 2005). In order to perform this balancing act we must "learn how to eavesdrop on the mental conversations we have with ourselves as we struggle to strike the right balance between preserving our existing worldview and rethinking core assumptions. This is no easy art to master. If we listen carefully to ourselves, we will often not like what we hear. And we will often be tempted to laugh off the exercise of introspective naval gazing. . . . But if I had to bet on the long-term predictor of good judgment, it would be individuals with a commitment, a soul-searching Socratic commitment, to thinking about how they think" (Tetlock 2005, 215).

A well cultivated critical thinker: raises vital questions, formulating them clearly and precisely; gathers and assesses relevant information, using abstract ideas to interpret it effectively; comes to well-reasoned conclusions and solutions, testing them against relevant criteria and standards; thinks open-mindedly within alternative systems of thought, recognizing and assessing, as need be, their assumptions, implications, and practical consequences; and communicates effectively with others in figuring out solutions to complex problems. Critical thinking is, in short, self-directed, self-disciplined, self-monitored, and self-corrective thinking. It requires rigorous standards of excellence and mindful command of their use. It entails effective communication and problem solving abilities and a commitment to overcome our native egocentrism and sociocentrism. (Paul and Elder 2008, 2).

In its truest form, critical thinking requires the application of "universal intellectual standards"—clarity, accuracy, precision, relevance, depth, breadth, logic, significance, and fairness—as guides to better reasoning (Paul and Elder 2008), either with oneself (in the case of metacognition) or with someone else. The questions in Table 3.1 demonstrate the application of critical intellectual standards with someone else, or in a group setting, such as the boardroom.

Although these questions are useful, and would certainly test the quality of one's own thinking, or that of a colleague, thinking critically in the boardroom in the governance-as-leadership context requires that board members get outside their comfort zone (especially if that is the fiduciary mode) and examine their own thinking and boardroom behaviors, which means "getting on the balcony."

TABLE 3.1　*Questions for the Application of Universal Intellectual Standards.*

Clarity	Could you elaborate further? Could you give me an example?
Accuracy	How could we find out if that is true? How could we verify or test that?
Precision	Could you be more specific? Could you give me more details?
Relevance	How does that relate to the problem? How does that bear on the question?
Depth	What factors make this a difficult problem? What are some of the complexities of this question?
Breadth	Do we need to look at this from another perspective? Do we need to consider another point of view?
Logic	Does all this make sense together? Does what you say follow from the evidence?
Significance	Is this the most important problem to consider? Is this the central issue on which to focus?
Fairness	Do I have a vested interest on this issue? Am I sympathetically representing the viewpoints of others?

Source: Adapted from Paul and Elder 2008, 10.

GETTING ON THE BALCONY

The notion of figuratively stepping out of the action around the boardroom table and "getting on the balcony" holds appeal from a consequential governance standpoint. What might you see differently from a higher or different vantage point? "Few practical ideas are more obvious or more critical than the need to get perspective in the midst of action. Any military officer, for example, knows the importance of maintaining the capacity for reflection, even in the 'fog of war.' Great athletes can at once play the game and observe it as a whole—as Walt Whitman described it, being both in and out of the game" (Linsky and Heifetz 2002, 51).

Getting on the balcony means: observing what is going on around you; staying diagnostic even as you take action; developing more than one interpretation; watching for patterns; and reality-testing your interpretation, especially when it is self-serving or close to your default (Heifetz, Grashow, and Linksy 2009, 126)—all important in the governance as leadership framework—but all easier said than done for most of us.

If critical thinking, metacognition, and getting on the balcony make so much sense and appeal to us as rational beings, what gets in the way of transferring these concepts into the boardroom? To answer requires that we first think about human beings as individuals who take mental shortcuts and are subject to cognitive biases, and then think about what happens to individuals in group decision-making situations, which are wrought with a host of other complications.

WAYS OF THINKING

At the extremes, there are two very different ways of thinking and approaching problems characterized as hedgehogs or foxes (Berlin 1953; Tetlock 2005) or as boardroom lions or humble hounds (Brooks 2010). Because the principles of governance as leadership are more likely to resonate with foxes and humble hounds (who will also be more skillful at and adaptable to a different way of governing) than with hedgehogs or lions, whether and how your board engages in trimodal thinking, and how it goes about its deliberations are, in part, a function of the numbers and types of these animals on the board.

Hedgehogs and Foxes

In his essay on Tolstoy's view of history, Isaiah Berlin (1953) quoted the Greek poet Archilochus, saying, "The fox knows many things, but the hedgehog knows one big thing" (3).

Berlin expanded upon this idea as he divided thinkers into two categories: hedgehogs, who viewed the world through the lens of a single defining idea (for example, Plato, Lucretius, Dante, Pascal, and Nietzsche); and foxes, who drew on a wide variety of experiences and for whom the world could not be boiled down to a single idea (for example, Aristotle, Erasmus, Montaigne, Molière, and Goethe).

In more recent times, Tetlock (2005), annoyed by the apparent intractability of most political disagreements and "how rarely partisans admit error, even in the face of massive evidence that things did not work out as they once confidently predicted" (xi), revealed how differently hedgehogs and foxes think within the realm of "expert" political judgment (see Table 3.2).

"Hedgehogs are like Churchill's definition of a fanatic: someone who cannot change his mind and will not change the subject. Once hedgehogs boarded a train of thought, they let it run full throttle in one policy direction for extended stretches, with minimal braking for obstacles that foxes took as signs they were on the wrong track" (Tetlock 2005, 100).

Although foxes have an advantage in decision making that resides in *how* they think, not in *what* they think (Tetlock 2005, 106), they can become entangled in self-contradictions because of their tendency to assign so much likelihood to so many possibilities (190). Foxes see explanation and prediction not as deductive exercises but rather as exercises in flexible "ad hocery" that require stitching together diverse sources of information (73).

TABLE 3.2   *Hedgehogs and Foxes.*

Hedgehogs	Foxes
Know one big thing	Know many things
Toil devotedly within one tradition	Draw from an eclectic array of traditions
Reach for formulaic solutions to ill-defined problems	Accept ambiguity and contradictions as inevitable features of life
Are characterized by hubris and self-confidence	Are self-critical and self-subversive
Are close-minded; rarely change their mind	Utilize a dialectical or point-counterpoint style of reasoning
Are certain of their views	Are skilled at self-overhearing
Crave closure; display bristly impatience with those who "do not get it"	Listen for doubt
Dismiss dissonant data	Entertain contradictory data
Eschew tentativeness and nuance	Elevate no thought above criticism; appreciate nuance
Do not admit mistakes	Recall but do not rationalize mistakes
Rely on grand schemes and broad generalizations	Are skeptical of grand schemes
Aggressively extend the reach of one big thing into new domains	Realize that a new domain is new and proceed cautiously

Source: Adapted from Tetlock 2005.

Boards practicing governance as leadership run smack up against the two ways of thinking that determine how they decide issues—how to best mix theory-driven and imagination-driven modes of thinking. "Theory-driven thinking confers the benefits of closure and parsimony but desensitizes us to nuance, complexity, contingency, and the possibility that our theory is wrong. Imagination-driven thinking sensitizes us to possible worlds that could have been but exacts a price in confusion and even incoherence" (Tetlock 2005, 214).

Boards, presumably composed of at least some hedgehogs and some foxes, are likely to face challenges as board members disagree about how to manage the trade-off between being theory- or imagination-driven. "Hedgehogs put more faith in theory-driven judgments and keep their imagination on tighter leashes than do foxes. Foxes are more inclined to entertain dissonant scenarios that undercut their own beliefs and preferences. If there are advantages to self-subversive thinking, foxes will reap them. If there are prices for suspending disbelief, foxes will pay them" (Tetlock 2005, 214).

Boardroom Lions and Humble Hounds

In a *New York Times* op-ed piece, David Brooks (2010) applied the hedgehog and fox ways of thinking to board leaders. He defined boardroom lions as superconfident, forceful, charismatic, and quick to reach decisions; they do not second-guess or look back. Lions are relentless for transformational change. By contrast, humble hounds combine extreme humility with intense professional will (Collins 2001); they will think less about their own mental strengths than their own mental weaknesses, spend a lot of time on metacognition, understand that the world is complex and unpredictable, spend more time seeing than analyzing, and sometimes construct thinking teams. For hounds, life is all about navigating uncertainty. Humble hounds try not to fall for the seductions that mark failing organizations: "the belief that one magic move will change everything; the faith in perpetual restructuring; the tendency to replace questions with statements at meetings" (Brooks 2010). In a governance-as-leadership context, where a premium is placed on asking questions rather than having answers, it follows that we would want more humble hounds than lions on our boards. But without solid practices in place to minimize dysfunctional behaviors, the lions can eat the hounds for lunch.

More Hedgehogs/Lions Than Foxes/Humble Hounds

Although ideally we may wish to fill our boardrooms with more humble hounds and foxes, there is no shortage of research describing why the sort of self-awareness, self-reflection, and self-criticism they exhibit are so rare. Most of us take mental shortcuts and we make mistakes. Indeed, a quick scan of the topic yielded a number of provocative titles and undoubtedly interesting reads (see Exhibit 3.1).

At this point, I should make clear some of my assumptions:

- If the world contained more foxes—careful, self-critical, and self-subversive thinkers—there would be fewer of these books.

- Even if more people wanted to be more foxlike, basic human nature and cognitive biases work against doing so.

- Boards are microcosms of the larger world; therefore, it is likely that many have either a preponderance of board members who are like hedgehogs or lions. Even if they are not a majority, then those few hedgehogs or lions—with their confidence and assertiveness—hold the most sway and wield the most power.

- Not all board members are *completely* hedgehogs or foxes (some may fall somewhere in between and vary in their thinking according to the issue).

- Regardless of your board's exact ratio of hedgehogs/lions to foxes/humble hounds, all boards have group dynamics issues.

> ## Exhibit 3.1: Readings on Mental Shortcuts and Cognitive Mistakes
>
> Blakeslee, S. 2010. *Sleights of Mind: What the Neuroscience of Magic Reveals About Our Everyday Deceptions*. New York: Henry Holt.
>
> Chabris, C., and D. Simons. 2010. *The Invisible Gorilla: And Other Ways Our Intuitions Deceive Us*. New York: Crown.
>
> Fine, C. 2006. *A Mind of Its Own: How Your Brain Distorts and Deceives*. New York: Norton.
>
> Gilovich, T. 1991. *How We Know What Isn't So: The Fallibility of Human Reason in Everyday Life*. New York: Free Press.
>
> Hallinan, J. T. 2009. *Why We Make Mistakes: How We Look Without Seeing, Forget Things in Seconds, and Are All Pretty Sure We Are Way Above Average*. New York: Doubleday.
>
> Kida, T. 2006. *Don't Believe Everything You Think: The 6 Basic Mistakes We Make in Thinking*. New York: Prometheus Books.
>
> Shore, Z. 2008. *Blunder: Why Smart People Make Bad Decisions*. New York: Bloomsbury Press.
>
> Tavris, C., and E. Aronson. 2007. *Mistakes Were Made (But Not By Me): Why We Justify Foolish Beliefs, Bad Decisions, and Hurtful Acts*. Orlando, FL: Harcourt Books.
>
> Van Hecke, M. L. 2007. *Blind Spots: Why Smart People Do Dumb Things*. New York: Prometheus Books.

Each of the next topics applies more directly—in the extreme—to hedgehogs and boardroom lions; by their very definition, they have big egos, are certain that what they think is right, refuse to admit they are wrong, view being wrong as a weakness, have delusions of rationality, and believe that their worldview applies to all contexts precisely because it is *their* worldview.

IMPEDIMENTS TO CRITICAL THINKING

Although the next several sections are designated with separate headings, their content is interwoven in ways that represent the complex workings of the human mind. Being wrong and being certain are two sides of the same coin. Diagnosis momentum flows from being certain and loss aversion is a subset of not wanting to be wrong. Thinking we are rational is part of being certain that we are not wrong. All serve as important considerations for implementing the principles of governance as leadership.

Being Wrong

Absolutely no one wants to be wrong. Why? It goes against human nature. It violates the ego. It insults the mind. Besides, being right is simply delicious. "The thrill of being right is undeniable, universal, and (perhaps most oddly) almost entirely undiscriminating" (Schulz 2010, 3). French playwright Molière captured the sentiment beautifully, "It infuriates me to be wrong when I know that I'm right."

Kathryn Schulz (2010) wrote: "In high-stakes situations, we should want to do everything possible to ensure that we are right which . . . we can only do by imagining all the ways we could be wrong" (13). That is extremely challenging for most people. "Our everyday actions are grounded in an essentially limitless number of implicit convictions" (91–92), so implicit that we hold them as beliefs—our own mental map or model of the world—and believe them to be true. When an implicit assumption is violated, it turns into an explicit one. "While many of our beliefs fall somewhere in the middle of the implicit-explicit spectrum, it is those that lie at the extreme ends that collapse most spectacularly in the event of error. If anything can rival for sheer drama the demise of a belief that we have adamantly espoused, it is the demise of a belief so fundamental to our lives that we never even registered its existence" (93).

It was Alan Greenspan's "absolutist" faith in the ability of free markets to regulate themselves that led to his "shocked disbelief" when the markets did the opposite and slid into chaos, argued Schulz, noting that it was not that Greenspan had never been warned about the possibility, because he had. "Nor was it because his own model had never been criticized (it had), or because alternative models had never been floated (they had) . . . Greenspan was as figuratively invested in unregulated markets as the rest of us were literally invested in them. He had a model of how the world worked, and his confidence in it was all but immoveable" (90). It is easy to examine the flaws in Greenspan's thinking (and in that of many others) but not so easy to examine our own "immoveable" and "right" mental models. Although we are "highly adept at making models of the world, we are distinctly less adept at realizing when we have made them" (99) and we are so "emotionally invested in our beliefs that we are unable or unwilling to recognize them as anything but the inviolable truth" (103–104).

Physician Jerome Groopman's eye-opening book (2007) about the practice of medicine reported on a study by Dr. E. James Pitchen at Michigan State University on the performance of over one hundred radiologists examining a series of sixty chest x-rays that included some duplicates. He compared the diagnostic accuracy of the top twenty (correct 95 percent of the time) with that of the bottom twenty (correct 75 percent of the time). "Most worrisome was the level of confidence each group had in its analysis. The radiologists who performed poorly were not only inaccurate; they were also very confident that they were right when they were in fact wrong. 'Observers' lack of ability to discriminate normal from abnormal films does not necessarily diminish their confidence,' Pitchen wrote" (180).

Turning back to Isaiah Berlin, hedgehogs especially hate to be wrong, preferring instead to dig themselves deeper into intellectual holes. "The deeper they dig, the harder it gets to climb out . . . and the more tempting it becomes to keep on doing what they know how to do: continue their metaphorical digging by uncovering new reasons why their initial inclination . . . was right. Hedgehogs are . . . prisoners of their own preconceptions, trapped in self-reinforcing cycles in which their initial ideological disposition stimulates thoughts that further justify that inclination, which, in turn, stimulates further supportive thoughts" (Tetlock 2005, 118).

This all becomes especially problematic in board decision settings; strangely, we (hedgehog or not) are so convinced that our own beliefs are right that we see no need to extend that assumption to others who disagree with us. Instead we feel utter disbelief when others' views differ from our own and first assume that they are ignorant (Schulz calls this the Ignorance Assumption)—they do not know the facts and I do, and once I inform them of the facts, they will agree with me. "When other people reject our beliefs, we think they lack good information. When we reject their beliefs, we think we possess good judgment" (Schulz 2010, 107). But when people "stubbornly persist in disagreeing with us even after we've tried to enlighten them—we move onto the Idiocy Assumption" (107–108); the person who continues to disagree with me must simply lack the brain power to comprehend my view—in short, she or he is a dolt. And if the person holding a different view is shown not to be ignorant or an idiot, then we can always fall back on a third possibility—the person is clearly evil (the Evil Assumption, 108). "If we assume that people who are wrong are ignorant, idiotic, or evil—well, small wonder that we prefer not to confront the possibility of error in ourselves" (110).

At the risk of oversimplifying Schulz's amazingly eloquent treatise, we become, over time, so entrenched in our own beliefs and are so blithely unaware of it that being wrong actually feels like being right; "our sense of certainty is kindled by a feeling of knowing—that inner sensation that something just *is*" (163). This is deadly in the governance-as-leadership context where boards need to frame problems before they solve them, and make sense before they make decisions. If board members are more interested in asserting their own opinions and seeing things from one vantage point—their own, that is, the "right" one—than they are in exploring the views of others, seeing possibilities, and thinking in three modes, then practicing governance as leadership is impossible.

Being Certain

Medical doctor Robert Burton shed light on the "inner sensation" of knowing by describing being certain as "neither a conscious choice nor even a thought process. Certainty and similar states of 'knowing what we know' arise out of involuntary brain mechanisms that, like love or anger, function independently of reason" (Burton 2008, xiii). Case in point: the *Challenger* Study. The day after the 1986 *Challenger* shuttle accident, psychologist Ulric Neisser asked 106 students to write down precisely where they were and what they were doing when they first heard about it. Two and a half years later, he interviewed them about the event and found that 25 percent gave very different accounts; however, when confronted with their own documentation, many students defended their beliefs including one who said, "That's my handwriting, but that's not what happened" (Burton 2008, 11).

We perceive the external world through our physical senses and our internal world through our feelings—feeling about what is correct or incorrect and what is strange or familiar. Without these inner feelings of knowing, reported Burton, we would all be constantly plagued by inertia—a perpetual "yes, but" reel of self-questioning— precisely because we *can* reason. Our logical and rational mind would want to weigh all the alternatives present in any situation were it not for the almost automatic and unconscious trigger of the feeling of knowing.

Like Lehrer, Burton (2008) argued that because our brains hold rational *and* irrational thoughts we would be well served to "distinguish between felt knowledge— such as hunches and gut feelings—and knowledge that arises out of empirical testing" (220). "We can't afford to continue with the outdated claims of a perfectly rational unconscious or knowing when we can trust our gut feelings. We need to rethink the very nature of thought, including the recognition of how various perceptual limitations are inevitable" (221). However much we crave certainty, in fact, "know" that we are certain, and hate to be wrong, in Burton's opinion, "certainty is not biologically possible" (223) because "feelings of knowing, correctness, and certainty aren't deliberate and conscious choices. They are mental sensations that happen to us" (218).

Lehrer (2008) acknowledged, "While our instincts and emotions can be astonishingly prescient, they can also lead us to disaster. And a more deliberative style brings its own set of problems, such as losing sight of the most relevant information and even a debilitating indecisiveness." He contended that "the best decisions occur when people take the time to study their decision-making process, and not just the decision itself. The end result is decisions that are made in the right frame of mind." Certainty is seductive; it is built into the brain at a very basic level (Lehrer 2009):

It feels good to be certain. Confidence is comforting. This desire to always be right is a dangerous side effect of having so many competing brain regions inside one's head. While neural pluralism is a crucial virtue—the human mind can analyze any problem from a variety of different angles—it also make us insecure. You never know which brain area you should obey. It's not easy to make up your mind when your mind consists of so many competing parts. This is why being sure of something can be such a relief. The default state of the brain is indecisive disagreement; various mental parts are constantly insisting that the other parts are wrong. Certainty imposes consensus on this inner cacophony. It lets you pretend that your entire brain agrees with your behavior. You can now ignore those annoying fears and nagging suspicions, those statistical outliers and inconvenient truths. Being certain means that you aren't worried about being wrong. (210)

American historian James Harvey Robinson (1921) said, "Most of our so-called reasoning consists in finding arguments for going on believing as we already do" (15). In the context of the boardroom, effective consequential governance requires that board members suspend logic from time to time as they think playfully and get outside of their own mental models that may prevent them from seeing alternative frames and listening to opposing views. Given what we now know about certainty, this presents an enormous challenge.

Diagnosis Momentum

Being certain leads to still another problem—diagnosis momentum (Groopman 2007). Once a particular diagnosis becomes fixed in a physician's mind, despite incomplete evidence or discrepancies in evidence, it is difficult to change, and it becomes even more pronounced when one physician passes a diagnosis along to others. "Diagnosis momentum, like a boulder rolling down a mountain, gains enough force to crush anything in its way" (Groopman 2007, 128). Indeed, "Once a senior physician has fixed a label to the problem, it usually stays firmly attached" (154). In many medical cases, the senior physician is "usually right" but what if he or she is not? The problem is that once a diagnosis is determined, various treatments are recommended—and in medicine, if wrong, the outcome can be severe, even fatal. Although our boardroom decisions do not have such consequences, we should try to guard against diagnosis momentum—when a particularly outspoken, perhaps quite intelligent board member insists on the diagnosis of the problem and the board rushes into "fixing" it without anyone saying, "What if we're wrong about the definition of the problem?"

Latching on to an idea or solution is problematic in another way. The first decision we make in what will be a long stream of decisions has a big and oftentimes snowball effect. "The power of the first decision can have such a long-lasting effect that it will percolate into our future decisions for years to come. Given this effect, the first decision is crucial and we should give it an appropriate amount of attention" (Ariely 2008, 44).

Unfortunately, "We are particularly bad at revisiting our initial assessment of a situation—our initial frame," or diagnosis. This happens, in part, because of two "hardwired" processes for decision making: (1) the use of emotional tags and (2) pattern recognition. Emotional tagging occurs when emotional information attaches itself to thoughts and experiences stored in our memory; this in turn tells us whether to pay attention to something or not, and it tells us what sort of action we should be contemplating as a result (Campbell, Whitehead, and Finkelstein 2009, 63). Pattern recognition allows us to integrate information from as many as thirty different parts of the brain. We make assumptions based on prior experiences and judgments; "when we're dealing with seemingly familiar situations, our brains can cause us to think we understand them when we don't" (62). That is, we fit what we encounter into a preexisting pattern that allows us to take mental shortcuts that may work fine, but may also mislead us. Normally, we would think that familiarity, practice, and experience would lead to better decisions; however, sometimes just the opposite can occur. Studies have shown that airline pilots can become complacent when doing a seemingly routine landing at a very familiar airport. As one pilot noted in a NASA report (1995), "Misidentification of the runway was probably caused by my (our) failure to study the airport diagram prior to arrival. The oversight was probably caused by a feeling of familiarity (complacency)." Edward Tufte, noted expert on visual displays of data, conducted a pro bono study of airport runway maps and how runway incursions might be reduced with better maps reported that "pilots familiar with an airport often pay little attention to the taxi diagram (map)" (2006). Why? Their mental map takes over. We see what we expect to see and often miss the unexpected or out of place.

Many of us have watched the minute-long video clip on YouTube of kids in white T-shirts and black T-shirts passing a basketball. Viewers are asked to count the number of ball passes between white-shirted players. About 50 percent of viewers fail to notice that an actor in a gorilla suit walked into the center of the action, pounded his chest, and walked off the stage; in fact, he is there for a full seven seconds! A key takeaway from this experiment is the power of framing and focusing on the task at hand; if we're focused on something—or when we are told to look at something in a certain way—we often miss other important information. (Incidentally, though not unimportantly, this research has been used to examine why talking on cell phones leads to accidents, and why people driving a car often miss seeing motorcyclists, bicyclists, or pedestrians. Some of their limited cognitive capacity is diverted, in the former case, and in the latter, humans often simply ignore data that does not fit; for example, people in cars tend to be watching for other cars.)

Ultimately, the result of pattern recognition and emotional tagging means that, as mentioned earlier in the discussion of Burton's work, much of the mental work we do is unconscious, which makes it difficult to check the data and logic we use when we make a decision. "Compounding the problem of high levels of unconscious thinking is the lack of checks and balances in our decision making. Our brains do not naturally follow the classical textbook model: Lay out all the options, define the objectives, and assess each option against each objective. Instead, we analyze a situation using pattern recognition and arrive at a decision to act or not by using emotional tags. The two processes occur almost simultaneously . . . our brains leap to conclusions and are reluctant to consider alternatives" (Campbell et al. 2009, 63).

People often feel pressure to solve problems quickly, and so they minimize the time spent in diagnosis, collecting data, exploring possible interpretations, and analyzing alternative courses or action; they do not spend enough time on the big question, "What is *really* going on here?" (Heifetz, Grashow, and Linsky 2009, 7).

The single most important skill and most undervalued capacity for exercising adaptive leadership is diagnosis. In most companies and societies, those who have moved up the hierarchy into senior positions of authority are naturally socialized and trained to be good at taking action and decisively solving problems. There is no incentive to wade knee-deep into the murky waters of diagnosis, especially if some of the deeper diagnostic possibilities will be unsettling to people who look to you for clarity and certainty. Moreover, when you are caught up in the action, it is hard to do the diagnostic work of seeing the larger patterns in the organization or community. People who look to you for solutions have a stake in keeping you focused on what is right in front of your eyes: the phone calls and emails to be answered, the deadlines to be met, the tasks to be completed. (Heifetz, Grashow, and Linsky 2009, 7).

CEOs and board chairs must, therefore, be willing to take the risk associated with slowing down the diagnostic process and "actively resist the urge to suppress the argument" (Lehrer 2009, 218). Better to endure the rolling of the eyes and the "harrumphs" from the usual suspects than to jump to solutions of the wrong problem. Einstein is quoted as having said that if he had one hour to save the world he would spend fifty-five minutes defining the problem and only five minutes finding the solution; to paraphrase, it is better to have the right problem than the right solution.

Loss Aversion

Being proven wrong means that we have lost. Loss aversion refers to the finding that people strongly prefer avoiding losses to acquiring gains (Kahneman and Tversky 1979, 1984) and, in fact, make rather silly decisions as a result. This phenomenon occurs in part because of loss frames—if one alternative is framed in negative terms, we want to avoid it, even if it means exactly the same thing framed in positive terms. Two simple examples make the point. People prefer to buy meat that is labeled as 85 percent lean as opposed to 15 percent fat. People react differently to being told that a medical procedure has an 80 percent chance of saving your life versus a 20 percent chance of failure, resulting in death.

When individuals are confronted with an uncertain situation, they do not carefully evaluate alternatives or calculate probabilities or even do much thinking at all; instead, they rely on emotions, instincts, and mental shortcuts as a way of skipping thinking altogether (Kahneman and Tversky 1984). "The desire to avoid anything that smacks of loss often shapes our behavior, leading us to do foolish things," commented Lehrer (2009, 77); "you can't avoid loss aversion unless you know that the mind treats losses differently than gains" (250). This is one reason why thinking about thinking is so important and we have to guard against the belief that being wrong is tantamount to losing.

When making decisions we think we are in control but, more often than not, we act in "predictably irrational" ways (Ariely 2008). Even when we become aware of our flawed thought processes, once a decision has been made, or we form a belief, we are unlikely to change our mind. Why? "Once we take ownership of an idea . . . we love it perhaps more than we should. We prize it more than it's worth. And most frequently, we have trouble letting go of it because we can't stand the idea of its loss. What are we left with then? An ideology—rigid and unyielding" (Ariely 2008, 137–138).

Delusions of Rationality

From the ancient Greeks and Romans to today, we believe that humans are rational beings who, when faced with a decision, seek factual information, sift fact from fiction, use data, consciously analyze alternatives according to their various pros and cons, and deliberate critically before deciding. "There's only one problem with this assumption of human rationality: it's wrong" (Lehrer 2009, xv). The either-or nature of human thought does not serve us well. The truth of the matter is that humans have irrational *and* rational thoughts; sometimes they rely primarily on gut instinct and sometimes they rely on statistics and data. As Lehrer's chapter titles (2009) aptly describe, we can as easily be "Fooled by Feeling" (Chapter Three) as we can "Choke on Thought" (Chapter Five). The key is to see that "The Brain Is an Argument" (Chapter Seven) and to understand that "different brain areas think different things for different reasons . . . sometimes largely emotional" (2009, 198) and sometimes more rational. In the end, Lehrer argued that the best decision makers think as much about *how* they are making a decision as the decision itself (discussed previously as self-overhearing); we make better decisions when we consciously think about whether to rely on gut instincts or decide to override them.

"We are far less rational in our decision making than standard economic theory assumes. Our irrational behaviors are neither random not senseless—they are systematic and predictable" (Ariely 2008, 239). We only *think* we are rational: "Business decisions . . . are frequently based on hope or fear, what others seem to be doing, what senior leaders have done and believe has worked in the past, and their dearly held ideologies—in short, on lots of things other than the facts" (Pfeffer and Sutton 2006, 5).

Pfeffer and Sutton (2006) also observe:

- Benchmarking against others is far too casual. "The logic behind what works at top performers, why it works, and what will work elsewhere is barely unraveled, resulting in mindless imitation" (6).

- We all too easily do what has worked in the past even though the new situation is different from the past and "what we 'learned' was right in the past may have been wrong, or incomplete in the first place" (9).

- And, most problematic of all, we "are overly influenced by deeply held ideologies and beliefs," which cause us to adopt some practice "not because it is based on sound logic or hard facts but because managers 'believe' it works, or it matches their (sometimes flawed) assumptions" (10).

These behaviors are especially apparent when decision making occurs in the context of a threatening situation; it is then that stress and anxieties induce a rigid cognitive response on the part of individuals, known as threat rigidity. "People tend to draw upon deeply ingrained mental models of the environment that served them well in the past. Individuals also constrict their information gathering efforts, and they revert to the comfort of well-learned practices and routines. This cognitive rigidity impairs a leader's ability to surface and discuss a wide range of dissenting views" (Roberto 2005, 24). This can be especially problematic if thinking generatively feels threatening, or if changing how the board governs feels like a forced proposition.

How Governance as Leadership Helps

Fortunately, several aspects of the governance-as-leadership model can actually help mitigate the factors described so far. Being wrong and being certain have no place when the board is involved in sensemaking rather than decision making, or when the board is asking questions rather than demanding answers. Generative mode means that "great minds think differently." It's all about perceiving and grappling. Sensemaking and framing—first-guessing upstream rather than second-guessing downstream—can help boards avoid diagnosis momentum. The idea with framing, after all, is to help ensure making the best diagnosis before treatment is applied. By working at the boundaries of the organization, the board is aware of the relevant views of various constituents, which also, if considered, helps ensure a better diagnosis and treatment plan. The context is more about win-win than loss. And the idea is to suspend Robert's Rules of Order and logic, as the board plays with concepts and ideas.

COGNITIVE BIASES AND BOARD WORKAROUNDS

Beyond these basic aspects of human nature, fully manifested in hedgehogs, everyone is subject to a variety of mental shortcuts and errors. Cognitive biases are mental errors caused by simplified information processing strategies that can affect critical thinking, board dynamics, performance, and decision making. The most common and relevant are these: (1) anchoring, arbitrary coherence (Exhibit 3.2), and ordering; (2) framing and loss aversion; (3) confirmation bias and cognitive conservatism; (4) false consensus bias; and (5) bounded awareness.

In the next sections I describe each bias and provide board examples, tools, and techniques to work around or through the issues. Importantly, it is impossible to completely avoid cognitive biases; but the more informed the board is, and the more consciously board members deliberate, the better the chances that someone will notice the potential for biases when they have crept into the discussions, and the board can talk about how to handle the situation. The more the board practices thinking and working in the three modes, the better its discernment will be, not only of the issues but also of the processes affecting governance.

Anchoring, Arbitrary Coherence, and Ordering

Anchoring is whatever serves as the base or reference point for what comes after. Anchors are "sticky" in that, once fixed in our minds, it is difficult to adjust from them at all or very far from them. "Analysts tend not to adjust from their starting point," as manifested by "analysts failing to account fully for situation-specific factors that make the likely magnitude of an event distant from that of past cases" (Woocher 2008, 408).

Arbitrary coherence means that we can set an anchor in people's minds in a completely arbitrary fashion; it may have absolutely nothing to do with the decision at hand, but it will be utilized and stick nonetheless. Shockingly, "irrelevant anchors affect peoples' estimates even where they know the anchor is not relevant" (Woocher 2008, 408). Because of anchoring, the order of information in a decision situation is also important; what comes first sets the tone and direction (see Exhibit 3.2).

Exhibit 3.2: Anchoring and Arbitrary Coherence in Action

Subjects are asked to write down the last two digits of their social security number. They are then asked whether they would pay this number in dollars for a bottle of Côtes du Rhône, 1998. *Would the mere suggestion of the last two digits of your social security number affect how much you would pay for the wine? Of course not, right? Wrong.*

In the experiment, a bottle of the wine is held up, its flavor is described, and subjects are told that it has received 86 points from *Wine Spectator*. Another wine, Hermitage Jaboulet La Chapelle, 1996, is displayed and described as being the "finest vintage since 1990," with a 92-point rating from *Wine Advocate* magazine and of which only 8,100 cases were made.

Subjects are then shown several other items including a cordless trackball, a cordless keyboard and mouse, a book on graphic design, and a box of Belgian chocolates and given a sheet of paper with all the items listed. Everyone is asked to write down the last two digits of their social security number on the page and then to write them again next to every item, adding a dollar sign to the numbers.

They are asked then to say—yes or no—whether they would pay that amount for each item, and then to jot down the maximum they would pay for each. In the experiment, whoever had the highest bid paid that for the item and took it with them.

When everyone was asked whether writing down the last two digits of their social security number in any way influenced their bids, they all dismissed that as preposterous.

However, when the data were analyzed, the results were quite clear. Participants with the highest ending number (from 80–99) bid highest, while those with the lowest ending numbers (from 1–20) bid lowest. The top 20 percent bid an average of $56 for the cordless keyboard; the bottom 20 percent bid an average of $16.

Those with the highest SS digits bid 216 to 346 percent more, on average, than those with the lowest SS digits (Ariely 2008).

"The significance of this is that once participants were willing to pay a certain price for one product, their willingness to pay for other items in the same product category were judged relative to that first price (the anchor)" (Ariely 2008, 29). Other experiments showed how difficult it is to budge from a first anchor that is set in our minds. Without conscious cultivation, "the first evidence we encounter will remain the last word on the truth" and "once that initial evidence takes hold, we are off and running. No matter how skewed it may be, it will form the basis for all our future beliefs. Inductive reasoning guarantees as much" (Schulz 2010, 132).

The Anchoring Cognitive Bias Applied to Boards

The anchoring cognitive bias, along with its associated issues of stickiness and arbitrariness, is troublesome to boards as they deliberate all sorts of issues because whatever number, strategy, problem statement, or solution is first thrown into a discussion drives the conversation. This is one reason why the quickest (and often the most outspoken) board members are able to steer the direction of board discussions and, thereby, affect the outcome.

Approaches to Dealing with the Anchoring Bias

- Have board members ask questions, rather than make declarative statements, as they think about an issue. Doing this in small groups is a good idea so to avoid even a single question driving what the entire board thinks.

- Have silent starts (Chait, Ryan, and Taylor 2005). Before the start of a major discussion, have board members anonymously write on an index card the most important question the board and management should consider relevant to the issue at hand. Collect and randomly distribute the cards. Have each board member read his or her card aloud. Board members are asked to raise their hand if they have a similar thought on their card, allowing a running tally. Continue until all the views are shared. This process effectively removes the anchoring effect in which the discussion all follows from the first statement uttered, and helps the board identify the questions most important to the most members, and to hear each other's individual thoughts.

- If there are multiple proposals, or alternatives, that the board is considering in small groups, ensure that each group deliberates a different one. If the organization wants all of the groups to deliberate each option, reorder them so that the same option is not always addressed first. Not only does this guard against the anchoring bias, it also helps ensure that all the questions will be fully addressed by at least one group.

- If the situation requires that the conversation begins with an explicit anchor, it is a good idea to provide context for that starting point by stating its origin, the thinking behind it; that is, to make assumptions explicit.

Framing and Loss Aversion

Framing, in the cognitive bias context, has to do with the language we use to describe a situation, which then shapes how we think about it and how we decide. We are typically unaware of how framing shapes our decisions because the "thinking" is automatic and below conscious thought. Loss aversion (our propensity to place a greater value on loss than on gains) is related to framing because if something is described in terms of loss—framed as a loss—we are more likely to act. For example, we are more likely to replace the windows in our home when told that we are "losing" money by not doing so than when we are told that we will "save" money by doing so (even though the decision is exactly the same). We prefer the status quo over a 50/50 chance for positive or negative alternatives with the same absolute value, and we prefer to avoid a certain loss in favor of a potential loss, even if we risk losing significantly more (Woocher 2008).

However useful frames may be for simplifying complex problems, they constrain the range of options that are considered and distort how people interpret data (Roberto 2005).

The Framing and Loss Aversion Biases Applied to Boards

These issues apply to board members in almost every setting; whether in committees or operating as a full board, board members are asked to interpret data, assess risks, and make decisions. How those conversations and decisions are framed can shape the outcomes significantly (a key point underlying the governance-as-leadership framework).

Approaches to dealing with the framing and loss aversion biases

- Have generative discussions. Framing is at the heart of generative discussions during which boards take time to decide how to cast an issue, problem, or opportunity. The very act of declaring something as a "problem" versus an "opportunity" sets the frame, shapes how people approach the issue, how they think about it, and how they eventually decide the issue. For example, when a university board met in 2008, it posed these questions for board discussion: "What sense do we make of the economic downturn? What does it mean for us? What are the 'hidden' opportunities the downturn presents?"
- Even when problems or opportunities have been framed, it makes sense to ask, "Before we go a lot further on this, how else might we look at this? Are we all agreed on the *framing* of the issue?"

Confirmation Bias and Cognitive Conservatism

Confirmation bias occurs when individuals interpret ambiguous information in ways that conform to their starting position, seek confirmatory evidence for what they think is true, and fail to search for disconfirming evidence. Confirmation bias is bolstered by the fact that looking for counterevidence requires time, energy . . . and "sufficient social capital to weather the suspicion and derision of the defenders of the status quo" (Schulz 2010, 130). In addition, when we do see counterevidence, we decide that it has no bearing on the validity of our beliefs (Schulz 2010). Experimental psychologists have shown that we apply more stringent standards to evidence that challenges our prejudices than to evidence that reinforces them (Tetlock 2005).

Cognitive conservatism is a close cousin of confirmation bias; it refers to our natural reluctance to admit mistakes or update beliefs (Tetlock 2005); and the more set we are in our beliefs, the more difficult it will be to change them.

The Confirmation Bias and Cognitive Conservatism Applied to Boards

These two biases are typical of, and indeed they define, the thinking of hedgehogs and boardroom lions. Busy board members only have so much time to devote to thinking about the materials sent in advance of meetings; for many, the best they give them is a cursory glance. Often, board members enter the boardroom having already made up their minds and no amount of information or discussion will sway them.

Approaches to dealing with confirmation bias and cognitive conservatism

- Practice predecisional accountability (Lerner and Tetlock 1999, 2002) whereby the board is told that two board members will be randomly selected to explain a decision about to be made at a board meeting to an unknown constituency waiting outside. This process not only helps with confirmation bias and cognitive conservatism, it is also a great "ego-leveler" because when board members are expected to justify their judgments, they want to avoid appearing foolish in front of an audience. They consider a wider range of views, listen more carefully, deliberate more fully, pay greater attention to various cues and clues, anticipate counter arguments, weight the merits with greater impartiality, and practice better metacognition prior to making a decision. Suddenly, the hedgehog is not quite so certain.

- Engage board members high on the generative curve. It is at that stage that board members are more likely to be especially thoughtful and even self-critical; it is at the diagnostic and framing stage where there is no known "accepted" view or perspective on the matter. There is no "evidence"—confirmatory or otherwise.

- Role play. "Ask subsets of the board to assume the perspective of different constituent groups likely to be affected by the issue at hand. How would these stakeholders frame the issue and define a successful outcome? What would each group regard as a worst-case scenario?" (Chait, Ryan, and Taylor 2005, 129).

- Advocacy panels and debates. Just as role playing makes board members think from a different point of view, so do panel discussion and debates. For example, if there are three alternatives under consideration, divide the board randomly into three groups; have each group convene to generate their best thinking to advocate for that alternative. Similarly, boards can form smaller groups to debate a topic.

False Consensus Bias

We fall prey to false consensus bias when we project the way we think onto everyone else and assume that everyone else must certainly agree with us. It can occur in groups when no one speaks up to challenge the prevailing view (more on groupthink and conformity later). However, "good decisions rarely arise from false consensus. Alfred P. Sloan, the chairman of General Motors in its heyday, once adjourned a board meeting soon after it began. 'Gentlemen,' Sloan said, 'I take it we are all in agreement on the decision here . . . then I must propose we postpone further discussion of this matter until our next meeting to give ourselves time to develop disagreement and perhaps gain some understanding of what the decision is all about'" (Lehrer 2009, 218).

The False Consensus Bias Applied to Boards

Whether because of congeniality, habit, time constraints, or groupthink, almost every organization faces the issue of false consensus bias. Before taking a vote, the CEO or chair wonders if apparent consensus is real or not.

Approaches to Dealing with False Consensus Bias

A board could certainly do as Sloan did; however, most nonprofit boards do not meet as frequently as corporate boards, so this solution might not be practical. Akin to having a triple-helix conversation, Charan (2001) suggested an effective strategy to avoid false consensus bias is to engage in *decisive dialogue*—"a process of intellectual inquiry rather than of advocacy, a search for truth rather than a contest" (76). Four characteristics mark an effective decisive dialogue:

1. Openness: There is no predetermined outcome; there is an honest search for alternatives. Questions like "What are we missing?" draw people in and signal interest in hearing all sides.

2. Candor: A willingness to speak the unspeakable, to expose what needs to be exposed, to air the conflicts that undermine consensus. People express their true opinions, not just what they think the group wants to hear.

3. Informality: Formality suppresses candor. Carefully scripted, formal presentations signal that an outcome is preordained. Informality encourages candor and reduces defensiveness. Group members feel more comfortable asking questions and reacting honestly.

4. Closure: Although informality is good for drawing everyone into a conversation, closure is needed to impose discipline. At the end of the meeting, everyone should know what was decided and what will happen next as a result, including who needs to do what by when.

Bounded Awareness

As the previous gorilla video example demonstrated, we see what we expect to see and miss the rest because of bounded awareness, a phenomenon that causes people to ignore critical information when making decisions. Learning to expand the limits of one's awareness before making an important choice will save us from asking, "How did I miss that?" What we see and consider in any given decision situation is bounded by "cognitive blinders" (Bazerman and Chugh 2006, 90) that prevent us from seeing, seeking, using, or sharing highly relevant, easily accessible, and readily perceivable information during the decision making process.

Failure to See Information.   There are several reasons why we fail to see information. First, focus limits our awareness. We overlook what we are not expecting. The Bazerman and Chugh (2006) article highlights a video similar to the gorilla one mentioned earlier about two teams in different colored jerseys passing a basketball into the midst of which a woman carrying an open umbrella walks. When people are focused on counting the number of passes, only 21 percent notice the woman; but when people have no such assignment, they see the woman. In another study, researchers Wolfe, Horowitz, and Kenner recreated in a lab the process of screening bags for weapons at airports.

Participants screened bags for dangerous objects after having been told how often those objects would appear. When they were told that the objects would appear 50 percent of the time, they had an error rate of just 7 percent; but when told that objects would appear only 1 percent of the time, the error rate jumped to 30 percent. "Since people didn't expect to see the objects, they stopped looking for them—or as Wolfe explains, 'If you don't see it often, you often don't see it'" (Bazerman and Chugh 2006, 91).

Second, we do not typically notice gradual changes. In yet another version of the gorilla and the basketball players on YouTube, "The Monkey Business Illusion" by Daniel Simon, the curtain behind them shifts subtly from red to orange; very few notice. One player in a black T-shirt actually leaves the game. Even fewer notice that. The researchers (Chabris and Simons 2010) call this unintentional blindness and the illusion of attention.

Third, we may see what is there, but fail to note what is *not* there. The study of radiologists discussed previously is revealing on this matter of bounded awareness. One film of the sixty was of a patient who is missing his left clavicle. Sixty percent of the radiologists failed to note the missing bone. When informed with more clinical data—that the x-rays were obtained as part of an annual physical, which primary care physicians perform in order to screen for serious diseases like lung cancer—58 percent of the radiologists still missed it and scored the film as normal. When they were told that the chest x-rays were obtained as part of a series of studies to find a cancer, 83 percent noted the missing bone. The radiologists' performance improved when they were provided specific clinical clues, rather than simply relying on a flash impression (Groopman 2007, 180).

Failure to Seek Information.   In addition to not seeing information that is presented to us, we often fail to seek information in the first place. "The *Challenger* disaster provides a tragic example of failing to seek relevant information. The day before the disaster, executives at NASA argued about whether the combination of low temperature and the O-ring failure would be a problem. But because no clear connection emerged between low temperatures and the O-rings in the seven prior launches when O-ring damage had occurred, they chose to continue on schedule. Tragically, the decision makers did not seek out the temperature for the 17 shuttle launches in which there was no O-ring failure. The data set of all 24 launches would have unambiguously pointed to the need to delay *Challenger.* Later analyses suggest that, given the low temperature, the probability of disaster exceeded 99 percent" (Bazerman and Chugh 2006, 92).

The problem is, we typically seek out information at hand, and we do not typically seek information that would argue against our preexisting view, preferring instead confirming evidence (confirmation bias). "Seeking disconfirming information is a powerful problem-solving approach, but it is rarely a part of our intuitive strategies" (Bazerman and Chugh 2006, 93).

Failure to Use and Share Information.   It is not uncommon to literally drown in data; when this happens, little of it will be used effectively. In addition, success can breed carelessness about existing information. However, research has shown that decision-making groups can benefit from pooling members' information, "particularly when members have partial and biased information but collectively can compose an unbiased characterization of decision alternatives" (Stasser and Titus 1985, 1467). Group members commonly fail to effectively pool their unique information because discussion is typically dominated by the information members hold in common before the discussion and information that supports members' existent preferences (Stasser and Titus 1985). Furthermore, the focus on already shared information increases as the group size increases (Stasser, Taylor, and Hanna 1989).

One reason group members do not share unique information is that it is simply easier to discuss common information; also common information is more positively rewarded as others chime in with their support (Bazerman and Chugh 2006, 96). But another, more troublesome reason for not sharing is that "the bearer of unique information, like the bearer of bad news, incurs some social costs . . . these social costs may include the necessity of establishing the credibility and relevance of the unique information" (Stasser and Titus 2003, 308). To compound the matter still more, lower-status group members feel an especially heavy burden in social costs related to surfacing private information (Larsen, Christensen, Abbott, and Franz 1996). In contrast, when the bearer of unique information was labeled an expert, the group seemingly paid more attention to the information (Stasser and Titus 2003, 308).

Overcoming Bounded Group Awareness

Although groups have an advantage over individuals because they collectively possess more information than any one person, groups are bounded by the information that becomes part of the group discussion (Bazerman and Moore 2009). Groups tend to "focus more on shared information (information previously known to all group members) than on unique or unshared information (information previously known by only one group member)" (Bazerman and Moore 2009, 50–51).

In order to overcome group bounded awareness, researchers Stasser, Vaughn, and Stewart (2000) suggest informing the group in advance of the unique knowledge of different members and identifying expertise in the group before discussions begin. The central idea is to make information known to individuals explicit to the group before the group deliberates rather than while discussions are already under way. At that stage, information can too readily be ignored or seen as self-serving to the individual rather than as relevant to the decision at hand.

Bazerman and Chugh (2006, 93) recommended several other steps that groups can take to seek, see, share, and use information, all of which should resonate with boards:

- Know what you're looking for and train your eyes by asking questions like, "What if our strategy is wrong?" "How would we know?" Simply asking the questions forces groups to pay attention to what is typically outside of the group's awareness.

- Develop (or pay for) an outsider's perspective. Insiders tend to see what they always see, while outsiders see other important and critical factors.

- Challenge the absence of disconfirming data. "Receiving recommendations without contradictory data is a red flag indicating that your team members are falling prey to bounded awareness. Assign someone to play the role of devil's inquisitor" (93).

- Undersearch in most contexts, but oversearch in important contexts. If the decision context is one in which an error would be extremely difficult to recover from, oversearch for information.

- Unpack the situation. Consciously consider the full decision context to ensure that the group is not overemphasizing one focal point and discounting others.

- Assume the information needed exists within the organization. It typically does and approaching it with that mindset helps ensure that the relevant information will be discovered.

- Everyone has unique information; ask for it explicitly. Meeting agendas should require relevant updates. If individuals are reluctant to be forthcoming about controversial or unpopular information, allow anonymous input.

- Create structures that make information sharing the default.

The authors encourage groups to locate useful information outside their bounds of awareness by simply asking, "Why not?" After all, the status quo is only a given as long as we accept it and fail to question our commonly accepted assumptions about the way things are or how things work. "We must learn to actively combat our inductive biases: to deliberately seek out evidence that challenges our beliefs and to take seriously such evidence when we come across it" (Schulz 2010, 131).

The cognitive biases discussed here apply not only to individuals confronting decision-making situations, but also to groups like boards. In addition to the phenomena and complications of bounded group awareness, boards face several other issues that may affect group behavior, process, and performance. At one end of the dysfunction spectrum is social loafing, where not all participants pull their own weight, and at the other is groupthink, where everyone goes along to get along; both are destructive to group performance.

SOCIAL LOAFING

Social loafing—also called the "free-rider" theory—is the tendency of people to put forth less effort when they are part of a group than when they are individually accountable. Researchers Steven Karau and Kipling Williams's meta-analysis (1993) of seventy-eight studies showed that social loafing is robust and generalizes across various tasks and populations. A German psychologist named Ringelmann conducted an unpublished study where he asked people to pull as hard as they could on a rope, alone or with one, two, or seven others, and used a strain gauge to measure how hard they pulled. He found that dyads pulled 93 percent of the sum of their individual efforts, trios at 85 percent, and groups of eight at only 49 percent (Latané, Williams, and

Harkins 2006, 298). Some argued that the reduction in effort was not the result of social loafing but instead a result of coordination problems or group inefficiency. To see what was actually happening, Ingham and colleagues first replicated Ringelmann's study. In a second experiment, individuals were blindfolded and led to believe that others were pulling with them, but in fact, they were always pulling alone. Similar results were found: people pulled at 90 percent their alone rate when they thought one other person was also pulling, and at 85 percent with two to six others believed to be pulling (301).

Social loafing is more likely to occur when: (1) individual effort and outputs cannot be determined or evaluated; (2) the task is not meaningful; (3) there is no comparison group; (4) members feel their inputs are redundant; (5) members expect the other group members to perform well without their input; and (6) the group is large.

Ways to preventing social loafing:

- Ensure that the task is challenging, appealing, and involving. Work high on the generative curve or work that gets the group into "flow" (Chapter One) tends to engage everyone.

- Build the board's capacity for team play (the subject of the next chapter).

- Form smaller work groups because it is tougher to hide with fewer people working on an issue.

- Practice predecisional accountability so board members understand that they might be called upon to explain the group's decision.

GROUPTHINK

Most everyone has heard of groupthink and has experienced it firsthand. It occurs when a cohesive group fails to consider alternatives in a decision-making situation in order to preserve group harmony. The group's desire to minimize conflict and reach a consensus decision is so strong that independent thinking is overlooked and overridden (Janis 1972). Some common conditions for groupthink are: (1) an amiable, cohesive group; (2) relative isolation of the group from dissenting viewpoints; and (3) a directive leader who signals the "right" decision—the one he or she favors. Groups are also more prone to groupthink when: (1) they are going through a particularly stressful period of time; (2) they have suffered a recent failure or major setback; (3) the decision-making task is especially arduous; or (4) the decision involves moral dilemmas.

But any group can fall victim to groupthink. It arises not only from disproportionate exposure to support for the group's beliefs, underexposure to the opposition, and a tendency to discount that opposition even if it is encountered, but also from the "suppression of doubt or differences of opinion within a community" (Schulz 2010, 153). Suppression can be subtle or self-imposed, such as shying away from anything seen as disruptive to the group, or overt and deliberate, as when enforced through ostracism or exile (153).

The primary symptoms of groupthink are: illusions of invulnerability and unanimity; unquestioned belief in the group's morality; rationalization; stereotyped views of the "opponents"; pressure to conform to the group; self-censorship of ideas that vary from the group's; and "mind-guarding," which occurs when some members protect the group from information that would call into question the effectiveness or morality of its decisions.

Ways to prevent groupthink:

- Leaders (the CEO and board chair) should take a neutral stance instead of stating preferences and expectations for outcomes at the start of the deliberation process (Janis 1971).

- Assign devil's advocates (who make counterarguments) and devil's inquisitors (who ask questions) (Bazerman and Chugh 2006, 93).

- Break the board into small groups to work on the same problem and then reconvene to discuss each group's deliberations. Then, examine all realistic alternatives. Ideally, allow key constituents not on the board to weigh in.

- Invite outside experts into the meeting to act as a sounding board and ensure that other perspectives are given full consideration.

- After reaching a preliminary consensus about what seems to be the best course of action, hold a "second-chance" meeting at which every member expresses as vividly as she or he can, all of her or his residual doubts, and rethinks the entire issue before making a definitive choice (Janis 1971).

The Abilene Paradox

The Abilene Paradox (Harvey 1988; Exhibit 3.3) is a common form of groupthink in which a group of people collectively decide on a course of action that is counter to the preferences of any individual in the group.

Exhibit 3.3: The Abilene Paradox

The July afternoon in Coleman, Texas (population 5,607), was particularly hot—104 degrees according to the Walgreen's Rexall thermometer. In addition, the wind was blowing fine-grained West Texas topsoil through the house. But the afternoon was still tolerable—even potentially enjoyable. A fan was stirring the air on the back porch; there was cold lemonade; and finally, there was entertainment. Dominoes. Perfect for the conditions. The game required little more physical exertion than an occasional mumbled comment, "Shuffle 'em," and an unhurried movement of the arm to place the tiles in the appropriate perspective on the table. All in all, it had the makings of an agreeable

Sunday afternoon in Coleman. That is, until my father-in-law suddenly said, "Let's get in the car and go to Abilene and have dinner at the cafeteria."

I thought, "What, go to Abilene? Fifty-three miles? In this dust storm and heat? And in a 1958 Buick with no air conditioning?"

But my wife chimed in with, "Sounds like a great idea. I'd like to go. How about you, Jerry?"

Since my own preferences were obviously out of step with the rest, I replied, "Sounds good to me," and added, "I just hope your mother wants to go."

"Of course I want to go," said my mother-in-law. "I haven't been to Abilene in a long time."

So into the car and off to Abilene we went. My predictions were fulfilled. The heat was brutal. Perspiration had cemented a fine layer of dust to our skin by the time we arrived. The cafeteria's food could serve as a first-rate prop in an antacid commercial.

Some four hours and 106 miles later, we returned to Coleman, hot and exhausted. We silently sat in front of the fan for a long time. Then, to be sociable and to break the silence, I dishonestly said, "It was a great trip, wasn't it?"

No one spoke.

Finally my mother-in-law said, with some irritation, "Well, to tell the truth, I really didn't enjoy it much and would rather have stayed here. I just went along because the three of you were so enthusiastic about going. I wouldn't have gone if you all hadn't pressured me into it."

I couldn't believe it. "What do you mean 'you all'?" I said. "Don't put me in the 'you all' group. I was delighted to be doing what we were doing. I didn't want to go. I only went to satisfy the rest of you. You're the culprits."

My wife looked shocked. "Don't call me a culprit. You and Daddy and Mama were the ones who wanted to go. I just went along to keep you happy. I would have had to be crazy to want to go out in the heat like that."

Her father entered the conversation with one word: "Shee-it." He then expanded on what was already absolutely clear: "Listen, I never wanted to go to Abilene. I just thought you might be bored. You visit so seldom I wanted to be sure you enjoyed it. I would have preferred to play another game of dominoes and eat the leftovers in the icebox."

After the outburst of recrimination, we all sat back in silence. Here we were, four reasonably sensible people who—of our own volition—had just taken a 106-mile trip across a godforsaken desert in furnace-like heat and a dust storm to eat unpalatable food at a hole-in-the-wall cafeteria in Abilene, when none of us had really wanted to go. To be concise, we'd done just the opposite of what we wanted to do. The whole situation simply didn't make sense.

Because no one is completely forthcoming or honest about the choice at hand, each member of the group believes that their own preference is counter to the group's and, therefore, does not raise the objection. By not "wishing to make waves," or "rock the boat," each individual does nothing and the group makes a bad decision about which no one is happy.

Social Conformity

Another prevalent problem with groups is social conformity—changing one's opinions or behavior as a result of real or imagined group pressure (Asch 1955; Aronson and Aronson 2007). In the Asch experiments, 123 Swarthmore College students were asked to participate in a "psychological experiment" in visual judgment. All but one participant in each testing group of 7 to 9 were confederates (who knew the true aims of the study) of the experimenter; the study was to see how the one "naïve" member of each group would react to the behavior of the confederates. Subjects are shown two side-by-side line drawings (see Figure 3.1).

The card on the left has the reference line and the one on the right shows the three comparison lines. Study participants were asked to say which of the three lines (A, B, or C) on the second card matched the line on the first card. In each round, the naïve subject answered last or second to last. For the first two trials, everyone gives the obvious, correct answer. On the third trial, the confederates give the same wrong answer. Over the course of eighteen trials, the confederates answered incorrectly for twelve, known as the "critical trials." The goal was to see if the naïve respondent would change his answer to conform to what the others said, even though his eyes were telling him it was wrong.

FIGURE 3.1 *Sample Cards in the Asch "Line Experiment"*

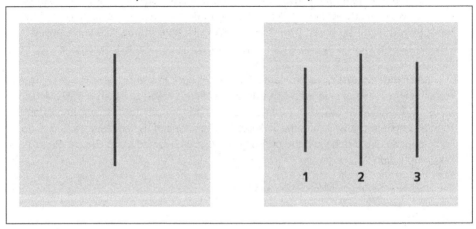

Source: Asch 1955.

Only 25 percent of the naïve participants did not conform on any trial; 75 percent conformed at least once and 5 percent conformed every time. On average, the minority subjects swung to acceptance of the majority's wrong judgments 37 percent of the time. The size of the majority mattered. When the naïve individual was confronted with only one person who contradicted his answers, he continued to answer independently and correctly. But when the opposition increased to two, the pressure to conform increased and minority subjects accepted the wrong answer 14 percent of the time. Under the pressure of a majority of three, the subjects' errors jumped to 32 percent. In subsequent tests, Asch found that the presence of one other supporting participant to the naïve individual depleted the majority of much of its power.

Conformity is not just an issue among families or college students. Sonnenfeld (2002) cautioned that even though boards are composed of directors who are "almost without exception, intelligent, accomplished, and comfortable with power . . . [and] if you put them in a group that discourages dissent, they nearly always start to conform. The ones that don't often self-select out" (111).

Whether the board of Albright College fell prey to groupthink, the Abilene Paradox, or social conformity does not matter so much as that the next example demonstrates how a board can reverse a course of action through thoughtful, albeit sometimes uncomfortable, deliberations.

Example 7: Albright College Board

Albright recently celebrated the grand opening of a "new" science center, a $35 million, 78,000-square-foot facility that includes the total gut renovation of the old 1929 building and a 1965 wing, plus the addition of a four-story, 41,000-square-foot state-of-the-art laboratory and undergraduate research building that was dedicated as Trustee Hall on the faculty's suggestion to recognize the extraordinary leadership of the board in making this long-deferred dream come true.

What is especially interesting about this achievement is the back story that reveals a board's ability to rethink and reverse a prior decision about the building's location after it had been designed. The president explained that when he took office, the plan was to build the science center on the corner of the main street that runs through campus, and attach it to the college's Memorial Chapel—a move that would have destroyed one of the most lovely tree-filled greens on campus. "It was an unpopular decision for some who felt it had been rammed through without sufficient deliberation or sensitivity to those who were objecting. They simply felt shouted down."

Despite the dismay of many about the location, no one—he and his wife included, having so recently arrived on campus—wanted to "upset the apple cart."

However, as the plans developed, the scope and scale of the building was outstripping the college's ability to finance it. The president suggested to the board that a new

(continued)

question be raised with the architects, "Rather than constructing another monumental building, how can we meet our desired academic objectives in the most cost-effective manner?" The architects suggested a gut-renovation of the old building and a major addition that would more than double the total size of the science center. The president noted that he discovered no feasible financial plan for the renovation of the old science building, but using it for academic purposes was part of the long-range plan. "So even if we could figure out how to afford the planned new building, which had grown to something like 90,000 square feet, we would still have a very old, dilapidated former science building and no funds with which to renovate it. It would be in danger of becoming a shell of its former stately self and another patched-up, broken-down structure with hundreds of thousands of dollars in deferred maintenance."

The president continued, "The board wrestled with the options in several sessions and finally came down on the side of the proposed addition/renovation, which we've now completed. I don't think this could have happened without the previous work the board had done on best practices and improved governance. It was a difficult decision and tantamount to reversing itself. It was interesting how many folks, including some board members, said how relieved and pleased they were that the initial plans had been abandoned." Not long afterwards, Albright completed a new campus master plan. The firm that did the plan pointed out the beauty and importance of the "Great Lawn," and made it a key component of the plan. "We never called it the 'Great Lawn' before, but you can be sure we do now," remarked the president.

Cascades (Social, Informational, and Reputational) and Group Polarization (Risky Shift)

These phenomena have been linked to yet another pervasive mental shortcut—the availability heuristic—whereby the perceived likelihood of any given event is tied to the ease with which its occurrence can be brought to mind (Kuran and Sunstein 1999, 685). The use of the availability heuristic is one reason, for example, why most people rate the chance of death by homicide higher than the chance of death by stomach cancer, even though death by stomach cancer is five times higher than death by homicide.

Because public discourse triggers the availability heuristic, social cascading occurs whereby collective beliefs—right or wrong—are formed and reinforced; a chain reaction is triggered that gives the perception of increasing plausibility. An informational cascade occurs when people with incomplete information base their own beliefs on the apparent beliefs of others (Kuran and Sunstein 1999). People follow the views of the opinion leaders and then others follow the followers (Sunstein 2003). With a reputational cascade, the motivation to accept the views of others stems from seeking social approval and avoiding disapproval. "In seeking to achieve their reputational objectives, people take to speaking and acting as if they share, or at least do not reject, what they view as the dominant belief" (Kuran and Sunstein 1999, 686–687). The consequence of these cascades is that group thoughts, attitudes, beliefs, and ultimately decisions are moved along not based on relevant facts, but purely because of the momentum of the discussion. A number of people appear to support a certain course of action simply because others appear to do so (Sunstein 2000). Cascades are also problematic when a series of decisions are being made because each subsequent decision is made in lemming-like fashion based on previous decisions which may have less validity than presumed.

Cascades also lead to group polarization—among the most robust patterns found in deliberating bodies (Sunstein 2002)—which occurs as group members come under the joint influence of their common group membership and beliefs. Collective decisions made under those influences can become more extreme than the position of any individual member of the group. Researchers have found that group decisions can become more risky (known as *risky shift*) or more cautious because of attitude polarization.

More generally, these shifts in thinking that occur as group members converse have become known as *choice shifts* because not all decisions where this occurs involve risk. A choice shift is said to occur when, after a group's interaction on an issue, the mean final opinion of group members differs from the members' mean initial opinion. Noah Friedkin (1999) showed that choice shift is the product of the group's social structure in which certain members have more influence than others during the opinion formation process; often, the opinions and decisions of a group shift toward the most confident or socially powerful member.

AVOIDING GROUPTHINK AND ITS CLOSE COUSINS

In order for boards to bypass the Abilene Paradox, problems of social conformity, and cascades (and related problems) they need to (1) resist the urge to suppress debate; (2) engage in dialogue and discussion; and (3) learn.

Resist the Urge to Suppress Debate

"Bad decisions happen when the mental debate is cut short" (Lehrer 2009, 247). Although it is human nature to resist cognitive dissonance (the discomfort of holding conflicting ideas simultaneously), or to let emotions rule the day (rather than spending more time going through a rational decision-making process), better decision making occurs when we let the debate continue. "The only way to counteract the bias for certainty is to encourage some inner dissonance. We must force ourselves to think about the information we don't want to think about, to pay attention to data that disturbs our entrenched beliefs" (Lehrer 2009, 217). Lehrer's advice is to: (1) always entertain competing hypotheses: "When you force yourself to interpret the facts through a different lens, you often discover that your beliefs rest on a rather shaky foundation" (247); and (2) continually remind yourself of what you don't know. As Lehrer reminds us,

Colin Powell is noted for saying to his intelligence officers: "Tell me what you know. Then tell me what you don't know, and only then can you tell me what you think" (248).

Resisting the urge to suppress debate will lead to better thinking and ultimately to better decisions. Remember hedgehogs and foxes? And being certain? The problem with thinking like a hedgehog is that "he is prone to bouts of certainty—the big idea is irrefutable—and this certainty causes him to misinterpret the evidence. If the amygdala [the part of the brain that regulates emotional responses, including fear] contradicts one of his conclusions . . . then the amygdala is turned off. Useful information is deliberately ignored. The inner argument is badly argued" (Lehrer 2009, 242). A better approach is that of the fox who is "skeptical of grand strategies and unifying theories. The fox accepts ambiguity and takes an ad hoc approach when coming up with explanations. The fox gathers data from a wide variety of sources and listens to a diversity of brain areas. The upshot is that the fox makes better predictions and decisions. . . . Because foxes pay attention to their inner disagreements, they are less vulnerable to the seductions of certainty" (Lehrer 2009, 242–243).

Because individual mental debate is crucial to critical thinking, it is in the best interest of organizations to help ensure that board members: (a) have time for mental debate well prior to board meetings, and (b) understand that spending time thinking prior to the meeting is part of what is expected of board members.

Engage in Dialogue and Discussion

Intellectual diversity in groups leads to better decisions, but only if real dialogue occurs during meetings. The purpose of dialogue is not to decide, but to strive to understand; "in dialogue, people become observers of their own thinking" and they "begin to observe the collective nature of thought" (Senge 1990, 242). The fifth habit of highly effective people described by Covey (1989) is that they "seek first to understand, then to be understood" (235). Covey continues, "We typically seek first to be understood. Most people do not listen with the intent to understand; they listen with the intent to reply. They're either speaking or preparing to speak. They're filtering everything through their own paradigms" (239). Seeking first to understand requires empathetic listening—with the intent to understand—that is, listening to get inside another person's frame of reference. This takes skill and practice.

Peter Senge (1990) describes the views of David Bohm (a contemporary physicist and leading quantum theorist who is a major contributor to the current thinking on team learning) who notes that dialogue occurs when a group "becomes open to the flow of larger intelligence" (239). There are three necessary conditions for dialogue. First, all participants suspend their assumptions; that is, they are stated and constantly accessible for questioning and observation by the team. Second, all participants must regard one another as colleagues in a mutual quest for deeper insight and clarity. "Colleagueship does not mean that you need to agree or share the same views. On the contrary, the real power of seeing each other as colleagues comes into play when there are differences of view" (245). Third, a facilitator "holds the context" (243) of

TABLE 3.3 *Discussions Versus Dialogues.*

Discussions	Dialogues
Different views are presented and defended.	Different views are presented as a means of discovering a new view.
Decisions are made.	Complex issues are explored.
Convergence on a conclusion of course of action occurs.	Divergence is the goal; not seeking agreement, but a richer grasp of complex issues.
Action is often the focus of discussion.	New actions emerge as a by-product of dialogue.

the dialogue. "In the absence of a skilled facilitator, our habits of thought continually pull us toward discussion and away from dialogue" (246). A discussion is like ping-pong with its back-and-forth qualities where "the subject of common interest may be analyzed and dissected" (240) from the point of view of whomever speaks up. The objective of a discussion is to win over others to our point of view, whereas the objective of a dialogue is to go beyond any single individual's view, to gain insights from all, so that everyone wins because of deeper, collective understanding and meaning-making. Based on the framework that Senge (1990) presents, Table 3.3 summarizes the differences between discussions and dialogues.

Part of Abraham Lincoln's brilliance, and success, has been attributed to the fact that he composed his cabinet of men who thought differently than he did and with whom he regularly entered into dialogues and discussions (Goodwin 2005). Ultimately, boards need to effectively balance discussion and dialogue in order to make informed decisions; they actually master movement back and forth between dialogue and discussion. When team members enter into dialogues regularly, they: develop trust that carries over to discussions, experience how larger understandings emerge by holding one's own view "gently," and they learn to master the art of holding a position rather than being held by it (Senge 1990).

Another strategy recommended by experts is called dialectical inquiry (DI), during which participants nurture cognitive conflict (Roberto 2005). DI recognizes that each group member has unique information, knowledge, experience, or perspective that may only be shared through dialogue. The focus is to seek consensus on an issue. The decision makers are divided into two groups. One group develops recommendations and supports them with all the key assumptions, facts, and data that they have; they provide a report orally and in writing to the other group. The second group develops plausible, alternate assumptions that negate those of the first, and then uses new assumptions to construct counter recommendations. The two groups then dialogue until they agree on a set of assumptions—and unite to develop recommendations. DI often leads to an entirely new option that no one had thought of previously.

Learn

Great boards, like great teams, learn how to learn together; it's not easy and takes practice. The problem is few boards practice learning. When they meet, they primarily listen to reports, and perhaps make some decisions or take a vote on some matter. Sometimes, the board is engaged in an intellectual debate of ideas and members learn each others' opinions. "The main product of the team's work is decisions about specific situations, often debated under great time pressure, and each decision is final as soon as it's made. There is no experimentation with decisions: worse still, there is little opportunity to form reasoned assessments of the wisdom of different decisions, and there is no opportunity to step back, as a team, and reflect on how we might arrive at better decisions together" (Senge 1990, 259).

Senge recommended the following conditions for team learning: (1) all members of the team are together; (2) the ground rules for effective dialogue are explained; (3) the ground rules are enforced (if someone cannot suspend his/her assumptions, the team acknowledges that this is "discussing" not "dialoguing"); and (4) the team is encouraged to raise the most difficult, subtle, and conflictual issues. Suggested ground rules are: (1) the suspension of assumptions (that is, rather than people taking a position and defending it while others take opposite positions, with the result of polarization, the group examines underlying assumptions); (2) acting as colleagues wherein everyone leaves their positions at the door (there is no hierarchy, and there is a facilitator); and (3) encouraging a spirit of inquiry where members explore their thinking and the assumptions held.

Scrutinizing the group's assumptions in any decision-making context is no easy task, but asking these questions (Roberto 2009) will help:

1. What are the facts of this situation?

2. What issues remain ambiguous or uncertain?

3. What explicit and implicit assumptions have we made?

4. Have we confused facts with assumptions?

5. How would an outsider with an unbiased perspective evaluate each of our assumptions?

6. How would our conclusions change if each of our assumptions proves incorrect?

7. Can we collect data, conduct a simple experiment, or perform certain analysis to validate or disprove crucial assumptions? (85)

The key for boards is to take the time needed to ask the questions, determine the answers, clarify that which can be clarified, and proceed. Then, in the true spirit of creating and sustaining learning, look back on decisions to see what actually happened and ask the following questions: What did we set out to do? What actually happened? Why did it happen? What will we do next time? (Garvin 2000).

The Boston Children's Chorus board made great strides forward not only in tackling a challenging issue, but also in bringing others effectively into the process. Through the inclusion of more voices, they (1) overcame the board's bounded group awareness, (2) resisted the urge to suppress debate, (3) engaged in true discussion, and (4) practiced group learning. Along the way, they built bridges with the community; ultimately, they most likely made a better decision on a controversial issue.

Example 8: Boston Children's Chorus Board

After its board retreat, the Boston Children's Chorus (BCC) decided to use more working groups for a couple of reasons. First and foremost, such groups would allow multiple constituencies to work more closely with the board and encourage a greater sense of community. The executive director noted, "As harsh as it sounds—but probably true of many boards—there was a feeling that the board was like some ghostly entity that met mysteriously and was untouchable. The board wanted to be more transparent about its activities and processes, and also be more a part of the community, not some entity sitting on high and dictating downward. They wanted to understand the realities of the young people we're serving and ensure that those kids know their voices are being heard, and they wanted to also connect more directly with the parents." The board chair commented that there had, historically, been some reluctance to engage the parents, "but they are a real asset."

Second, working groups of board members and constituents would help the board focus its attention on truly critical issues, one of which was a signature event for the BCC—its nationally televised Martin Luther King Jr. concert—but not in isolation. The executive director commented, "We've had numerous, very emotional conversations at the full board level about the MLK Concert for a couple of years. We decided to pull the conversation out of that venue and give it to a smaller group to discuss to see if progress could be made—to move the conversation from the emotional to the more analytical— because the reality is that the entire event required enormous staff time and effort over the course of four or five months. The MLK Concert involved dinner, a VIP reception, celebrities, and the like. Televised productions are very expensive. The financial and human capital expenditures were vast and we didn't even know if the event had impact."

And so, the MLK Concert Working Group was formed, composed of board and staff members, alumni, current singers, and parents. The group was charged with gathering information, presenting to the board, and engaging the board in a dialogue. In order to do that, the group grappled with several difficult fiduciary, strategic, and generative questions including:

- How can we best celebrate King's legacy?

- Is television the best way to do so or is there an alternative?

(continued)

- What would be lost to the organization if we don't do the concert?
- If we change things, what would be the effect on fundraising?
- Does this event need to be national or might it be regional or limited to Boston?

Said the director, "Everything was on the table." At a meeting with the full board, the working group brought forward the following questions that helped unearth people's deeply help beliefs, values, and underlying assumptions about the BCC and one of its most revered programs:

- What role does the MLK event play in the life of BCC now, and what role would we like it to play in the future?
- What outcomes for the MLK event would make you feel it's been worth the energy and time?
- What questions, if answered, could make the most difference in the success of our future MLK events?
- What could happen that would enable us to feel fully engaged and energized about the new direction of the MLK activities?

"A rich discussion ensued. We heard from the usual loudest voices who argued passionately, but we also heard from those who are typically fairly quiet or even silent. And, importantly, we heard from newer board members, who didn't have a particular view coming in; they were instrumental in asking a lot of great questions," said the executive director. "Yes," said the board chair, "I can no longer be just one of the loud ones; it's my job to draw everyone into the conversation and ensure that everyone's voice is heard. Sure, it takes time, but it's worth it because you ultimately get better decisions with greater buy-in."

The upshot on the issue was that the board accepted the recommendation of the working group (to not produce a lavish televised event and go with radio instead) but the outcomes for the board and the organization are quite profound, as they extend well beyond this one situation.

"This was a first big step in creating a really strong board, coalescing as a team, along with parents and singers. I give a lot of credit to our board chair for his leadership. Governance is a work in progress, and we're made great strides forward. We now are partnering parents with board members for fundraising efforts, which is really exciting," remarked the executive director. The board chair concurred, adding, "Now that we have a model for how ad hoc groups can work effectively, we've formed another one to consider our 10th Anniversary, so stay tuned. Engaging all the constituents, especially giving the singers—the young people—a voice, and recognizing that they all have roles to play and a stake in what we decide as a board, has been very gratifying. It is good to know that, in this process, we are building stronger community and a better, stronger organization."

With all the challenges to getting board members thinking critically and engaging in productive dialogue at board meetings, it is easy to wonder if it can ever really happen. But if thinking about our thinking and self-overhearing are as important to good decision making as the research suggests, and as experience confirms, then it behooves us to try.

CHAPTER THREE HIGHLIGHTS

- **Boards are bored; they are passive 67 percent of the time at board meetings.** Time at typical board meetings is apportioned as follows: 32 percent listening to reports or presentations by the CEO, staff, or committee chairs; 24 percent conducting regular business; and 11 percent getting educated. Boards are actively engaged as follows: 20 percent of time is spent discussing or debating ideas of courses of action; and 13 percent of time is spent making sense (for example, framing issues, thinking from the perspectives of constituents).

- **While governance as leadership requires critical thinking, there are numerous "human-nature" impediments.** Various aspects of human nature—not wanting to be wrong, being certain, not wanting to lose, thinking we are rational, and wanting to size up a situation and get to solutions—can impair critical thought processes.

- **Individual cognitive biases (for example, anchoring; framing; confirmation bias; false consensus bias; and bounded awareness) and group dysfunctions (for example, social loafing; groupthink; social conformity; and group polarization) can also impede governing more effectively.** This chapter offered a variety of techniques and tactics to work around, avoid, or overcome the complications these biases and dysfunctions cause for board members and for driving the board to higher performance.

CHAPTER

4

TURNING YOUR BOARD INTO A HIGH-PERFORMING TEAM

*If a board is to truly fulfill its mission . . . it must become a robust team—
one whose members know how to ferret out the truth, challenge one
another, and even have a good fight now and then.*
—Jeffrey Sonnenfeld (2002, 113)

*Boardroom effectiveness has less to do with structure than with the
quality of the directors themselves and how they interact.*
—Jay W. Lorsch, Professor, Harvard Business School, and
Robert C. Clark, Distinguished Service Professor,
Harvard School of Law (2008, 108)

When most people think about high-performing teams, they think of athletics, military tactical units like the Navy Seals, or perhaps emergency room or trauma center staff. Though building high performance through teamwork makes sense to people, and board members regularly talk about the management team, and even teamwork, most do not consider their board to be a team; it is not a concept that's commonly invoked in this context. If board members want the organization to be high performing, with the staff, the faculty, the doctors, or the curators all pulling together, then board members should lead the way and model the behaviors they seek in others. However, "the very idea that boards should operate as high-performing, work-oriented teams is relatively new, and in some ways, fairly radical. It contradicts the traditional view of boards as ceremonial appendages to the apparatus of corporate governance, and as collections of dignitaries who would assemble infrequently to place their obligatory stamp of approval on management's predetermined decisions" (Nadler, Behan, and Nadler 2006, 105).

The elements of high-performing teams—common purpose and goals, trust, respect, mutual accountability—are not required of ceremonial (Charan 2005) or Type I (Chait, Ryan, and Taylor 2005) boards. Those boards operate in "hub and spoke" fashion where board members attempt to influence the CEO and other decision makers directly and individually. Board meetings offer a pretense for governance; everyone knows that the real power is wielded privately or by a small inner circle, or clique, to advance special interests and personal agendas. If this behavior is tolerated, governance is back-channeled and team play does not matter. Organizations survive and board members go quietly about their business.

Few would argue that nonprofit "governance as usual" will continue to serve organizations well in the volatile, uncertain, complex, and ambiguous world in which we now operate. The governance-as-leadership model demands more of organizational leaders and board members to truly partner in successfully leading the nonprofits they serve. Governance as leadership moves from the Type I "hub and spoke" board to the "think tank" board, and in doing so, places a premium on effective group dynamics. "Generative work thrives on deliberations among participants with different perspectives and different frames for noticing different cues and clues. The more hypotheses and angles of vision, the more likely the perceptive reformulations and keen insights will materialize. . . . Generative work benefits from the interplay of ideas" (Chait et al. 2005, 99–100). The collective view matters more than any one individual's point of view. Therefore, governance as leadership boards are well served to understand another crucial, though rarely discussed ("invisible") dynamic—the board as a social system.

SOCIAL SYSTEMS

A social system (Parsons 1951) consists of two or more individuals interacting directly or indirectly in a bounded situation, meaning that the individuals are oriented, in a whole sense, to a common focus or interrelated foci. The major units of a social system are collectivities and roles (that is, not individuals as such); the major patterns or relationships linking these units are values (ends or broad guides to action) and norms (rules governing role performance in the context of system values).

In his examination of corporate boards, Jeffrey Sonnenfeld (2002) pondered the meltdowns at Enron, Tyco, and Worldcom and asked whether the boards were asleep at the wheel, in cahoots with corrupt management teams, or simply incompetent (106). Although it seems "inconceivable that business disasters of such magnitude could happen without gross or even criminal misconduct" on the part of boards, a close examination revealed no pattern of incompetence or corruption (106). In fact, scary as it is, these boards all passed the test of what would normally be seen as accepted practices for board operations: members showed up for meetings; they had money invested in the company; the boards were not too small or too big; nor were they dominated by insiders (106). Sonnenfeld's point is that most of the suggested remedies for failures of governance have been structural rather than cultural, and therefore, miss the mark. "What distinguishes exemplary boards is that they are robust, effective social systems" (Sonnenfeld 2002, 108).

Wayne Cascio (2004) reflected upon the plethora of evidence of poor boards—complacency, conflicts of interest, cronyism among board members and the CEO, and boards comprised of insiders who are afraid to challenge the status quo—and noted the typical structural responses, for example, having independent outsider directors, effective committees including one for audit with outside directors, and CPA-certified quarterly financial reports. Though prudent and sensible, these steps are "far from sufficient" (97). A board is a work group—"an intact social system, complete with boundaries, interdependence among members, and defined roles" (97).

GROUPS AND TEAMS

If we agree that boards are social systems, then when their individual members meet together they form either a group or a team or something in between. According to two leading consultants on teams and workforce performance, Katzenbach and Smith (2006, 91–92), the following definitions are instructive:

1. Working group: This is a group for which there is no significant incremental performance need or opportunity that would require it to become a team. The members interact primarily to share information, best practices, or perspectives and to make decisions to help each individual perform within his or her area of responsibility. For example, a manager might bring his or her direct reports together to discuss an upcoming project with a focus on each individual's responsibility rather than an overarching one for which they hold themselves mutually accountable. A group of teachers might meet together to talk about pedagogy but not necessarily about each teacher's specific role in a child's development.

2. Pseudo-team: This is a group for which there could be significant, incremental performance need or opportunity, but it has not focused on collective performance and is not really trying to achieve it. It has no interest in shaping a common purpose or set of performance goals, even though it may call itself a team. Pseudo-teams are the weakest of all in terms of impact, because the interactions detract from each member's individual performance without delivering any joint benefits. Pseudo-teams are formed when managers are required to meet together periodically—oftentimes for the simple purpose of updates—but there is no higher purpose and the meeting only serves to take people away from their job.

3. Potential team: This is a group for which there is significant, incremental performance need, and that really is trying to improve its performance impact. Typically, however, it requires more clarity of purpose, goals, or work products and more discipline in hammering out a common approach. It has not yet established collective accountability. Managers of various organizational units are potential teams—they understand their individual roles, but are not focused on the collective's responsibility for a higher, common goal. IBM's management "team," prior to Gerstner, was notorious for competing against each other for turf and resources.

4. Real team: This is a small number of people with complementary skills who are equally committed to a common purpose, goals, and a working approach for which they hold themselves mutually accountable. Katzenbach and Smith (2006) feel that size matters when it comes to producing effective teamwork, but say that small is "more of a pragmatic guide" (45) than anything else. They concede that larger numbers of people, fifty or more, can "theoretically become a team" (45) but that there are logistic and behavioral constraints such as "crowd or herd behaviors that prevent the intense sharing of viewpoints needed to build a team" (46). Large groups "tend to settle on less clear statements of purpose that, typically get set by the hierarchical leaders, and they look to teamwork values as their working approach. Then, when teamwork values breakdown, the group reverts to formal hierarchy, structure, policies, and procedures" (46). In addition, large groups will give up on the team concept sooner than small groups, especially if members feel they are meeting as a group for the sole purpose of getting along better (considered by many in a workplace setting as a waste of time). Katzenbach and Smith also acknowledge that even small groups can fail to become teams.

5. High-performance team: This is a group that meets all the conditions of real teams, and has members who are also deeply committed to one another's personal growth and success.

According to the Katzenbach and Smith model, nonprofit boards, more often than not, resemble working groups or pseudo-teams rather than real or high-performing teams. Typically, they lack an understanding of the collective and there is often no sense of common purpose; even if board members can recite the mission of the organization it does not mean that they understand what they should do in support of it. In addition, some boards are not composed of people with complementary skills; frequently, there is little or no collective accountability beyond basic fiduciary oversight and even then, management is typically ultimately responsible for organizational performance. Katzenbach and Smith (2006), in fact, believe that extended teams are not, by definition, real teams, and cannot ever be. "Large numbers of people usually cannot develop the common purpose, goals, approach, and mutual accountability of a real team. And when they try to do so, they usually produce only superficial 'missions' and well-meaning intentions" (47). The authors say, therefore, that it is better to break the large group into smaller ones "to tackle significant performance goals and then help those subgroups become real teams" (47). This might be one reason why board members who sit on large boards enjoy working in small ad hoc groups at board meetings, tackling specific issues, and why board members often say that their committees are where the "real work" gets done. My conviction is that boards governing consequentially—utilizing the principles of governance as leadership—do in fact coalesce as high-performing teams, even those with many members who only meet periodically.

BOARDS AS TEAMS

According to Charan (2005), corporate boards may evolve through three phases— from ceremonial groups to liberated boards to progressive teams. On ceremonial boards, there is very little dialogue. Meetings are very tightly scripted, focused on compliance, and the board mostly rubber-stamps management's agenda. Liberated boards are those that developed post-Sarbanes-Oxley boards to consider performance and compliance. They are marked by more active board member participation, but are still too often a collection of individuals rather than a high-performing team. Charan refers to the third stage as progressive—a collectively high-performing team where individuals maintain their independent viewpoints; board meetings are marked by robust dialogue and debate on critical issues, leading to consensus and closure; and directors do not get sidetracked by tangential issues. The board-CEO relationship is constructive and collaborative, but "board members are not afraid to confront hard issues" (9). The board "adds value on many levels without becoming a time sink for management" (10). Board members "challenge each other directly, without breaking the harmony of the group and without going through the CEO. Directors find the give-and-take in board meetings energizing. They enjoy the intellectual exchange, and they learn from each other. They look forward to meetings" (9).

Charan provided a set of diagnostic questions (11–13) to help boards identify where they score on a number of factors that signify a "progressive" board, including:

- Effective group dynamics: The board brings dialogue on critical issues to closure with consensus; directors speak their minds; board meetings include a lot of give-and-take among directors and not just through the CEO or chair; dialogue is focused on important issues and does not wander into minutiae or off on tangents.

- Supportive architecture: Information is timely, focused, regular, and digestible; management anticipates the board's need for information; and board members "learn the business." There is enough time for dialogue on key matters; information is presented in a way that leads to productive discussion; and the CEO discusses the good and the bad news.

- Focus on substantive issues: "Lack of focus has an insidious effect on group dynamics. Boards become frustrated because their discussion time is lacking on the central issues on which they believe they should devote their scarce time. Directors feel rushed and leave board meetings knowing they have not covered the right things. They lose confidence in the board's ability to add any value at all"

(Charan 2005, 68). Charan suggests that the board and CEO jointly set a twelve-month agenda (an outline of key topics for the year ahead—a list of "very specific, forward-looking discussion points that the board and management jointly decide must be addressed at some point in the coming year") (69).

Challenges for Boards Performing as Teams. In their book about corporate boards, David Nadler, Beverly Behan, and Mark Nadler (2006) state unequivocally that high organizational performance demands an effective board team. "No team is more vital to the organization's success than the board, but at the same time, no other team faces so many unique obstacles to team performance" (106); those challenges are summarized in Table 4.1.

TABLE 4.1 *Characteristics Differentiating Boards from Other Teams.*

	Typical Teams	**Boards as Teams**
Affiliation	Members work for the same organization.	Outside directors may be members of more than one board; this is not their "day job."
Interaction	Members spend considerable time together; experience intense personal interaction.	Directors spend little time together, making it difficult for them to build working relationships.
Time and information	Constantly immersed in company's business.	Limited time available to devote to mastering issues of complex company.
Leaders as members	Most members are not accustomed to sitting at the head of the table.	Majority of members may be CEOs, who are used to leading, not following.
Authority relationships	Members' roles on the team often reflect their status in the company.	Lines of authority complex and unclear; chairmen/CEO both lead and report to boards.
Changing expectations	Usually created with reasonably clear charter—such as completing a project—in mind.	Difficult to achieve consensus in a climate of unprecedented scrutiny and pressure.
Formality	High degree of formality is rare; generally reflects the culture of the company.	Physical setting and social rituals reinforce aura of power and privilege.
Meeting focus	Work of teams continues between meetings.	Little time devoted to board's work between meetings.

Source: Nadler, Behan, and Nadler 2006, 107. Reprinted with permission of John Wiley and Sons, Inc.

Ram Charan's book on corporate governance (2005) also reported that it can be "challenging for directors to gel" (18) because boards are not like most other social bodies in two respects similar to the "authority relationships" issue (see Table 4.1): (1) boards consist of individuals who are assembled without a final arbiter whereas most teams have a defined manager, captain, "or at least someone who, at the end of the day, makes final decisions and is held accountable for them" (18) and (2) boards as a collective have a great deal of power but each director has little individual power so the group needs to try to form consensus (without an arbiter). But Charan sheds light on a third important consideration: although boards are composed of highly respected peers who are typically leaders in their own fields, and in which they tend to be strong and confident, when gathered together on a board they sometimes hold a lot back for fear of losing respect. "Unless directors learn to proffer dissent productively, the 'code of congeniality' can suppress debate as directors avoid contradicting one another directly" (18).

EFFECTIVE BOARD TEAMS IN THE CONTEXT OF GOVERNANCE AS LEADERSHIP

A number of conditions are common to all high-performance teams including: skilled members, explicit values and norms, clarity of high purpose, clear and compelling performance goals that are measured and for which members are held mutually accountable, and effective leaders. Translating those conditions to the context of governance as leadership means that boards should take the following steps discussed in this section: (1) pay attention to board composition, including the mix of minds; (2) ensure a shared sense of high purpose and meaningful goals by having the board discuss its mission and what it needs to do in support of that purpose; (3) make values and norms explicit through a board code of conduct or statement of mutual expectations; (4) provide new board member orientation and mentoring; (5) measure team performance; and (6) ensure effective leadership for consequential governance by utilizing an inclusive and transparent board chair selection and succession process and elevating the role of a governance committee well above nominating new members.

Board Composition

The CEO of every organization wonders about the right mix of people to have on the board and every leader must pay attention to board member succession—that is, it is a good idea to always cultivate potential board members. There are no simple answers to the questions: "Who should we put on our board? What should their skill sets be? What's the right mix?" But who is on the team is crucial to the team's performance.

It is essential to get the "right people on the bus . . . those who are productively neurotic, self-motivated and self-disciplined, who wake up every day compulsively driven to do the best they can because it is simply part of their DNA" (Collins 2001, 15). Collins noted that this first principle is especially important in the social sector where, because board members are volunteers, getting people *off* the bus is typically more difficult than in the private sector. "It is the *collective* strength of the directors that gives the board its capability for judgment—the capability that translates into a distinct additive role. The challenge of this paradox is to forge a set of relationships among a group of strong individuals that will permit information to be shared, recommendations challenged, and actions evaluated, while at the same time avoiding the trap of becoming a group so trusting, familiar, and comfortable with itself that judgment is undermined by cozy self-satisfaction" (Demb and Neubauer 1992, 131). The problem is that when new board members come onto the board, there is no trust yet, and conversations can be guarded. However, as the board works together over a period of years, "familiarity may lead to complacency and a tendency to seek new members who 'fit' with existing members. Slowly, and very incrementally, the board's critical ability, its collective ability to challenge, deteriorates" (Demb and Neubauer 1992, 131). Mueller (1989) cautioned boards to guard against "concinnity bias" that occurs when, in selecting new members, internal harmony and being "clubbable" is placed ahead of objectivity and independent judgment.

Board Composition in the Context of Governance as Leadership. It is common practice to examine the board's composition according to demographic variables and diversity of, for example, gender, age, race/ethnicity, and geographic location; profession, for example, lawyers, educators, investment bankers, entrepreneurs; and resources such as the ability to give and access to others who can give. This way of building the board may work especially well for covering fiduciary/Type I issues.

Another approach is to think beyond members' areas of expertise and to build the board team with an eye toward bringing on diverse perspectives, as the following example details.

Example 9: United World College USA Board

The United World College USA has had great success in its approach to finding new board members—something that many nonprofits find challenging. Common refrains are: "There just are not enough potential board members out there" and "It seems like we're all competing with each other for board members."

The president commented on governance and finding board members: "The better we get, the better we want to be. And that means bringing on the very best board members we can—those who will bring some combination of intellectual, political, and financial capital to the table." The institution had, in the past, used a common approach which involved "friend finding." Said the chair, "We would talk about people we knew, make the occasional ask, and recruit a new member; it wasn't a very efficient or necessarily effective process."

So UWC USA decided to try something completely different and did so with great success. The chair described the process, "We hired a headhunter (an alum of UWC

(continued)

USA) to make cold calls. We honestly thought if we found one wonderful new board member this way it would be a home run. In the first year we had a list of 180 names to choose from—more than we ever could have generated on our own. These were people who were interested in possibly serving! We interviewed twelve people and brought in four new board members the first year, three the next, and three the next. Our board is now, in a word, stellar."

The United World College USA now counts among its board members a former school head and professor, one of the Middle East's economic, defense, and energy strategists, an entrepreneur, a former senior partner at McKinsey, a former senior administrator from Princeton University, a director of sales and marketing for a hospital, an architect, the former head of Philips Exeter, and several others.

"I never would have believed it was possible," remarked the president. "But if your mission and vision is bold enough, people will join you regardless of prior affiliation. The same can be said of donors—the vast majority of whom have no prior association with the school. It wasn't so long ago that I was thinking this could not be done. I'm so glad I was wrong."

Some boards are thinking about their areas of organizational focus when discussing board composition and recruiting new board members. A hospital board chair commented on the fact that their board has gotten more sophisticated about looking at its current composition and thinking about gaps that it may have not just in terms of demographic variables and board member profession, but also by thinking about the areas of institutional focus—quality, customer satisfaction, finance, and employee turnover—and whether and how new members can add value on those issues. The CEO said, "We're being much more strategic about whom we invite onto the board; we're looking hard at the skill set required and trying to ensure that our board has a composition that meets our needs in this day and age—in this era of healthcare, which is more complex than ever."

Centenary College, showcased in the next example, has begun seeking new board members based on their ability to add value to various elements of the strategic plan.

Still less common than trying to find board members with a good fiduciary or strategic fit, but perhaps most essential, is to consider what the potential board member will bring to the board team from a critical thinking, behavioral, and disposition point of view; for example, is he or she primarily an idealist or pragmatic, assertive or deferential? Does he or she rely on logic or intuition? See Table 4.2 for some selected questions from a "board member trait and preference inventory" that Richard Chait and I developed for this purpose. In addition to using it to gauge the "fit" of potential new board members, it is also a useful tool for seeing how current board members think and to determine where there might be a preponderance of board member preferences that tip the scale in one direction or the other; for example, a board full of consensus-builders might want to bring on or develop a few devil's advocates.

Example 10: Centenary College Board

The board of Centenary College has spent time recently rethinking an extremely important role of the board: how it finds, cultivates, vets, and engages prospective trustees.

The president and board chair recruited a very talented trustee to chair a newly constituted Trusteeship and Governance Committee (TGC). The president said of this person, "He is a go-getter, but not a steamroller. His approach to chairing the committee is quite elegant and has been crucial to us as we change the culture from historic ways of doing things to being more thoughtful. It's not that the old ways didn't serve us well in the past; they did. But we found that those old ways wouldn't get us where we want to go in the future. We never had a formalized process through which new trustees were vetted. It was very informal, say, a lunch with the president. The names came from current board members. That's not unusual with boards, but because of our culture of politeness, people were hesitant to say what they really thought about a potential board member who was a friend of someone else's on the board."

Under the leadership of the committee chair, supported by the board chair, the bylaws now state that the TGC shall: (1) be staffed by the president's designee; (2) ensure that the membership and leadership of the board consist of highly qualified and committed individuals; (3) ensure that the regular programs of new trustee and in-service education are maintained; and (4) periodically recommend initiatives by which the Board shall assess its performance. In addition, the TGC "shall maintain a list of qualified candidates for possible nomination, consider cultivation strategies for promising trustee candidates, and propose and periodically review the adequacy of the statement of trustee responsibilities as adopted by the Board and manage issues related to Board governance."

Under the new guidelines for trustee selection, names of candidates are submitted in writing to the TGC. The nomination letter includes the candidate's résumé or a statement of their professional and personal background as it relates to the strategic plan and the nominator's own comments about why and how the college would benefit from having this person on its BOT.

Potential candidates have conversations with members of the TGC, the board chair, and the president of the college. These conversations are to explore fit with the culture of the board and where the college wants to go strategically, as well as to ascertain the person's interest in possibly serving on the board. "We ask potential trustees why they want to serve on the board, what they hope to get from the board service, and what the college can expect in return. We are really looking for the right skill set and mind set so we can build the best team," remarked the president.

The chair of the TGC explained his philosophy as follows: "It is my belief that Centenary's success in implementing the very forward-thinking and creative strategic plan . . . will depend in great part on a forward-thinking and creative Board of Trustees. As part of the TGC's contribution to the successful implementation of this strategic plan, I believe that we should take those actions that will enhance the possibility that every new member who is added to the board will contribute to making the board equal to the required task."

TABLE 4.2 *Board Member Trait and Preference Inventory (Extracts).*

Item	Choice Options	Response
I prefer:	A. What's possible	
	B. What's practical	
I am primarily:	A. A divergent thinker	
	B. A convergent thinker	
I tend to be:	A. Task-oriented	
	B. Process-oriented	
I most enjoy:	A. Starting new projects	
	B. Seeing projects through to the end	
I am typically:	A. A provocateur	
	B. A consensus-builder	
I participate:	A. On most issues	
	B. Selectively	
	C. Rarely	
I prefer to:	A. Define and frame problems	
	B. Solve problems	
I tend to:	A. Speak my mind	
	B. Bite my tongue	

Source: Richard Chait and Cathy Trower 2008.

Although the old checklists many organizations use that show what potential board members bring in terms of professional and financial background have some utility and a certain appeal, governance as leadership suggests a new approach to board member recruitment that augments the standard way, "one that stresses quality of mind, a tolerance for ambiguity, an appetite for organizational puzzles, a fondness for robust discourse, and a commitment to team play" (Chait et al. 2005, 178). After all, nonprofits are not just seeking board members to fill a seat and fulfill the basic fiduciary oversight; they need board members who can "contribute to leadership through the practice of governance" (178).

Shared Sense of Compelling Purpose

One of the single most important characteristics of every high-performing team is that they have a shared purpose—they know *why* they're doing *what* they're doing. For the social sector, as elsewhere, a compelling purpose is to deliver superior performance and make a distinctive impact over time (Collins 2005, 6). A common, meaningful purpose sets the tone for the group; it supplies both meaning and emotional energy (Katzenbach and Smith 2006). Clayton Alderfer (2001) wrote that only a small proportion of corporate boards pay explicit attention to the board as a group and to the board-management relationship. The boards that do so develop and rewrite as necessary a mission statement *for the board.*

One reason boards don't always resemble great teams is that they lack a common purpose, an issue more complex than it seems initially. First, although board members certainly understand, support, and indeed, typically feel passionate about their organization's mission, that mission statement does not necessarily lead to a common understanding about what the board should do in support of it. Second, boards are collections of individuals, all with their own reasons for serving as board members. Thus, they differ tremendously from sports teams where athletes all join to play the same game and, presumably, to win as often as possible. Nonprofit boards differ, too, from corporate teams formed to design a product or a building. While sports team members may disagree about strategies to beat the opponent, and the engineers or architects may disagree about the best approach to use, they have a common purpose for being on the team. Not so with board members. Some are there to give, some to give back, some for something to do, some to build a résumé, or for another self-serving interest. Third, it's likely that those who serve together on boards have less in common with each other than those on athletic or corporate teams. This can cause them to look around the boardroom and wonder, "Why is he here?" or "What does she get from this?" Sitting around the nonprofit board table are stay-at-home-moms, CEOs, investment bankers, real estate developers, lawyers, physicians, accountants, salespeople, and retirees. Are they simply a potpourri of individuals with little in common, or do they form a collective that works?

Shared Sense of Purpose in the Context of Governance as Leadership.
Governance as leadership is based, in part, on the simple fact that higher purpose drives higher performance. "Many board members are ineffectual not just because they are *confused* about their role but because they are *dissatisfied* with their role. They do not do their job well because their job does not strike them as worth doing well" (Chait et al. 2005, 16).

An effective technique to guide the board to a shared sense of higher purpose is to have board members write a *board* mission statement.

Board members also should each answer a key legacy question. Here are some from which to choose:

- For what do board members want to be remembered?
- Five years from today, what will this organization's key constituents consider to be the most important legacy of the current board?
- What is it that this board provides to this organization that no other board can?
- Why do we exist as a board?

Once everyone has written their answers, board members should form small groups to share the individual responses and then produce one statement that reflects the collective view. Have each group display and read aloud its mission statement and invite discussion by asking:

- Are there common elements to the mission statements?
- Are there unique elements?
- Is there something about unique aspects that the board wants to be sure to include in its final mission statement?

Next, write one succinct statement that best captures/synthesizes the analysis discussion. This process yielded the following board mission statements:

- The board supports the fulfillment of the university's mission by ensuring:
  - An effective leadership team;
  - The development of a strategic plan that anticipates the changing needs of its constituencies and that delivers on it promises;
  - Financial integrity and sustainability;
  - Transparency; and
  - Effective advocacy for the university. [Large Public Research University]
- Our board mission is to partner with management to lead the School into the future with integrity and vision, never forgetting that we exist for the students and their families. [Independent School]
- Our mission is to initiate, create, implement, and maintain an evolving strategic planning and thinking process that will strengthen: (1) collaboration with our partners, and (2) identity and brand awareness, while incorporating advances in technology, without losing compassion for our patients and their families. [Hospital Auxiliary]
- The board's mission is to ensure the long-term ability of this organization to provide best in class services by focusing on long-term funding sources and by

enhancing the public recognition. This requires us to position the organization strategically to best respond to the critical needs of children and families. [Community Service Organization]

The board may wish to keep not only the organization's but also the board's mission statement front and center at meetings and to periodically revisit their mission statement to ensure that it still motivates and focuses members appropriately. The board's mission statement should be included in new board member orientation and board assessments (both discussed later in this chapter).

The process of writing a board mission statement serves several aims of governance as leadership:

- The exercise emphasizes "our" legacy—a shared vision—not just that of a single board member whose name may be on a building.

- The stakes are raised significantly above fiduciary oversight.

- The view is elongated well beyond the meeting, the quarter, or even the year.

- The process takes the responsibility for effective governance out of the realm of the technical expertise of any single board member and places it squarely with the collective.

- Board values are revealed.

After the board has made its purpose clear, the next step is to concretize the implicit values and normative behaviors that underscore the mission.

Values and Behavioral Norms

High-performing teams, work groups, and boards share similar values and characteristics (Axelrod 2007; Charan 2005; Katzenbach and Smith 2006; Lencioni 2002; Nadler et al. 2006; Senn and Hart 2006; Sonnenfeld 2002) that shape behaviors and that become normative—"the way we do things around here." The core values of high-performing teams include respect, trust, candor, integrity, independence, and open-mindedness.

Core Team Values. High-performing teams value mutual respect, trust, inclusiveness, and candor among members and between members and management. Mutual trust and respect are marked by confidentiality inside and solidarity outside the boardroom; respect for individual expertise and diversity of opinion; and active, respectful, charismatic listening.

Independence, integrity, and open-mindedness are demonstrated through a healthy spirit of inquiry and constructive debate in which everyone participates, engaging in "unfiltered conflict around ideas" (Lencioni 2002). Axelrod (2007) described these values as the capacity to explore divergent views in a respectful rather than adversarial manner. Members feel free to challenge one another's assumptions and conclusions, and management encourages lively discussion of strategic issues (Sonnenfeld 2002). This second requirement for high performance builds on the first because teams that lack trust are incapable of engaging in unfiltered and passionate debate of ideas, resorting instead to veiled discussions, guarded comments, and posturing.

"Well-functioning, successful teams usually have chemistry that can't be quantified. They seem to get into a virtuous cycle in which one good quality builds on another. Team members develop mutual respect; because they respect one another, they develop trust; because they trust one another, they share difficult information; because they have the same information, they can challenge one another's conclusions coherently; because a spirited give-and-take becomes the norm, they learn to adjust their own interpretations in response to intelligent questions" (Sonnenfeld 2002, 109).

Whether because of a historical relationship between a board and its CEO, changes in leadership and new board members, or concerns about vulnerability, building a base of candor and trust can be challenging and yet is absolutely essential to board team performance. Some excerpts from interviews with CEOs and chairs about these issues are presented in Exhibit 4.1.

Exhibit 4.1: CEOs and Board Chairs Talk About Candor and Trust

Because of internal strife and a crisis at the organization prior to her arrival, and the board's response of micromanaging, one CEO admitted that, "I was hesitant to trust the board and the executive committee completely. I didn't ask for their help because it felt dangerous. Historically, the organization had a pattern of blaming and scapegoating as solutions to problems. That's a powerful dynamic that can be difficult to break because sometimes that's all people can see." Being explicit about the past tensions and creating a new culture of candor has "gone a long way to break out of those old patterns." The board chair echoed her CEO, saying, "Now that we've learned how to be more effective as a board, the CEO has felt more confident and less protective; she can now really look to the board for support in ways not really possible before working through this process and getting beyond some of the baggage from the past—especially the trust issues."

You have to have mutual trust between the board and the CEO. Without that, it would be really challenging to work through some of the squirmy moments with the board, especially as we practice generative thinking. The CEO can feel really vulnerable bringing questions rather than answers to the board and to opening up about what keeps him awake at night. Let's face it; his job is the one on the line, not any particular board members' or the board chairs'. There needs to be alignment between what the CEO and

Exhibit 4.1: CEOs and Board Chairs Talk About Candor and Trust (*Continued*)

board want to achieve through governance and to achieve alignment, there has to be trust. [Board Chair]

We encouraged our CEO to be completely candid with the board and to not be afraid to disagree with us. We've encouraged a stronger management style; we've asked the CEO to be straight up with board members—good and bad. This has been critical to building a better organization and better CEO-board relationship. The CEO used to be hesitant to bring us the bad news, but he has really turned it around and the board has more confidence in him as a result. [Board Chair]

There's always tendency for CEOs to put a positive spin on things in an effort to ensure that the board has confidence in their leadership. But to really add value the board has to be able to look at things critically and they have to understand the big picture. Once our CEO realized that she could open up with the board, making herself vulnerable, the board has been able to be more supportive and accept more ownership of organizational direction and outcomes. The success of the organization depends on the CEO *and* the board, and to be fully functional there has to be trust. [Board Chair]

It all comes down to the honesty thing. Tell the truth to each other. The hardest thing for people to do when being strategic is face the brutal facts. You have to start with the brutal facts and not sugarcoat them; you have to stare the monster in the face. Who are we? What are we? What do we have? What do we need to have? Where are we going and how are we going to get there? You have to do this honestly and candidly. It's the hardest and most rewarding thing to do. [CEO]

Making Values and Norms Explicit. It is one thing for boards to discuss team values like trust, candor, integrity, and open-mindedness and quite another to make those values normative by writing them down. An effective way to get started is to give all board members a marker and several 5×7 sticky notes and ask them to complete the sentence, "To fulfill our board mission, it is essential that we . . . [fill in the blank]" by writing one to five words on each of the notes. Board members have suggested: trust each other and management; communicate effectively; engage in robust discourse; participate at meetings; work between meetings; work closely with management; fundraise; focus on what matters; provide leadership and critical thinking; be accountable; work together as a team; collaborate.

Have each board member read their notes and stick them up front horizontally for each new idea and vertically underneath an idea that has already been mentioned.

Once all ideas have been shared, ask board members to further group like ideas until there are five or six key topics or themes. For example, "work together," "collaborate," and "trust" might all fall under the general category of "teamwork" or "be a team." Next, assign small groups to each of the themes to discuss and create indicators for measuring progress on the topic, then discuss as a large group and agree to the steps the board will take to fulfill its mission. These steps can then become a set of guidelines for board responsibilities and actions. The Life University board engaged in this process and created the material shown in Exhibit 4.2.

Exhibit 4.2: Life University Board Mission and Board Agreements

Board Mission: The Life University Board of Trustees will provide the leadership and accountability that fosters the highest standards of academic excellence and fiscal responsibility and that produces successful graduates who live with "Lasting Purpose."

To fulfill our mission it is vital that we:

- Are accountable
- Participate actively
- Have the right people on the bus
- Tell the "Life" story
- Collaborate
- Communicate effectively
- Plan ahead and lead

As part of the follow-up process to setting its mission and what it needed to do in support of it, the board:

1. Agreed to conduct a 360 assessment* where each trustee rated all other trustees on 22 performance dimensions that spanned attendance, engagement, teamwork, and collaboration;
2. Agreed to work on moving upstream from providing primarily legal oversight (the focus for several years) to inquiry and strategic foresight;
3. Designed an overall dashboard to gauge institutional performance;
4. Sets aside a minimum of ten minutes at each board meeting to discuss breakdowns and challenges; and,

*For sample "360" questions for boards, see Table 4.3.

Exhibit 4.2: Life University Board Mission and Board Agreements (*Continued*)

5. Schedules a board dinner the night before each board meeting (three times per year) that includes celebrations of trustees and staff.

   In addition, trustees created a large placard containing the board's commitment to excellent governance, which is displayed at all board meetings. It states:

We agree to:

- Wholly commit to the vision of the university.
- Set aside personal agendas to make decisions for the sake of internal and external stakeholders.
- Take a leadership role in fundraising activities.
- Remain in a cohesive partnership with senior administration.
- Periodically revisit our mission to accomplish the vision.
- Stay at 50,000 feet.
- Make clear decisions after careful deliberation.
- Stand by decisions and remain in consensus when we leave the boardroom.
- Have the maturity to argue passionately but reasonably, acknowledge contributions, and leave meetings with everyone feeling energized.

The idea behind a 360 review is that each individual learns, anonymously, how others view his or her performance. In business, for example, individuals would be rated by their supervisor, their same-level peers, and by their subordinates. For boards, the idea is that each board member rates all other board members along any number of *observable* dimensions. The use of 360 review processes is controversial and should not be carelessly applied in any setting. Although this sort of assessment holds a certain appeal to those wanting to learn about how they personally are viewed by others, and by those seeking a mechanism to help troublesome board members "see the light," such feedback can be divisive and cause anxiety, tension, or friction, and can even be explosive. Those who wish to conduct a 360 board review will need a mechanism, such as an outside third party, to ensure confidentiality and anonymity. Table 4.3 shows a sampling of questions that can be used for this purpose, with a four-point scale. Some boards use a five-point scale with a neutral—"neither agree nor disagree"—rating or add an answer of "don't know."

Although not all boards have used the process described above, many have found it useful to begin with clarifying what is expected of board members in terms of board

TABLE 4.3 *Sample 360 Questions for Boards.*

	Strongly Agree	Agree	Disagree	Strongly Disagree
X is a real team player.				
X is open to input from other board members.				
X communicates effectively at board meetings.				
X brings needed skills and expertise to the board.				
I find it easy to communicate with X.				
X has the ability to consider the entirety of the organization in an unbiased fashion.				
X engages fully in board meetings.				
X behaves consistently with integrity.				
X is an effective leader.				
X demonstrates respect for other board members.				
X listens carefully to other board members at meetings.				

service. A good example of this is the MGH Institute of Health Profession's "Trustee Expectations and Statement of Commitment" (Exhibit 4.3). The statement speaks to "evidence" of trustee commitment to the organization's mission, including guidelines about: attendance at meetings, retreats, and events; committee service; preparation for meetings; philanthropic and advocacy support; conflict of interest; confidentiality; appropriate constituency representation; and participation in board assessment. Board members get a good sense of what they are supposed to do, but not necessarily how they are supposed to comport themselves.

The next example, from Cedar Crest College (Exhibit 4.4) states trustee responsibilities and norms (similar to MGHIHP's), and goes one step further toward mutuality, by including some responsibilities of the president and senior staff.

At the other end of the responsibilities-behaviors spectrum, is a third example (Exhibit 4.5). Entirely about board member comportment, rather than board member responsibilities, these board "Operating Agreements" set a very high bar for how board

Exhibit 4.3: MGH Institute of Health Professions, Trustee Expectations and Statement of Commitment

Members of the Board of Trustees of the MGH Institute of Health Professions serve as ultimate fiduciaries in their oversight of institutional affairs in accordance with the MGH Institute's charter, bylaws, evolving mission and purpose, and institutional plans. In serving in this critical capacity as a governing board, the board members hereby clarify for themselves, and for those invited to join them, what is expected of individual members.

All trustees are expected to have a deep and abiding commitment to the Institute's mission, goals, values, and heritage, and to uphold and strengthen the organization's commitment to prepare clinical leaders in the health professions, as well as the Institute's commitment to diversity and a community that considers all people equally.

Individual trustees are expected to be actively engaged members of the Board and the Institute community as evidenced by:

1. Attending a minimum of three of the four annual meetings, with at least two in person, although preferably attending all meetings, and in person whenever possible.

2. Serving on at least one board member committee, attending a majority of the committee's meetings, and accepting other assignments from the board chair from time to time.

3. Attending board retreats.

4. Demonstrating familiarity with the materials distributed in advance of board and committee meetings.

5. Supporting the Institute through the Annual Fund and other fundraising initiatives at a level that is personally meaningful and that sets a leadership example for others to emulate.

6. Assisting in identifying individual and institutional major gift prospects, and aiding in their solicitation whenever possible.

7. Participating in other board and institute activities to the extent time and interest permit, such as commencement, honors convocation, and special events.

8. Promoting and advocating for the Institute to alumni, prospective students, the health care and business communities, officials, donors and prospects, foundations, and the public at large.

9. Referring substantive information or concerns from the above groups to the president or board chair, recognizing that only the president and board chair are authorized to speak for the institute or its board.

10. Serving the institute as a whole, rather than any particular internal or external constituency.

11. Avoiding any situation that could cause the appearance of a conflict of interest, in accord with the institute's conflict-of-interest policy.

12. Maintaining confidentiality of information conveyed in the board's executive sessions.

13. Participating in individual board member self-assessment and collective assessment of the board's effectiveness.

Holding a trusteeship at the MGH Institute of Health Professions offers many rewards. They come from being an important participant in efforts to advance the MGH Institute's reputation among outstanding health professions schools and enhance its impact, as well as the personal gratification that comes with dedicated service to current and future generations of students and practicing health professionals.

Exhibit 4.4: Cedar Crest College, Board of Trustees Responsibilities/Norms

Responsibilities

1. Board members will attend either in person or via phone all sessions of the three formal board meetings in their entirety in each academic year, October, February, and May. Exact schedules are set two years in advance; future dates appear with the materials for each board meeting. If unable to attend, the board member will inform the board chair and president.

2. Board members will serve on at least one board committee. These meetings are usually by conference call and every effort should be made to attend. If unable to attend, the committee chair will be informed.

3. Board members are expected to attend the May graduation. They will be informed of other campus events and are welcome to attend those. An effort should be made to participate in the life of the college by selecting an additional event(s) to attend. Notification of attendance at any event is done through the assistant to the president so that the president's office knows you are on campus.

4. Board members are expected to contribute financially to the college during each academic year. While there is no set amount for trustee giving, each member is asked to support the college at the maximum of his or her capability.

Exhibit 4.4: Cedar Crest College, Board of Trustees Responsibilities/Norms (*Continued*)

5. Board members are expected to provide support for fundraising. This may include building relationships, individual solicitation, helping with or hosting special events, writing mail appeals and the like.

6. Board members carry fiduciary responsibility for the college including setting policy and monitoring operations and performance.

Norms

1. Board members will be ambassadors for the college and advance its mission and goals.

2. Board members will act with care and loyalty in their responsibilities to the college and at all times with the highest integrity.

3. Board members are expected to read all material prior to meetings to facilitate participation. Preparation for board and committee meetings will occur through [the board portal] where all board documents are posted.

4. All discussions at the board meetings are confidential. All materials will be considered confidential unless designated differently.

5. All board members make a valuable contribution to the board. The board places a priority on wide participation and conversation during meetings, assuring candid and rigorous discussion of all points of view. However along with this goes respect for fellow board members points of view.

Responsibilities of the President and Senior Management to Cedar Crest Board Members

1. Cedar Crest management will be available to interact and respond to the board as required for execution of board responsibilities.

2. Provide all required and relevant information to the board to conduct his/her job as a board member.

3. To the extent possible, board members will be indemnified from liability for a board member's reasonable and necessary actions. All board members will be covered by D&O liability insurance coverage.

Cedar Crest management has the responsibility to inform the board and/or the executive committee in a timely manner of any actions/information to ensure that the board has complete information to conduct the business of the board in a responsible and timely manner.

Exhibit 4.5: Daniel Webster College, Board Operating Agreements

During Meetings

1. Commitment
   - Fully shared responsibility for the achievement of the team charter
   - Collective, positive effort to make meaningful progress and to achieve the goals of the agenda

2. Selflessness
   - Commitment to the team charter transcends personal and individual interests, egos, and politics
   - The tendencies of your personality are subordinated to the requirements of team-appropriate behavior
   - Prioritize team progress over self-interests
   - Actively contribute to team effectiveness

3. Professionalism
   - Courtesy and tactfulness; emotions under control
   - One speaker at a time; active listening
   - Question to understand, not to challenge
   - Guard against emotional responses (self-orientation) including impatience, frustration, irritation, boredom, aggressiveness, defensiveness, withdrawal

4. Participation
   - Team commits to active and balanced participation in meetings; environment of openness and candor
   - Members inclined to dominate must hold themselves back
   - Members inclined to listen must force themselves to talk
   - Other members must monitor and encourage each of the above

5. Constructive intent
   - Presume good intent; seek win-win relationships
   - Question to understand, not to challenge
   - Challenge the idea, not the person
   - Offer alternatives, not just criticisms
   - Don't personalize others' comments

Exhibit 4.5: Daniel Webster College, Board Operating Agreements (*Continued*)

6. Consensus decisions
   - Allow time as needed to ensure effective, inclusive problem solving and to make decisions that can be fully supported by all members
   - Seek solutions that transcend conflicts
   - Are essential to buy-in and follow-on commitment
   - Require the team to be patient while people reach a fuller understanding of issues and options

7. Learning
   - Be open to new ideas and willing to make the effort to understand issues and others' points of view
   - Effective teamwork skills are as important as technical knowledge
   - Help others to understand; seek knowledge from others

8. Helpfulness
   - Team shares responsibility for each others' success; positive feedback and constructive suggestions are encouraged and appreciated
   - It's not enough to be responsible for your own performance
   - If the team has shared responsibility, members must accept that others are dependent on them and have expectations of them
   - Appreciate help when it's offered, don't resist it

9. Direct dealing
   - Issues with individuals will be dealt with directly; can't be a fractioned team
   - Be willing to put topics that impact team success on the table for team discussion, even when it focuses on a single individual
   - Don't confuse individual issues with personal issues
   - Addressing issues off-line with selected individuals can create cliques and lead to "organizational politics"

10. On-task
   - Arrive on time, come prepared; time and efforts aligned with priorities; one conversation at a time, no off-line conversations, no distractions, cell phones, PDAs, pagers, etc.
   - Allocate time appropriate to the priority of the activity
   - Don't let interaction dynamics (personal feelings and behaviors) rob time and energy from meaningful work

Outside of Meetings

1. Confidentiality

   • Be aware that much of the information we view and discuss is privileged and confidential

   • Keep confidential conversations and information in the board room and within designated committees

2. Integrity

   • Be consistent with what you say, in and out of the board room

   • If you have disagreements, bring them to the team and directly to the individuals involved

3. Discretion

   • Protect information, channel inquiries to the board chairman or president

   • Be aware that there is a coordinated, strategic effort under way to market the image of the college

   • Understand that press exposures are often hazardous as reporters seek topics (or spins) of controversy

4. Truthfulness

   • Seek and promote facts, expose and squelch rumors

   • Refuse to participate in rumors and speculation

   • Ask appropriate parties for information (data) to clarify issues

   • Share valid information with the entire team to clarify issues and dispel rumors

5. Inclusion

   • Don't operate outside the team, don't create or participate in team factions

   • Be aware of potential team conflicts and encourage others to engage in constructive resolution

   • Make the team aware if you see conflicts that may undermine team trust and effectiveness

6. Reliability

   • Do what you say you'll do

   • Follow through with action items

   • Let the team know in advance if you're not going to be able to meet a commitment

Source: Prepared by Rod Conard, President of Conard Associates, Inc. and former board chair of Daniel Webster College prior to its purchase by ITT Educational Services, Inc., 2008.

members should act and treat each other; the board felt that such clarity and specificity would help ensure greater team performance, and higher board performance.

Making Values and Behavioral Norms Explicit in the Context of Governance as Leadership.   The governance as leadership approach "requires more self-discipline and collective responsibility of board members than traditional governance does. . . . Board members need to come prepared, rise to the occasion, work diligently as a group, and expect to be intellectually taxed by complex and consequential questions" (Chait et al. 2005, 180).

Because the rules of engagement are different, governance-as-leadership boards will find it useful to make quite explicit what is expected of board members and what board members can expect in return.

The following sample, from the Trinity College Trustee Code of Conduct (Exhibit 4.6), is especially noteworthy in the context of governance as leadership because it

---

Exhibit 4.6: Trinity College, Trustee Code of Conduct:
Standards for Dissent, Participation, and Interaction with Campus Constituents

Dissent

An essential ingredient of participation in a meeting is that participants benefit from a full discussion of the pros and cons of issues proposed for decision by vote. In fact, the absence of healthy debate and dissent in discussions frequently leads to faulty decisions. By advocating responsible dissent, leaders create a climate where passive acceptance of issues will be challenged. Accordingly, trustees are encouraged, without fear of reprisal, to offer alternative points of view to the prevailing sense of the meeting, the status quo, or to decisions previously made or to policies in place. Honest dissent is welcomed in an environment of mutual trust that encourages an open and free exchange of ideas.

Registering Dissent

There are several appropriate ways to register dissent. In all cases, in strict confidence, dissent may be registered:

1. In the meeting where the discussion is taking place (most appropriate);
2. With the board chair;
3. With the board member chair of the appropriate committee;
4. With the president or the secretary of the college;
5. With another board member.

Participation

The effectiveness of the board is only as good as the participation of its members. The effective trustee will prepare for all meetings by:

1. Analytically reading and reviewing all correspondence to the board and responding when appropriate;

2. Thoughtfully and thoroughly preparing for each meeting of the full board, standing subcommittee, or charter committees;

3. Actively participating in each meeting of the full board, standing subcommittee, or special project team by asking provocative questions, providing insight, opinions, and alternative viewpoints;

4. Proactively offering or applying individual talents and desires to the work before the board; and

5. Proactively and immediately addressing miscommunication or conflict by approaching the board chair or working within the subcommittee when such scenarios may arise.

Interaction with the President, Administration, Faculty, Staff, and Students

Trustees are encouraged to interact freely with all of the college's constituencies and especially the president, administration, faculty, staff, and students. It is especially important that trustees share their feelings and ideas with the president and other members of the administration as part of the ongoing responsibility of being an effective trustee. Nonetheless . . . Trinity trustees are expected to be mindful of their pledge of confidentiality to the board and to utilize sound judgment when interacting with any member of the Trinity College community. At all times, trustees must refrain from discussing any pending board business or policy issues with the various Trinity constituencies unless such outreach is endorsed by the chair or the board itself. Lastly, trustees need to be sensitive, in dealing with the administration, that they enjoy special access and that this is a privilege not to be abused by promoting personal agendas or by being insensitive to demands on administrative time.

makes explicit the "standards" for board member comportment in three critical areas—dissent, participation, and interaction with campus constituents.

In addition to its comportment standards for dissent, participation, and interaction, the Trinity College code delineates standards for attendance, confidentiality, and conflict of interest. In a second section, the code briefly highlights expectations for philanthropy (trustees are expected to make the college "one of their primary philanthropic obligations" through gifts to the annual fund, capital campaigns, and special projects) and development (trustees are expected to "play an active role in development activities by identifying possible donors, personally soliciting donors typically with an officer of the college, and personally arranging meetings for an officer of the college with potential donors").

The last example of clarifying board member expectations (Exhibit 4.7), which Richard Chait and I developed for a client, utilizes a process of asking (and then answering) those questions "frequently asked" by prospective or new board members about board service, including issues of organizational history, structure, and mechanics as well as mutual behavioral expectations inside and outside the boardroom.

Exhibit 4.7: Questions Frequently Asked by Board Members About What to Expect from Board Service

The first section lists questions that prospective and new board members, and sometimes seasoned board members, often have about a board's operations. The second section poses questions about what board members should expect of each other. The answers to these questions, once codified and adopted, comprise a social compact that should be honored by all board members and, as necessary, enforced by the governance committee and the chair of the board as appropriate.

Different boards will, naturally enough, have different answers to the same questions. All boards should come to these answers through thoughtful and inclusive discussions among board members and with senior officers.

Part I. Frequently Asked Questions

1. Board Member Selection
   - What personal attributes do we seek in prospective board members?
   - What expertise and experience do we seek?
   - What is the nomination and election process?
   - How may I recommend possible candidates?

2. Board Organization and Structure
   - What is the board's committee structure?
   - How are committee assignments made?
   - Can non–board members serve on board committees?
   - Who names committee chairs?
   - How do we select the board chair?
   - What attributes do we seek in the board chair?
   - Is there an executive committee? If so, what does it do?
   - Do we ever use task forces or ad hoc groups?

3. Past, Present, and Future Challenges

- What were the most important decisions that the board has made in the last few years?
- What are the most important decisions on the horizon?

4. Board Meetings Logistics/Operations

- If I am unable to attend a meeting, should I let someone know?
- Whom should I contact if I want to be updated on a meeting I missed?
- How often do the board and committees meet?
- May I attend any and all committee meetings?
- Who, beside board members, attends our meetings?
- Are our meetings open to the press?
- How may I suggest agenda items for committee or board meetings?
- Do we meet in executive session with the CEO? Without the CEO?
- What are the ground rules for these sessions?
- Is there a dress code for meetings?
- Are there assigned seats?

5. Other Matters

- What are the expectations for giving?
- Am I expected to help with fundraising?
- Is there an orientation process for new board members?
- Is a "board buddy" or "mentor" assigned to new board members?
- Is there a conflict of interest policy in place for board members?
- What expectations do we have about personal giving?
- Are board members expected to help identify and cultivate development prospects?
- What process do we use to evaluate the CEO?
- Do we participate in the evaluation of any other senior officers?

Part II. Mutual Expectations

1. Inside the Boardroom

- Are there attendance requirements?
- Is it acceptable to arrive late or leave early?
- Is everything confidential?

Exhibit 4.7: Questions Frequently Asked by Board Members About What to Expect from Board Service (*Continued*)

- How do I raise or discuss sensitive issues?
- What should I do if I disagree with a committee or management recommendation?
- How do I balance a constructive partnership with a culture of accountability?
- What happens if there is a split vote on the board?
- Should I keep quiet in meetings for the first year or two?
- Are there discussion guidelines? (for example, how often I can speak, expressing disagreement, calling for a vote)
- Are there other points of etiquette? (for example, may I check my PDA? Cell phone? Have sidebar conversations?)
- How can I best prepare for board and committee meetings?
- Do we evaluate the board's performance? Individual board members? If so, how often? What do we do with the results?

2. Outside the Boardroom

- Can I contact the CEO directly?
- Can I contact senior management directly for information or to offer suggestions?
- What should I do if I am approached by the press, or other constituent representatives with questions or requests for information?
- What do I do with grapevine information or gossip?
- Are board members expected to attend functions in addition to board and committee meetings?
- Is there a special process to follow regarding health services for board members and family members?

Source: Prepared by Richard Chait and Cathy Trower, 2009.

If your organization has no formal statement of board member expectations, it might be wise to discuss the idea at a board retreat, or ask a task force or the governance committee to make recommendations to the full board. When the organization has a statement of mutual expectations for board members, it can be used when testing the waters with a possible recruit to ensure understanding, when orienting new board members (discussed in the following section), and in evaluating team performance (addressed later in this chapter).

New Board Member Orientation

New board members are typically given a "Board Handbook" that includes standard factual information including: the organization's mission, history, products, and services; the bylaws; a list of board officers and board committee structure; a directory of staff members and board members (that designates officers and committee chairs); a calendar of meetings and important organizational events; the budget and latest audit statements; a report on the endowment; the strategic plan; minutes from the past year's board meetings; policies about, for example, endowment investment and spending; and forms, for example, conflict of interest; annual goals for the CEO, board, and committees; and other materials deemed relevant to understanding the organization and good board membership.

If there is an orientation at all, new board members hear about the organization and its financial condition and board roles and responsibilities, anchored in the bylaws. They meet with senior officers and are taken on a tour of the physical plant, and that is usually the extent of things.

New Board Member Orientation in the Context of Governance as Leadership. Effective boards orient new board members not only to the organization and to the responsibilities of board members, but also to the culture of the board and the major issues it faces while governing the organization. An orientation should: (1) help new board members understand the board's norms and preferred protocol of behavior; (2) explain how the board *really* works; and (3) illustrate that there are no secrets or forbidden questions (Chait, Holland, and Taylor 1996, 74).

An effective new board member orientation in the context of governance as leadership would include the following components:

- An introduction to governance as leadership which might include the first chapter of this book.

- A careful, explicit, and thorough review of the board's norms, rules of engagement, and characteristics and behaviors of effective board members for *this* board. This review could be built, in part, around the answers to the questions presented in Exhibit 4.7.

- A brief history of major changes the board has made in recent years in the way it does business and why those changes were made.

- Discussion of recent decisions that best illustrate core values of the organization—the values that may currently be under stress with issues on the horizon—and the processes the board uses to discern the issues on which to focus, how the board discusses them, and how it makes decisions.

- If the board utilizes a Web portal, orientation should include a lesson on its use.

- A glossary of terms and sector acronyms.

- Background briefing on upcoming deliberations so new board members are informed and ready to participate.

- Briefing on how the board evaluates itself and its members with an eye to team play, group dynamics, board member engagement, and board effectiveness.

- Some time with the new member's mentor. Because governance as leadership demands more of board members, and is likely to be foreign even to those who have served on many nonprofit boards, it is especially important to provide a mentor or board "buddy" for a board member's first year who can help answer questions and privately explain things that happen in the boardroom which might be unclear to a newcomer.

As with determining board norms, the conversations a board has about what should comprise new board member orientation have big payoff not only in terms of clarity and focus, but also in building the board as a team.

Accountability

"No group ever becomes a team until it can hold itself accountable as a team" (Katzenbach and Smith 2006, 60). Effective boards accept shared responsibility *and* leadership; "it's no longer good enough for directors to sit back and leave the heavy lifting to a handful of people filling formal leadership roles" (Nadler et al. 2006, 115). Board members are responsible for their own behavior (self-management, that is, attending, being on time, being prepared, asking good questions) and for shaping the behavior of other members (peer-management, that is, not allowing an individual to be abusive, inconsiderate, overbearing, or negligent); "it takes only the dysfunctional behavior of a single director to undermine the entire board's ability to do good work" (Nadler et al. 2006, 116). Each board member should feel a responsibility to contribute meaningfully to the board's performance (Sonnenfeld 2002). Without commitment to mutual decisions, even the most focused and driven people often hesitate to call their peers on actions and behaviors that seem counterproductive to the good of the team (Lencioni 2002).

Lencioni (2002) recommended an exercise to help build team performance whereby each member identifies the single most important contribution that each of their peers makes to the team, as well as one area that they must either improve upon or eliminate for the good of the team. Focusing on one person at a time, everyone reports their responses. This process may seem risky or difficult for some, but if the focus is truly on the team, and improving collective performance, the outcomes can be very positive. If it still seems too risky, the responses about each person could be collected anonymously so that no one is put on the spot or feels pressure to hedge their true beliefs about a colleague.

Accountability for Individual and Team Performance in the Context of Governance as Leadership.   Governance as leadership requires that board members be thoughtful participants at board meetings as they engage in critical thinking and constructive discussions, and remember that team play is essential to high performance. In order to ensure a key characteristic of high-performing teams—accountability—it is essential that there be

ways to measure and account for individual board member and board team performance. For individual performance, there is the 360 review, discussed previously. Because that process can be problematic and ill-advised for some boards, another approach is to have board members think about and rate their own performance (Exhibit 4.8).

Exhibit 4.8: Individual Board Member Performance Self-Assessment

Item	Strongly Agree	Agree	Disagree	Strongly Disagree
I understand the principles of governance as leadership.				
I understand the practice of governance as leadership with our board.				
I understand what is expected of me as a board member.				
I am reasonably well-informed about the organization.				
I am reasonably well-informed about trends affecting the organization.				
I have received feedback on my performance as a board member.				
I serve on a committee(s) that makes use of my talents.				
I understand the organization's mission.				
I understand the board's mission.				
I participate fully at board meetings.				
I give to the organization in accordance with expectations.				
I usually leave board meetings feeling it was important for me to be there.				
I have a good working relationship with the CEO.				
I have a good working relationship with the board chair.				
I understand how I can take on greater leadership responsibilities (for example, chair a board committee or task force).				

Exhibit 4.8: Individual Board Member Performance Self-Assessment (*Continued*)

- You have many commitments, perhaps including volunteering on other boards. Why are you this board?
- What do you find most fulfilling about serving on this board?
- What do you find most frustrating about serving on this board?
- Are there specific ways we could make better use of your time and talents? Please describe.

An individual's specific ratings and comments should be considered privately in one-on-one meetings with the chair of the governance committee. Aggregated average ratings, however, could provide excellent fodder for a full board discussion where board members make sense of the findings. For example, the board could discuss what accounts for low averages on any given item as well as the range of scores for items, especially those with the least congruence (for example, a bimodal distribution with a number of board members "strongly agreeing" and "strongly disagreeing"). What might account for that? Depending on how often the board does such assessments, changes over time could be analyzed by the board, again with an eye toward what accounts for improvements or worsening scores.

To measure team performance, Richard Chait and I designed a survey instrument (Exhibit 4.9) that allows anonymous input after meetings. Results can be tallied and shared for discussion at the next meeting to discern what went well and did not go well with respect to teamwork and to discuss possible approaches to improve.

Not only does the board assess its team performance, but it also makes sense of what the assessment reveals, and discusses how to capitalize on strengths and ways to improve weaknesses.

Skilled Team Leadership

Another key ingredient to high team performance is effective leadership. Leaders have the power to change and shape an organizational culture by what they pay attention to and reward; by acting as a model for the desired behaviors; and through the selection of senior staff members and board members. Leaders set the tone for the entire organization by modeling open, honest, and decisive dialogue (Charan 2001).

In the typical boardroom, there are two primary leaders: the CEO and the board chair. The chief executive sets the tone by the kind of issues he or she brings to the table, the quality and timeliness of the information he or she provides to the board, by the nature of his or her presentations to the board, and by how he or she responds to

Exhibit 4.9: Board Team Assessment Survey

Item	Strongly Agree	Agree	Disagree	Strongly Disagree
Meeting goals were explicitly stated.				
Board members were respectful of one another.				
Dissent was encouraged.				
Board members listened carefully to one another.				
Board members were open to different viewpoints.				
There was ample dialogue between board members.				
There was good give-and-take with senior staff members/executives.				
There was widespread participation.				
No one exercised undue influence.				
The atmosphere was collegial.				
No one was marginalized.				

- On a scale of 1 to 9, where 9 is best, how do you rate our overall performance as a team today?
- Were there any major infractions of group norms?
- If so, were the infractions explicitly addressed?

questions that board members ask (Alderfer 2001). The board chair is first among equals around the table. He or she has a long list of responsibilities including: facilitating the board's involvement in policymaking; guiding the board in its fiduciary oversight role and in support of the strategic plan; leading and facilitating board meetings; overseeing the board's committee structure; cultivating and orienting new board members; cultivating donors; overseeing the hiring, compensation, and evaluation of the CEO; and serving as a chief advocate for the organization in a variety of settings. Together, the CEO and chair "shape the culture through their own behaviors and actions, inside and outside the boardroom. They set the tone, manage interaction, and both clarify and reinforce norms by rewarding behavior that is appropriate and sanctioning behavior that isn't" (Nadler et al. 2006, 119).

Skilled Team Leadership in the Context of Governance as Leadership. Chapter Six will focus on what governance as leadership requires from the CEO and board chair that goes beyond the usual ways we think about those roles. For the purposes of this chapter on the board as a high-performing team, two issues are of primary importance: first, implementing an inclusive chair selection and succession process; and second, elevating the role of the governance committee beyond nominating new board members.

Chair Selection Process and Succession Planning

The caliber of the board chair enormously influences the quality of governance. Unfortunately, it is not uncommon for nonprofit board members to be unclear about how chair selection happens; someone is seemingly "anointed." The selection process is either improvised or reinvented each time the need arises. Failure to plan for chair succession can lead one board member to remain in that position for too long and concentrate too much power in the same hands, which serves to reinforce the corrosive idea that the board lacks depth of leadership (Chait et al. 1996, 81).

Because of the crucial role that the board chair plays in building, energizing, motivating, and leading the board as a team that engages effectively, meaningfully, and forthrightly at meetings, the process to select that person should be:

- Transparent: All board members should understand how the process works.

- Inclusive: All board members should have the opportunity to offer input.

- Contextualized: The decision should take account of institutional circumstances.

- Institutionalized: The process should be codified so that it is consistent over time.

As with the search for a CEO, the selection of a board chair should begin with: (1) a position description that delineates roles and responsibilities; (2) a set of paramount goals and objectives to achieve; and (3) a set of desired attributes, skills, and experiences.

To get started, it may be desirable to poll the board as to their thoughts about which group or individual (for example, all board members, the governance committee, the executive committee, the current board chair) should: (1) determine the chair's roles and responsibilities with respect to the board and to management (if not part of the bylaws or if only vaguely discussed therein); (2) set the goals and objectives for the next chair; (3) determine the desired attributes and skills of the next chair; (4) propose chair candidates; (5) decide the suitability of chair candidates; (6) make the recommendation; and (7) make the selection.

Steps 1 and 2: It is common practice to delegate the first two steps to the governance committee or committee on trusteeship. Regarding the job description and goals, the committee might ask a subset of the board, "What are the chair's most important functions, roles, and responsibilities?" and "What does the board and the organization need the chair to do over the next year or two?" As appropriate, goals might be related to transitioning to a new CEO, thinking through the next strategic plan, fostering more board engagement, focusing the board's deliberations, ensuring more effective committee work, promoting greater teamwork, developing an annual board work plan, or motivating more philanthropy. The governance committee could then take the job description and goals to the full board for approval.

Step 3: Given the job description and the goals for the chair, all board members can then be polled to determine the set of attributes, skills, and personality traits that it feels are "essential" and "highly desirable" in its next board chair.

Step 4: To determine a slate of potential candidates, members of the executive or governance committee should be asked to interview, in person or by phone, those who are determining the slate and ask:

- Do you have any further reflections or comments on the list of attributes previously developed?

- Are there any particular individuals whom you would recommend for consideration as board chair?

- Would you consider serving as board chair, if asked? (This question might be asked only of board members with a certain number of years' service, say three or more.)

Those conducting the interviews should use a common interview protocol and input collection form which would be collected and analyzed or tallied by the governance committee. Board members and senior staff should be invited to contact a member of the governance committee to add or delete names for consideration.

Steps 5, 6, and 7: The governance committee should review the recommended candidates against the stated job description, goals, and desired attributes and skill set to identify a preferred candidate whose name should then be shared with the executive committee and the CEO—not for approval but for comments and observations. Assuming the enthusiastic support of the CEO and the executive committee, and no overriding objections, the governance committee would place the candidate's name in nomination for review and approval by the board.

Elevate the Importance of Governance

Most nonprofits boards have, by tradition and bylaws, a "Committee on Trusteeship" with the primary responsibility of cultivating and nominating new board members. A typical set of duties would involve: (1) identifying board needs (usually using a template showing gaps in terms of demographic or professional skill sets); (2) generating a list of possible candidates (often by asking fellow board members and the CEO for names); (3) targeting certain prospects to interview; (4) proposing a set of nominees to the board for a vote; (5) conducting new board member orientation; and (6) proposing a set of officers and committee chairs to the board.

Although those activities are certainly important, governing consequentially requires much more of the board, which translates into spreading the responsibility for the quality of governance beyond the board chair and a handful of board officers and committee chairs, and expanding the role of a committee that is solely focused on nominating new board members and recommending a slate of officers into one that considers governance more broadly.

A charter for a governance committee would include the functions described in this chapter, including: (1) considering board composition not only in traditional terms but also by taking into account the diversity of thought and the mix of minds; (2) ensuring a shared sense of high purpose and meaningful goals by having the board discuss its mission and what it needs to do to support the mission; (3) making values and norms explicit through a board code of conduct or statement of mutual expectations that speaks to board roles, cultural norms, and appropriate behaviors; (4) providing new board member orientation not only about the organization but also about what service on the board entails and the standards for performance; (5) measuring individual and board team performance (as well as evaluating board meetings, committee, and overall board performance, discussed in Chapter Seven); and (6) ensuring an effective chair selection and succession process.

In addition, board education should be part of the governance committee's charter. With the senior staff, it should:

- Determine what is essential for board members to know such as "Financial Statements 101" and "Understanding Our Budgeting Process," and ensuring that board members have the basics. Some boards have a staff member or board member (or one of each) present optional mini-workshops (sixty to ninety minutes) on such matters.

- Determine ongoing education needs by having management identify a list of key trends board members should know about and have each board member rate, anonymously, their knowledge level on each. The committee can then, along with management, create short education sessions to address the knowledge gaps.

- Identify newsletters or magazines from the sector that all board members should read and then ensure subscriptions.

- Selectively mine such publications for especially relevant articles and assign them as reading (along with discussion questions) prior to board meetings.

CHAPTER FOUR HIGHLIGHTS

- **Effective boards pay attention to the board as a social system.** As attractive as it is to work on board structure, discuss the number of times a board should meet, or whether or not to have term limits, the fact is that the board is a social system composed of individuals coming together periodically to govern. The better those individuals work together, and with the organization's CEO and senior staff, the better the governance.

- **Boards can move from being groups to being high-performing teams.** Groups have no significant incremental performance need; they interact primarily to share information and make decisions. Teams share a common goal and sense of purpose for which they hold themselves mutually accountable. High-performing board teams have effective group dynamics and leadership, a supportive architecture, and focus on substantive issues.

- **In the governance-as-leadership context, effective board composition involves more than professional expertise.** In addition to considering board member background, expertise, and demographic characteristics, building a governance-as-leadership board requires understanding the personal qualities, skills, interpersonal style, and ways of thinking that each board member brings to the table, as well as the constellation formed by the individual stars.

- **Boards that embrace the governance-as-leadership framework ensure high purpose and effective teamwork by:**

  - Having a board mission statement that reflects the board's long-term legacy.

  - Developing a statement of behavioral norms and mutual expectations for board service that reflects the ideals of governance as leadership.

  - Orienting new board members to the way the board does business, including that it thinks and works trimodally.

  - Holding itself accountable for individual and team performance by assessing and discussing both.

  - Elevating the role of the governance committee and ensuring skilled team leadership (especially the board chair).

CHAPTER

5

CREATING A GOVERNANCE-AS-LEADERSHIP CULTURE

Make no mistake: it is the board's culture—the shared values and beliefs that delineate acceptable behavior—that ultimately determines how effective the board can be. Unless you have a culture that supports the active and independent participation of every director, nothing else matters.

—David A. Nadler, former chairman of Mercer Delta Consulting (2006, 104–5)

Social norms, introduced simply in the previous chapter as "the way we do things around here," are the written and unwritten rules that specify acceptable behaviors of a group; they are acceptable because they reflect shared values. Herb Kelleher, former CEO of Southwest Airlines, once said, "Culture is what people do when no one is looking"—a vivid reminder that norms, reflective of shared values, are the foundation of a group's culture. As we shall see, though, the normative assumptions driving group culture are so taken for granted that, over time, they become invisible—that is, below conscious thought.

Traditional governance is practiced in ceremonial fashion in tightly scripted meetings focused on compliance with culturally accepted norms like formality; deference to management; congeniality among board members; and individual influence, power, and status accorded by virtue of title, position, and wealth. The critical thinking and teamwork demanded by governance as leadership require a very different set of underlying assumptions about board performance that form the basis of a very different culture—the third subsystem—and subject of this chapter.

CULTURE

In technical terms, a group or organization's culture is: "A pattern of shared basic assumptions that the group learned as it solved its problems of external adaptation and internal integration, that has worked well enough to be considered valid and, therefore, to be taught to new members as the correct way to perceive, think, and feel in relation to those problems" (Schein 1992, 12).

A board's culture "consists of a combination of informal rules, agreements, and traditions that have developed slowly and unconsciously over time. Culture determines who makes the decisions, who speaks to whom and in what manner, how board and staff members relate to one another, and even where board members sit around the table. Culture also drives decisions about what role the chief executive has in board meetings, where the board invests the lion's share of its time, and what issues are considered sacred cows" (Axelrod 2007, 1).

To fully understand a culture, it is necessary to examine its three layers: (1) artifacts (visible structures and processes); (2) espoused values (stated strategies, goals, and philosophies); and (3) basic underlying assumptions (unconscious, taken-for-granted beliefs, perceptions, thoughts, and feelings—the ultimate sources of values and actions) (Schein 1992).

Artifacts

Artifacts in the boardroom include the physical trappings such as the table around which board members sit, the board chair's gavel, the board members' chairs, and engraved nameplates; and the observable processes such as where the CEO and board chair sit, how board members are called upon to speak, the role of the CEO and other staff members, and how voting occurs. Though observable, artifacts can be difficult to decipher; it is "dangerous to infer deeper assumptions from artifacts alone because one's interpretations will inevitably be projections of one's own feelings and reactions" (Schein 1992, 18). To understand a culture beyond what one can observe, one must go deeper to examine the values that group members say are important.

Espoused Values

Group learning is a reflection of "someone's original values, someone's sense of what ought to be as distinct from what is" (Schein 1992, 19). Over time, the values that are acted upon and achieve desired results become part of a group's shared meaning and understanding. Eventually, the most successful strategies become shared assumptions of what is good and correct; the prevailing espoused values are transformed into "non-discussable" assumptions supported by sets of beliefs, norms, and operational rules of behavior (Schein 1992, 20).

There is an important distinction between what people *say* they value (espoused values) and those values that have actually transformed into basic assumptions; therefore, espoused values predict well what people *say* but may not gel with what people actually *do* (Schein 1992). For example, board members may *say* they value dissent, but then squelch the dissenting voice. Espoused board member values depend on the type of organization and board, as well as on the individuals themselves. If the board has a codified statement of board member expectations (discussed in Chapter Four), the espoused values are quite clear. But not everything that governs behavior is, or can be, written down.

Underlying Assumptions

Underlying assumptions are the ultimate source of values and actions. If a basic assumption of a group is strongly held, members will find any other premise to be "inconceivable" (Schein 1992, 22). Argyris (1976) called these basic assumptions the "theories-in-use" and found that they actually guide behavior. Because basic assumptions are so widely held, group members neither confront nor debate them; they truly are taken for granted and are therefore extremely difficult to change. To change would require group members to "resurrect and reexamine" strongly held assumptions which is destabilizing. To "destabilize our cognitive and interpersonal world" (Schein 1992, 22) goes well beyond producing cognitive dissonance—the uncomfortable tension which comes from holding two conflicting thoughts in the mind at the same time—to causing great anxiety (discussed in Chapter Two). "Rather than tolerating such anxiety levels we tend to want to perceive the events around us as congruent with our assumptions, even if that means distorting, projecting, or in other ways falsifying to ourselves what is going on around us. It is in this psychological process that culture has its ultimate power" (22).

These three aspects of culture—artifacts, espoused values, and underlying assumptions—are intertwined: "Culture springs from shared values, a consistent view that certain things are axiomatically either good or bad in a given social context. Based on those values, people develop a set of beliefs—expectations that a particular form of behavior will inexorably lead to certain consequences, either positive or negative. Those beliefs, in turn, give rise to *norms*, unwritten yet powerful rules that define acceptable and unacceptable behavior. Those norms often result in *artifacts*, the observable evidence of culture at work" (Nadler et al. 2006, 109).

In summary, group cultures are pervasive, stable, and extremely resistant to change because:

- The human mind needs cognitive stability which comes, in part, from basic underlying beliefs about what is good and right.

- Challenges to such stability produce anxiety and defensiveness for individuals and for groups.

- Defense mechanisms kick in that can distort data by denial, rejection, rationalization, or other defensive means; we would rather *defend* than *change* basic assumptions.

- The power of culture is that assumptions are implicit, unconscious, and shared, and therefore mutually reinforced.

- Even if assumptions are somehow surfaced, or exposed, they still operate (Schein 1992).

THREE TOXIC CULTURES

Although not specifically about boards, Michael Roberto's description (2005) of three cultures that are particularly toxic to good decision making are certainly applicable.

Culture of Maybe

Especially in highly analytical cultures, management strives to gather extensive amounts of objective data prior to making decisions, applies quantitative analysis whenever possible, and makes exhaustive attempts to evaluate many different contingencies and scenarios. "Analysis paralysis" can occur as individuals strive to resolve all uncertainty and engage in costly searches for new information.

In a culture of maybe, people find themselves endlessly pursuing every unresolved question without regard to the costs of those searches for more data. How many times have you seen board members ask management for more information, more data? And management dutifully provides it, only to be asked for still more data. Roberto noted three primary reasons for the prevalence of cultures of maybe: (1) many members' personality and cognitive style favor seemingly rational and objective problem-solving methods; (2) many members have been educated and trained to value systematic, analytical techniques; and (3) when making critical decisions, anticipatory regret (Janis and Mann 1977) is common. People become anxious, apprehensive, and risk averse when they imagine the negative emotions that they may experience if a decision they make is wrong. High anticipatory regret can lead to indecision and costly delays (Roberto 2005, 154).

Culture of No

Former IBM CEO Lou Gerstner encountered a culture of no which he called a "nonconcur" system. Cross-functional teams could spend months working together on a solution to a problem but if any single manager objected because of some perceived negative effect on his or her unit, he or she could obstruct or prevent implementation. A lone dissenter could issue a "nonconcur" and stop a proposal dead in its tracks. A culture of no enables those with the most power or the loudest voices to impose their will on the group, typically by offering critiques rather than positive pronouncements about proposals and ideas under consideration (Roberto 2005, 147).

Stanford scholars Jeffrey Pfeffer and Robert Sutton (1999) referred to this "insidious inhibitor of action" as the "smart talk trap"; their research showed that all too often people are "rewarded for talking—the longer, louder, and more confusingly the better" (135). Those who talk frequently are more likely to be judged by others as influential and important and are seen to be the leaders (think hedgehogs and boardroom lions). But Pfeffer and Sutton also found that when people strive to impress others in meetings, they tend to explain—in unnecessarily complex or abstract language—how and why a proposal will *not* work, rather than describing why it might succeed. The former lapses into criticism for criticism's sake; the latter confuses people. Both tendencies can stop action in its tracks.

Roberto (2005, 146) made important distinctions between a "culture of no" and devil's advocacy in terms of what dissenters do, shown here in Table 5.1. Ensuring dissent through effective devil's advocacy is an important element in good decision-making processes.

TABLE 5.1 *Two Types of Dissent: Devil's Advocacy Versus Culture of No.*

Devil's Advocacy	Culture of No
Objective is to encourage divergent thinking and open new lines of inquiry.	Objective is to block proposals that conflict with one's own interests and objectives.
Dissenters have the ability to affect the decision process, but not dictate the outcome.	Lone dissenters have virtual veto power.
Dissenters have more impact if they present unbiased perspectives and if they provide equal levels of critical examination for all options under consideration.	Dissenters with more power and status, or who "pound the table harder than others," have more clout.
Dissenters share information freely with others so that others may form their own conclusions.	Dissenters horde information that might enable others to engage them in a productive dialogue.
Dissenters seek to generate many new options.	Dissenters tear down existing proposals without offering alternatives.
Dissenters focus on the extent to which assumptions underlying each option may be overly pessimistic as well as overly optimistic.	Dissenters focus only on downside risks associated with the specific proposals that they oppose.

Source: Michael A. Robert, *Why Great Leaders Don't Take Yes for an Answer: Managing for Conflict and Consensus,* 1st ed., © 2005. Reprinted by permission of Pearson Education, Inc., Upper Saddle River, NJ.

Culture of Yes

In a culture of yes, group members appear to agree by smiling and nodding, but some or many are secretly thinking "no." Board members may suppress objections during meetings, but then work behind the scenes (often in one-on-one, sidebar or parking lot conversations) to undermine the apparent consensus. This culture can develop when raising objections during meetings is not only frowned upon but is actively discouraged. All too often, board meetings are a race against time and any dissension can cause board members or senior staff members to roll their eyes, sigh heavily, and frown a lot. Over time, these highly dysfunctional behaviors lead to groupthink, where everyone goes along even though they disagree, just for the sake of being agreeable and not standing out as a "troublemaker."

In a *Harvard Business Review* article, Charan (2001) discussed a "culture of indecision," similar to Roberto's "culture of yes." It happens like this. A two-inch-thick proposal is reviewed at a board meeting. When the presentation is over, the room is silent as board members look down, look left or right, waiting for someone to open the discussion. The presenter may even ask, "Are there any questions?" When no one says anything, or a few simple questions are asked and answered in perfunctory fashion, the CEO asks a few mildly skeptical questions to show he has done his due diligence, but it is clear he backs the project. Soon, those around the table chime in dutifully with positive comments so that it appears that everyone supports the proposal. However, several around the table have real reservations and concerns; others are only lukewarm about the idea. But everyone keeps their opinions to themselves and the meeting ends inconclusively. "Over the next few months, the project is slowly strangled to death in a series of strategy, budget, and operational reviews. It's not clear who's responsible for the killing, but it's plain that the true sentiment in the room was the opposite of the apparent consensus" (Charan 2001, 76). Constrained by lack of trust and formality, the group failed to engage with one another meaningfully at the meeting. Without emotional commitment to the proposal, the project is doomed to fail, mostly because of a failure to truly decide after considerable dialogue and debate during which all views are aired.

If these are examples of poor cultures, what are the good ones? For Charan (2005), that would be a culture of the "progressive" board (discussed in Chapter Four); for Axelrod (2007), it is a culture of inquiry—"a climate that fully enlists multiple skills, differences of opinion, and informed questions" (vii), where board members look at issues from all sides and are not afraid to question complex, controversial, or ambiguous matters (2). A culture of inquiry is one where:

- Dialogue, candor, and dissent are all part of group dynamics; board members master the skills of listening, dissecting the issues, and responding thoughtfully in the best interests of the organization.

- Learning and information gathering are important ingredients because decision making and accountability depend on board members' confidence that they are knowledgeable about various sides of an issue.

- Vigilance is part of the culture, and board members are aware that difficult questions need deliberation; even situations that seem trouble-free may encompass deeper, more complicated issues.

These dimensions of a culture of inquiry provide a nice segue to thinking about the culture required to help boards put governance as leadership into practice.

CULTURE CHANGE

Because the research and literature on organizational culture and how to change it are so vast, I will not attempt to report it here, but perhaps a short distillation by John Kotter, Harvard Business School professor, author, and authority on the subjects, would be helpful here. Kotter (1995, 1996) has written that there are eight steps that leaders should take in order to oversee an effective cultural change process. Those steps are to:

1. Establish a sense of urgency. Kotter believes that 75 percent of an organization's leaders need to be convinced that the organization needs to change for the eight-step process to work. One way to light that fire is to identify the cost and consequences for not taking action; see Chapter Two's Getting Started section about calculating the cost of the status quo and about creating Anxiety II (Schein 1993).

2. Form a powerful coalition. No change process is successful if only one person wants to do it; therefore, it is good practice to create a team of leaders who champion the change. See Chapter Two's Getting Started section on building support.

3. Create a change vision. According to Kotter, this step begins with getting clear on values and using those values to create a vision statement. See Chapter Two about reflecting your sector's values and best practices in the boardroom.

4. Communicate the vision. The keys here, according to Kotter, are to keep the message simple and clear, and repeat it often.

5. Empower others to act on the vision. This step involves cultivating change leaders (see Chapter Four about elevating the importance of governance and establishing a governance committee).

6. Plan for and create short-term wins. Because success breeds success, it is a good idea to start small, showcase successes, and recognize those who make positive contributions.

7. Consolidate improvements and produce more change. Kotter recommends setting targets, measuring, and reporting on progress (see Chapter Five on organizational dashboards and Chapter Seven on governance and board dashboards).

8. Make change stick. Kotter reminds us that it is easy to fall back to old ways of doing business, so leaders need to persist, embed new values when hiring, and

constantly reinforce and model the desired behaviors. These topics are covered in Chapter Four on board composition, this chapter on norms, Chapter Six on leadership, and Chapter Seven on sustaining governance as leadership.

CULTURE CONDUCIVE TO GOVERNANCE AS LEADERSHIP

There are three overarching "genetic markers" of "governance as leadership-friendly" cultures: (1) the board plays a central role in discernment and sense-making; (2) the board and management collaborate effectively; and (3) diligence through productive engagement. These are each discussed in the following sections.

Collective Discerning, Learning, and Sensemaking

Lew Platt, former CEO of Hewlett-Packard (HP), famously said, "If only HP knew what HP knows, we would be three times more productive." The same is true of boards. But for many reasons discussed in prior chapters—impediments to critical thinking, individual or group cognitive biases, or dysfunctional group dynamics—learning is difficult in organizations. Learning requires that groups spot and frame problems and opportunities and work their way up the knowledge hierarchy to unleash the collective wisdom needed to solve or capitalize on them, which requires group sensemaking—all easier said than done. Although these concepts—discerning, sensemaking, and learning—represent another triple helix in that they are intertwined rather than separate or linear, each is described separately here for ease of discussion.

Discerning.   A major premise of the book *Know What You Don't Know* (Roberto 2009) is that successful organizations must change their mindset from problem *solving* to problem *finding*, much as Chait, Ryan, and Taylor (2005) said that better governance requires *sense* making before *decision* making and problem *framing* before problem *solving*.

Because good governance starts with good judgment about what matters most to the organization, boards and management must sift through information, read signals, pay attention to cues and clues, and ultimately discern what really matters. Some boards have practiced a managerial version of governance; that is, "instead of identifying problems, framing issues, or making sense of the organization, most boards address the problems that managers present to them. . . . When trustees and executives describe what would happen if the board 'hibernated' for several years, no one worries that the organization would be deprived of powerful ideas, keen insights, or important perspectives on problems. Even when vigorous debate does occur, board discussion invariably remains embedded within the initial frame constructed by management" (Chait et al. 2005, 92–93).

In addition to the issues of board member boredom and dissatisfaction resulting from not being invited into conversations upstream, and the dysfunctional behaviors that can result (for example, micromanagement, disengagement), there is another big concern with leaving the problem finding to the CEO or members of the staff: organizational problems may remain invisible—unidentified and undisclosed (Roberto 2009, 6). Organizational problems tend to remain hidden because: (1) people fear being marginalized or punished for speaking up to name them; (2) structural complexity keeps them obscured—that is, people cannot see the forest for the trees; (3) there are gatekeepers who filter or insulate leaders from hearing bad news; (4) organizations overemphasize formal analysis and underappreciate intuitive reasoning; and (5) people are not typically trained to spot problems (Roberto 2009, 9).

Finding and Framing the Issues. Roberto (2009) recommended several steps to becoming better problem finders. One is especially germane in the context of governance as leadership: the best problem finders are not isolated from their constituents. Good problem finders "reach out to the periphery of their business, and they engage in authentic, unscripted conversations with those people on the periphery. They set out to observe the unexpected, while discarding their preconceptions and biases" (20).

Because discerning important issues—such as problems and opportunities—and learning to spot triple-helix issues is "more a matter of cultivating awareness, than instituting procedures" (Chait et al. 2005, 110), having the board work at the tightly coupled boundaries of the organization is, in fact, essential to generative governance. "If one wanted to create an environment hostile to generative thinking, the typical boardroom would be a good start. It isolates trustees from cues and clues, features only information that is already framed, makes debate about the frames off limits, and discourages encounters with outsiders that inspire generative thinking" (111). The authors recommended having the board members work between the board and the organization (internal), for example, university board members having lunch with students or going on a retreat with faculty and deans; and between the board and the wider environment (external); for example, hospital trustees meeting with agencies that rate or accredit health care facilities (116).

In addition to talking with internal and external stakeholders, another good way to determine what matters most, and to help discern where the board should focus its attention, is to have board and staff members answer one of two questions: (1) What is the single most important question the board and management need to address in the next twelve to eighteen months? or (2) What three topics should be high on the board's agenda in the year ahead? The idea is to understand the collective views about what constitutes the most consequential subject matter for the board's attention. After the input has been gathered, engage the board in conversation about what they see and select the questions and issues around which there is the most agreement. As former Netscape CEO Jim Barksdale once said, "The main thing is to keep the main thing the main thing"; keeping focus is essential. Some boards can get sidetracked by the idea du jour or a current business trend. This doesn't work any better for nonprofits than it does for corporations.

Once the crucial issues have been identified, discuss possible ways to frame them by asking: "How do we see the problem or opportunity?" At this stage, the board and management together generate insight and understanding about a question, problem, challenge, opportunity, or the environment, *and* a sense of the organization's identity by thinking through "our way" of responding.

Learning.   If we accept the Merriam-Webster definition of learning as "knowledge or skill acquired by instruction, study, or experience," and wisdom as "accumulated learning," we can think about how groups learn and how boards improve governance. An examination of the Knowledge Management (KM) literature yields an important concept for boards—the Knowledge Hierarchy, introduced by systems theorist and professor of organizational change, Russell Ackoff (1989). The Knowledge Hierarchy involves moving from *data* (raw, unprocessed information) to *information* (processed data that has been giving "meaning" by way of relational connection, answering "who," "what," "where," and "when" questions) to *knowledge* (the application of information into something useful, answering "how" questions) to *understanding* (defined as mentally grasping, comprehending, appreciating the "why," thus requiring diagnosis and prescription) to *wisdom* (evaluated understanding or insight). Milan Zeleny (1987) referred to data as "know-nothing"; to information as "know-what"; to knowledge as "know-how"; and to wisdom as "know-why."

Although consequential governance demands that organizations tap the collective wisdom of the board members at board meetings, and despite the simplicity of the KM hierarchy, it would be naïve and erroneous to think that groups of people move systematically from observing data to making connections that define information, to appropriate application, and then to insight. Because sensemaking is complicated, without a clear beginning and end, it is critical to good decision making to understand more about how groups make sense of what they experience—the subject of the next section.

Sensemaking.   Simply stated, sensemaking is how we give meaning to experience. "Sensemaking is a motivated, continuous effort to understand connections (which can be made among people, places, and events) in order to anticipate their trajectory and act effectively" (Klein, Moon, and Hoffman 2006, 71). It involves turning circumstances into something that is comprehended explicitly in words and serves as a springboard into action; it involves the ongoing retrospective development of plausible images that rationalize what people are doing (Weick, Sutcliffe, and Obstfeld 2005, 409).

In organizations, group sensemaking often happens when the current state differs from the expected state and people come together to ask such questions as "What is going on here?" or "What happened?" or "What should we do about it?" Decision makers need to make sense of the past—retrospective sensemaking—in order to move forward; "people actually make sense by thinking about the past, not the future. By the time they are framed, the cues and clues we rely on for sensemaking are in the past" (Chait et al. 2005, 87). In the governance-as-leadership framework, it is the cues, frames, and retrospective thinking that enable sensemaking, where goal setting and direction setting originate and on which mission setting, strategy development, and problem solving depend.

Sensemaking starts with chaos and organizes flux through noticing and categorizing cues or clues based on our background, training, and experiences (Weick et al. 2005, 411). This is, in part, why two heads are better than one; different people will see, pay attention to, and assign meaning differently to different cues and clues. The distinguishing features of sensemaking are that:

- Its genesis lies in disruptive ambiguity
- It begins when people notice and categorize cues and clues
- It encompasses a mixture of retrospect and prospect
- Its presumptions guide action
- It recognizes the interdependence of variables
- It culminates in acting *thinkingly*

"Answers to the question 'what's the story?' emerge from retrospect, connections with past experience, and dialogue. Answers to the question 'now what?' emerge from presumptions about the future, articulation concurrent with action, and projects that become increasingly clear as they unfold" (Weick et al. 2005, 413).

Sensemaking serves numerous important functions: (1) satisfying a need to comprehend; (2) helping us test plausibility; (3) clarifying the past, but not necessarily making it completely understood; (4) anticipating the future; (5) unleashing a process of deliberations about plausible explanations of what is happening; (6) guiding the exploration of information; and (7) helping groups find common ground and shared meaning (Klein, Moon, and Hoffman 2006, 72).

There are two very important things to keep in mind about group sensemaking. First, it is not about truth or getting it right; rather, group sensemaking is about continued redrafting of an emerging story so that it becomes more comprehensible, incorporates more of the observed data, and is more resilient in the face of criticism; and, second, it is more about plausibility than accuracy (Weick et al. 2005).

In its truest sense, sensemaking is learning in action. "To deal with ambiguity, interdependent people search for meaning, settle for plausibility, and move on. Increased sensemaking should occur when people are socialized to make do, be resilient, treat constraints as self-imposed, strive for plausibility, keep showing up, use retrospect to get a sense of direction, and articulate descriptions that energize. These are micro-level actions. They are small actions, but they are small actions with large consequences" (Weick et al. 2005, 419).

Exhibit 5.1 shows how a foundation board "sense-makes" and "learns what it thinks" by utilizing different approach to making critical decisions.

Board-Management Collaboration

A common lament from CEOs is that the board micromanages; if only board members better understood their roles and responsibilities vis-à-vis management, all would be

Exhibit 5.1: Board Sensemaking in Action

In the past, the CEO presented a decision situation to the board, explained how the staff planned to respond, and asked the board if there were any questions. Typically, there were a few scattered, almost random and inconsequential questions, and the board would vote to approve management's decision.

Now, when the organization is facing critical decision situations, management takes the scenario to the board and asks these questions:

- What do you think our decision should be? Why?
- In formulating your answer, what constituents did you consider?
- How might this decision be viewed by which constituents?
- What are the intended consequences of the decision?
- What might be some unintended consequences (positive and negative)?
- What criteria or factors did you consider in making the decision?
- Did certain criteria weigh more heavily than others in making your decision? Why?

The CEO reported, "This method has produced far better board decisions than anything we tried in the past. How the board thinks is revealed by the answers to these difficult questions and the organization learns so much about itself. The board applies critical thinking and is engaged. Staff members have greater buy-in and constituents feel like they matter. This is truly win-win-win all around."

The board chair said, "We are much more deliberative now as we consider not only the upside of a decision, but also what might go wrong—the unintended negative possibilities. And even though we can't prevent them from happening, at least we've made a conscious decision to go forward—or not—with our eyes open. In addition, we are actually doing our job as board members, not just sitting passively on the sidelines watching to see what happens and then blaming management, which gets us nowhere."

well. It is almost as if some proverbial line could be drawn in the sand between management and the board and, once drawn, the organization would be well governed and board performance would soar. With Type I boards, in fact, such lines of authority are important. In fact, there are many "reasons" that boards "manage" rather than "govern"—most of them related to viewing governance as primarily a fiduciary matter, including the following circumstances (Trower 2010, 5–8):

- Legal requirements
- Fiduciary oversight of operational areas

- Lack of staff
- Loss of confidence in the CEO
- The board's committee structure mirrors management's lines of responsibility, which draws board members into those areas
- The board meets too often; in order to have something to do, board members delve into operations
- Some board members feel more comfortable managing than governing
- Board members are recruited for their business and managerial skills, and they want to use them
- Board members feel a sense of accomplishment from managing.

Sometimes the reason for micromanagement actually rests with the CEO; this occurs when he or she invites the board into "downstream" management or operational issues, withholds information so that the board feels compelled to pry into details and operations, or shows an inability to effectively lead the organization.

Despite these commonly occurring circumstances that lead to board member micromanagement, the requisite culture for governance as leadership rests more squarely with a meeting of the minds rather than a division of duties. In strategic mode, where thinking is emphasized over planning, the lines of authority between management and board become blurred; "Like partners in doubles tennis, neither party . . . can afford to be particularly territorial or both will lose" (Chait et al. 2005, 69). In generative mode, there are still fewer questions of turf precisely because framing issues, by definition, means that no one in particular "owns" them; they do not "belong" to a staff member or management, or to the board or a specific committee. The conversation is less about who call the shots—jurisdiction, authority, distribution of power—and more about whether the board and management, together, have taken aim at the right target and discussed the implications of doing so. Clearly distinguishing the board's "job" from that of management may mean more clarity and comfort, but they come at the cost of governance and impact. "Neat divisions of labor succeed by *relieving* boards and staff of the challenge of working together on important issues. Few partnerships, none less than trustees and their chief executive, succeed on the strength of clear boundaries. When trustees and staff share the labor, the complexity of board-staff interactions is not eliminated. But the results do make the tensions worth bearing" (Chait et al. 2005, 99).

In the true spirit of partnership and collaboration, former Tufts University president Larry Bacow started every board meeting by saying, "My problems are your problems," and his board chair would remind the board, "We are here to help the President better the University." In the next example, another university president compares his journey with his board to being great doubles tennis partners.

Example 11: University of New Haven

When Steve Kaplan interviewed for the position of president of the University of New Haven (UNH) in February 2004, he quickly learned from faculty and staff that the board had become so involved in management issues in recent years that many on campus were deeply demoralized. Faculty sat on board committees whose members would call for the elimination of tenure; and a board committee was making decisions on such things as the brand of overhead projectors being installed in classrooms. The board's executive committee had been meeting monthly for several years and was even involved in such matters as the hiring and firing of senior management.

"Much of this behavior grew out of the board's commitment to pulling the university through a few years of financial difficulties. Nevertheless, something dramatic with regard to governance needed to happen at UNH, and it did. The board agreed to a full external review shortly after I arrived. As a result, the bylaws were rewritten; the membership changed significantly from mostly local to the inclusion of trustees from across the country; and the board moved entirely away from management or operational issues," remarked the president.

In the subsequent years, enrollments doubled, the quality of the student body improved immensely, large sums of money for infrastructure and endowment were raised through substantial operating margins and fundraising, and the university began to thrive. The president said, "As the university became increasingly more successful, the board seemed to lose all interest in operational matters. Board meetings became dominated by unilateral presentations by management to board members without much board uptake or engagement. Things like new buildings still aroused extensive discussion, but presentations about important matters of academic and student life never seemed to move beyond the level of reports. It was at that point, about four years into my presidency and, ironically, just as the global economy was about to unravel, that we decided to bring in an outside consultant to reinvigorate our board meetings and reengage board members. The result: We redesigned our quarterly meetings so that a significant block of time is reserved for substantive board discussions in small groups on major topics, and ever since, board engagement has flourished."

The board, through its own deliberations, has moved from a "dogmatic call for ever-increasing operating margins to a flat 4 percent annual margin," which has enabled management to identify funds each year to invest in board-debated and approved investments in such important areas as experiential education, career services, student life, and large numbers of new faculty and staff in support of the student body.

At its most recent retreat, in 2012, the board engaged in retrospective sensemaking as it discussed what it said it would do in 2008 and what it had actually done to govern more effectively and to advance its stated legacy. A lively discussion ensued about where the board and university were in 2008, what drove those conversations, and where things stand in 2012 by comparison. The board grappled with these questions in triple-helix fashion: Where has the university made progress? Where has it not? What do we think accounts for that? What does the president need from the board? How do board

(continued)

> members and management see and define the most pressing, systemic, long-term issues? The president said, "I think we continue to grow and better understand the board-management partnership. If there is a 'perfect' equilibrium, or collaboration, I think we're close to it. Finding it requires constant vigilance for the board and the administration."
>
> *Source:* Printed with permission from Steve Kaplan.

Diligence Through Productive Engagement

Traditionally, nonprofit organizations sought trustees of "social stature, moral integrity, refined lineage, and wealth" (Chait et al. 2005, 137), which made perfect sense for ceremonial and Type I boards. As nonprofits became more strategic, focusing more on Type II work (in addition to Type I), they logically began to also consider technical expertise that various types of professionals might bring to the board (for example, financial, legal, marketing, and public relations). As we have seen, governance as leadership demands more of boards; as they govern most effectively, they are a source of "multiple forms of capital" (Chait et al. 2005, 139) extending well beyond the financial. The trilogies about board members supplying "work, wealth, and wisdom" or "time, treasure, and talent" support this way of thinking, and yet, many organizations underutilize the wisdom and talent around the table. Boards are most productive when meaningfully engaged in meaningful work. If fully engaged and utilized, board members bring forth crucial forms of capital other than money, including intellectual, reputational, political, and social capital (see Table 5.2).

TABLE 5.2 *Four Forms of Board Capital.*

Form of Capital	Resource Optimized	Traditional Use	Enhanced Value
Intellectual	Organizational learning	Individual trustees do technical work	Board as a whole does generative work
Reputational	Organizational legitimacy	Organization trades on trustees' status	Board shapes organizational status
Political	Organizational power	External heavyweight: Trustees exercise power on the outside	Internal fulcrum: Board balances power on the inside
Social	Efficacy of the board	Trustees strengthen relationships to gain personal advantage	Trustees strengthen relationships to bolster board's diligence

Source: Chait et al. 2005, 141. Reprinted with permission of John Wiley and Sons, Inc.

While the various forms of capital are all important, it is social capital that is most critical for promoting the norm of diligence required for a culture conducive to governance as leadership.

Social Capital.   Defined by Douglas S. Massey in a *Chronicle of Higher Education* article as the "productive value that can be extracted from social networks and organizations," few concepts are more familiar or more misunderstood than "social capital" (Massey 2002, as quoted in Chait et al. 2005, 155). Although boards necessarily involve social relationships, those relationships do not always produce the kind of social capital that improves governance, but "like a top-notch management team, athletic squad, musical ensemble, or law firm, a board of trustees can translate personal relationships and mutual trust into social capital that stresses personal responsibility, collective industry, and improved performance" (157)—that is, the norms of diligence.

Chait et al. (2005) detailed four actions that boards can take to build social capital and foster norms of diligence. Three of these have been described in this book: (1) adopt a code of conduct; (2) place trustees in high-stakes environments—at the boundaries of the organization—where they need to interact with stakeholders; and (3) have boards, in small groups, go to work on high-stakes issues. The fourth idea—having the board meet in executive session without the CEO present to engage in constructively candid conversations, especially about the board's performance—is addressed later in this chapter.

Environment and Evidence

Effective sensemaking, collaboration, and productive engagement require an environment in which: board members are collegial, not just congenial; dissent is encouraged by leaders; discussions are robust and driven by questions, not answers; codified board norm violations are sanctioned.

Collegiality, Not Just Congeniality.   Too often the predominant norm in the boardroom is congeniality where like-minded board members are pleasantly agreeable at all times. A strong congeniality norm can lead the compliant majority to treat critics and skeptics as troublemakers and to subtly sanction outliers with less air time, fewer important assignments, curtailed information, and social isolation (Chait et al. 2005, 156). The board then suffers from unexamined (and possibly false) consensus, lack of discourse, and little sense of shared responsibility. Shifting the norm from congeniality to collegiality may seem a subtle shift, but it is very important. Where congeniality is passive, collegiality is active. True colleagues respectfully push each other's thinking; they can respectfully disagree, sometimes just for the sake of argument, without damaging the relationship—to the contrary, such disagreement ultimately leads to better thinking. At the heart of generative governance, in fact, is convergent thinking as boards deliberate frames—What other ways might we look at this issue? How might others see it? What are our underlying assumptions? What if we are wrong? Collegial board members will govern more effectively and more consequentially than those who are just congenial.

Dissent Is Encouraged and Expected.   Chapter Three discussed the criticality of dissent in group decision making. Getting dissent into the boardroom is easier when board members understand their role as collegial and not just congenial partners. As true colleagues, with each other and management, board members realize their responsibility is much greater than smiling for the sake of getting along and voting "aye" for the sake of a unanimous vote. Governing more purposefully demands that board members think critically about the substantive issues before them and speak up appropriately in the spirit of ensuring better outcomes and preventing groupthink, where unless *one* trustee raises doubt, *no* trustee raises doubt (Chait et al. 2005, 125). The CEO and board chair actively encourage dissent by voicing opposing views themselves or calling on a board member to do so. (Recall that the Trinity College Trustee Code of Conduct, Exhibit 4.6, declares the importance of dissent in board meetings and as an expectation of good trusteeship.) Some boards legitimize and spread around the role of devil's advocate by having board members draw cards prior to meetings; two cards are labeled "D.A." and the rest are blank. Those who draw the D.A. cards play that role during the board meeting.

Robust Discourse Driven by Questions, Not Answers.   Because the "very point of Type III governing is to delve into sensitive subjects, [trustees need to] promote dialogue right where both the stakes and anxieties are high" (Chait et al. 2005, 124) as they trade up from harmony and congeniality to productivity and candor. In order to bring about robust dialogue, discussion leaders ask questions—as opposed to seeking answers—to elicit different points of view such as: Who sees the situation differently? What are we missing? How does the situation look from the vantage point of constituents most affected by the decision at hand? What is the best possible outcome? What is the worst-case scenario? What is the next question we should discuss? No one expects instant agreement; everyone expects to appreciate more deeply the complexities of the situation (Chait et al. 2005, 125).

Renegades Are Sanctioned.   One jerk can prove toxic to an otherwise productive team culture. Once the board has taken the step to codify board member norms and expectations, it must not allow renegades to violate what everyone agreed to do. If the actions of board bullies, flame throwers, or air hogs (see Exhibit 5.2) are tolerated, the board may as well tear up its code of conduct because it will have effectively undercut the culture required for governance as leadership.

Though some of these designations are more caricatures than true descriptions, and some are amusing, the fact remains that these people do exist and do serve on boards and the problems they create should be addressed.

There are a variety of ways to deal with renegades, depending on how egregious the behaviors. Sometimes a casual conversation in the form of an aside or simple observation from the board chair, chair of the governance committee or an assigned mentor is all that is needed. In other situations, a more serious, in-depth conversation with the board chair or chair of the governance committee is called for. Some boards

Exhibit 5.2: Board Member Personality Types Ranging from Destructive to Benign

- Bully: Verbally assaults fellow board members and staff members with complete disregard to affect and effect
- Grenade launcher or flame thrower: Has no self-control and enjoys maximum disruption
- Dominator or air hog: Will not let anyone else share airtime; interrupts and talks over others
- Naysayer: Pessimistic and full of ideas about why something will not work; seems to take pleasure in shooting down the ideas of others
- Bloviator: Speaks at length and in a pompous manner
- Loose cannon: A slight variation of the grenade launcher—is completely unpredictable, but not necessarily vicious
- Handler: Forms alliances and coalitions outside the boardroom to orchestrate a personally desired outcome
- Micromanager: Intrudes into operations and often seeks out private conversations with members of the senior staff
- Clueless wonder: Makes completely off-the-wall comments that have no bearing on anything the board is trying to address
- Bobblehead: Nods and smiles in apparent agreement with everything
- Passive: Participates minimally and is unwilling to engage when views are challenged
- Disengaged: Sits silently throughout meetings, adding no value whatsoever

utilize a more formal midterm, written review followed up by a conversation with the chair of governance committee. At the other end of the response spectrum is a decision not to reappoint a board member—one liberal arts college decided not to reappoint the most generous donor due to repeated violations of group norms (for example, bullying board members, violating confidences)—or to dismiss a board member midterm.

Some boards make use of routine reminders at the start of sessions by the board chair, or a committee chair, about confidentiality, constructive dissent, prohibitions against cell phones, and the like. This can be done with a light touch, for instance, when someone's cell phone rings or someone interrupts someone else. Just as many boards expect 100 percent participation in philanthropy, boards should reasonably expect 100 percent compliance with major mutual expectations.

TOOLS TO SUPPORT A "GOVERNANCE AS LEADERSHIP–FRIENDLY" CULTURE

The following sections highlight six things boards can do to support a culture conducive to governance as leadership: (1) design better agendas; (2) evaluate meetings and experiment; (3) evaluate committee performance; (4) consider the most effective use of an executive committee in your organizational context; (5) create dashboards to gauge organizational performance (this chapter) and board performance (see Chapter Seven); and (6) make use of executive sessions for reflective practice.

Agendas

Because the board's time together is limited, it is essential that it be well spent; a critical driver of how time is spent is the agenda. As much as boards want one, there is no "perfect" board meeting agenda, but there are certainly agendas that are preferable to others and that reflect governance as leadership principles. "Agendas are artifacts of bureaucracy designed to control and organize discussions that might otherwise meander unproductively. Imperfect as they are, agendas are valued precisely for this reason. But leadership creates value by *interrupting* such routine" (Chait et al. 2005, 47).

One way to "interrupt" the usual board agenda thinking is to consider first what makes for great meetings, something all of us know because we all attend so many—good and bad. Ask yourself, "What makes for an interesting meeting?" and "If a goal for board meetings was to elicit better thinking from board members, what would the agenda look like?" CEOs and board chairs reported that the most interesting meetings are those where:

- There are honest exchanges; people can be vulnerable (and not "know everything"); people trust each other.
- Multiple perspectives are shared openly and people challenge each other respectfully.
- There is intensely rigorous debate on critical issues facing the organization.
- People are focused on important and compelling topics, issues, and problems.
- There is bold and creative thinking; there is time to imagine the future.
- People learn new things; there is deeper understanding.
- There is a lot of interaction; there are no reports and no long, "mind-numbing" PowerPoint slideshows.
- There are high expectations and high standards for real content and substance.
- People are well prepared in advance so no time is wasted.
- There is clarity of purpose and outcomes; everyone knows why they are in the room and where the group needs to go; and "you actually get to the 'so what.'"
- There is effective leadership and facilitation to keep the group on purpose, on task, and on time.

One independent school board member conveyed all this especially well, saying:

The meetings I find most interesting in my professional life are those in which com-plex, often intractable issues are confronted by smart, dedicated people working in a cooperative, analytical and "truth seeking" mode. The nonprofit board on which I sit has both ingredients—extremely difficult issues (often multiple issues that are inter-woven in various ways) and fine minds—administration and board—assembled to tackle them. But we necessarily spend much of our time together dealing with nor-mal, recurring issues that boards typically address, in particular, those issues which are largely within our control, leaving perhaps too little time for the thorniest, longer-term issues such as the inevitable crisis of affordability.

Most CEOs and board members would agree with this assessment of the ideal and the reality. Although smart, well-intentioned board members want to grapple with big ideas in the boardroom, too often their time is consumed by trivial or operational mat-ters or in passive, listening mode rather than thinking and discussing matters of strate-gic import. CEOs and chairs would like to: ensure more discussion about what topics matter most and framing them; have more time for deeper discussions, dialogue, and debate; spend time on strategic and generative discussion; challenge assumptions and underlying beliefs; draw out all board members (be more inclusive of diverse per-spectives, ensure divergent thinking); and strike a healthier balance between discussion, planning, and action. The best agendas take all that into consideration and they:

1. Are designed with the thought that form follows function by considering the answers to three questions: What do we want to achieve at this meeting? How do we best structure the meeting to get those results? On what can board members add value?

2. Have clearly articulated goals (see Exhibit 5.3).

3. Include a consent agenda for routine business (for example, prior meeting min-utes, committee and staff reports, announcements) to conserve precious time (see Exhibit 5.4).

4. Reflect the strategic priorities of the organization by placing the most important material early, before people are tired, and by allotting a significant share of time to what matters most. An outsider should be able to peruse the past two board meeting agendas and discern what was important to the organization at that time.

5. Contain at least one question mark. The board should be provided a question or two for consideration and discussion, preferably without the need to make a deci-sion at the same meeting.

6. Provide blocks of time for the thoughtful discussion of important issues. Ideally, PowerPoint slide decks, written reports, and other materials should be sent well

Exhibit 5.3: Liberal Arts College, Board Meeting Goals

Over the course of this meeting, we will:

1. Get a sense of the collective views of the board about the information and issues surrounding offering master's degree programs.

2. Apply thinking in three modes to an issue of strategic importance to the college.

3. Begin the conversation about the role of athletics at the college.

4. Learn and think critically about the campaign feasibility study and discuss the board's role in the campaign.

5. Foster relationships with faculty (at dinner Thursday) and students (at lunch Friday).

Exhibit 5.4: Sample Consent Agenda

8:30 – 8:35 Consent Agenda

- Minutes of the January 23, 20XX Meeting (TAB 2)
- President's Report (TAB 3)
- Diversity Task Force Update (TAB 4)
- Development Committee Report (TAB 5)

in advance of the meeting along with guidelines for what board members should be reading for and thinking about.

7. Build in time for summarizing what happened, next steps, and meeting evaluation.

Agenda Design in Action: Cabrini Green Legal Aid. What follows next is information about one nonprofit's focus on better governance by holding a board retreat to examine organizational impact and redesigning board meeting agendas. The information, including a "before" and "after" agenda, was provided by and used with permission from Cabrini Green Legal Aid's then executive director, Robert Acton.[1]

---

[1]Mr. Acton is now executive director of NYC at Taproot Foundation. He attended sessions on board engagement and building a high-performance board team that I conducted for the BoardSource Leadership Forum in 2009 and 2010, and was kind enough to e-mail me regarding how CGLA transformed board meetings for greater director engagement.

First, a note on the board's retreat: it was held at one of the organizations that CGLA serves and started with a community presentation panel discussion and question-and-answer session. It also included a tour of one of the neighborhoods that CGLA serves. That tour was followed by a forty-five-minute board dialogue session about one of the organization's guiding principles: "deep involvement in our community, especially in connection with local churches," recognizing that "the trust and relationships built in the community . . . have been integral to the success and effectiveness of our work." The board discussed four critical questions:

1. What does our community engagement look like today?
2. What should it look like?
3. Are we living up to this guiding principle?
4. Are there underserved communities on which we should be focused?

Later in the retreat, the board spent twenty minutes talking about giving and they were asked, among other questions:

1. How well cultivated do you feel by the organization?
2. What do other organizations do well that CGLA does not?
3. Where does CGLA shine in comparison?

It is difficult to imagine that board members could have left that retreat feeling like they didn't make a difference or that their time was not well spent, or that the organization didn't benefit from the time spent.

Next, compare the CGLA's typical board meeting agenda (Exhibit 5.5) and a revised agenda (Exhibit 5.6). My purpose in providing these agendas is not to denigrate the "before" agenda because, in fact, it actually looks a lot like many (dare I say most?) nonprofit board meeting agendas that I see; rather, my intention is to show how one board changed its agenda to govern better.

Exhibit 5.5: CGLA Board of Directors "Before" Agenda:
CGLA Board Meeting Agenda: June 2008

6:30 p.m.	Call to Order, Prayer, and Introductions [Board Chair]
6:32 p.m.	Approve Prior Board Meeting Minutes [Tab A]
6:34 p.m.	Board Development Committee [Committee Chair]

- Update item
- Action: Re-elect Directors
- Action: Nominate officers slate
- Action: Re-elect Advisory Board Members
- Action: Nominate new Directors
- FY09 scheduled meetings [Tab B]
- Updated FY09 Board and Advisory Board contact lists, committee assignments, and terms [Tab B]

6:50 p.m.   Executive Director's Report [Executive Director]

- FY08 Highlights & Accomplishments [Tab C]
- Update on building project (schedule, issues, sources & uses) [Tab C]
- FY09 Outlook

7:00 p.m.   Program Committee [Committee Chair]

- FY08 Year End Program Reports [separate attachment]
- FY09 Program Goals [separate attachment]

7:15 p.m.   Strategic Planning Committee [Committee Co-Chairs]

- Planning Worksheet: Draft [handout]
- Update on FY08 Plan Progress (Executive Director) [Tab D]

7:30 p.m.   Development & Marketing Committee [Committee Co-Chairs]

- FY09 Fundraising Plan
- Report on Benefit Kick-Off Reception
- Report on potential grant

7:40 p.m.   Personnel Committee [Committee Chair]

- Update on planned changes to benefits structure
- Executive compensation

8:05 p.m.   Finance Committee [Treasurer]

- FY09 budget and narrative [Tab E]
- FY09 (with in-kind included) [Tab E]
- *Action:* Approve FY09 budget

8:30 p.m.   New Business & Adjourn [Board Chair]

- Next Board Meeting (Date, Time, Place: TBD)
- Annual Benefit Reception and Dinner (Date, Time, Place)

As the "before" agenda shows, a typical board meeting was a series of updates and reports from committee chairs squeezed into two hours. Judging from the time apportioned to each item, one might assume that reports from the personnel and finance committees were the most important (twenty-five minutes allotted to each); however, they are placed last on the agenda when directors are likely to be tired and when it's entirely possible that time might be running short. The last item, prior to adjournment, is approval of the FY09 budget, undoubtedly, without time for discussion.

The "after" agenda (Exhibit 5.6) reflects changes to better engage board members and draw more from them during the meeting.

Exhibit 5.6: CGLA Board of Directors "After" Agenda:
CGLA Board Meeting Agenda: October 2009

6:30 p.m.	Call to Order, Prayer, and Introductions [Board Chair]
6:32 p.m.	Approve Prior Board Meeting Minutes [Tab A]
6:35 p.m.	Board Development Committee [Committee Chair]

- *Action:* Nominate new directors

- *Discussion & Possible Action:* It is the recommendation of the Bylaws Committee that the Board develop and adopt a member description. The new bylaws will describe board service in a very general manner and will rely on a member description that articulates expectations and responsibilities of board service. The Board Development Committee recommends the attached "Member Description." Having reviewed the draft member description, what changes (if any) should be considered?

- Committee membership changes [Tab A]

- Save the dates: FY10 scheduled meeting [Tab A]

6:55 p.m.	Consent Agenda [Board Chair] [Tab B]

1. Amend bylaws to increase number of directors from 17 to up to 22.

2. Pass resolution adopting the amended and restated document for CGLA's 403(b) Plan

Request to remove any items for discussion?

Action: Vote on consent agenda

7:00 p.m.	Development & Marketing Committee [Committee Co-Chairs] [Tab C]

| | • *Discussion:* Feedback on 2009 Annual Benefit (strengths and areas of concern) |

- *Discussion:* Feedback on 2009 Annual Benefit (strengths and areas of concern)
- Benefit outcomes, prior year comparisons
- Benefit budget to actual; prior year comparisons
- FY10 IQ revenue report

7:25 p.m.   Bylaws Committee [Committee Chair]

- Presentation of amended version of CGLA's Bylaws. Pursuant to Bylaws Article XI, Section B, notice date is October 14, 2009. Vote to adopt amended bylaws will be January 30, 2010. [Handout at meeting]
- *Action:* Vote on articles of amendment to formally remove "Clinic" from name of organization.

7:35 p.m.   Strategic Planning Committee [Committee Co-Chairs] [Tab D]

- *Discussion & Action:* It is the recommendation of the Strategic Planning Committee that we adopt the following mission statement: *"Our purpose is to answer God's call to seek justice and mercy for those living in poverty by providing legal services that strengthen lives, families and communities."*
- CGLA's current Mission, Values and Vision Statement
- Five-Year Strategic Plan
  - Review five strategic priorities
  - Update on current activities related to plan
  - Update on plan mileposts already accomplished
- Scope of multi-layered report related to community expansion & next steps

8:10 p.m.   Finance Committee [Treasurer] [Handouts under separate cover]

- Review of FY10 IQ financials and six-month cash flow projections
- Status of FY09 audit & preliminary FY09 financials
- Update on line of credit, sliding scale fee service

8:20 p.m.   Executive Director's Report [Executive Director]

- Quarterly Board Dashboard Report [Handout under separate cover]

8:30 p.m.   New Business & Adjourn [Board Chair]

- Events (Dates, Times, Places)
- Next Board Meeting—Retreat (Date, Time, Place: TBD)

The "after" agenda reflects several positive changes from the "before" agenda. First, there were three "discussion" items and more time was allotted to those segments; for example, twenty minutes for discussing a draft description of what is expected of board members, twenty-five minutes for directors to provide feedback about the annual benefit, and thirty-five minutes for discussing a change to the mission statement. Second, not all committees made reports; only those with important business did so. Third, there was a consent agenda for routine business and a line noting that something can be removed from the consent agenda for discussion. Fourth, the ED's report was to highlight the dashboard indicators, also a new development for the organization. Rather than the usual updates, the ED focused the board's attention on how the organization was doing on the areas that matter most. The one-page dashboard (see Exhibit 5.7, spread across three pages 151–153 for optimum clarity in this book) includes: (1) key performance indicators, or metrics, and their status as green (shaded in this book) (up), red (unshaded in this book) (down), or = (unchanged), as well as projections and benchmarks for those indicators; (2) "alerts" for the quarter; (3) progress on the strategic plan, projected cash flow, revenue and expenses, and revenue sources; and (4) a block of text with an "Impact on Lives" organizational story (a wonderful idea to keep mission ever-present in the minds of board members).

Although CGLA's "after" agenda reflects several good practices, still more could be done to make it even better. Minimal changes would be to: (1) add goals and a purpose statement (Exhibit 5.3); (2) provide more time for the critical discussions (by sending questions in advance and having breakout sessions; see Exhibit 5.8) and limit still further the reporting time (by utilizing technology for advance clarification protocols; see Exhibit 5.9); and (3) add time at the end to summarize what happened, lay out next steps, and to evaluate the meeting (see Exhibit 5.10).

Meeting Evaluation

Because of the time involved, and their criticality, all retreats should be assessed by those in attendance—board members and staff alike. It is also a good idea to assess all board meetings at the time and then periodically, once the board has established good baseline data and trends of board effectiveness. Meeting assessment can take a variety of forms: ratings, open-ended written comment, or verbal feedback (Exhibit 5.10); it can be collected on site or electronically afterwards. Whatever way it is collected, it is important for the board to take a few minutes, as a collective, to discuss the findings.

Committee Evaluation

Committee performance and leadership should also be periodically evaluated with an eye toward measuring how members view the committee's central purpose, the criticality and strategic relevance of the work (past year and year ahead), and what members most and least enjoy about serving on the committee. Some open-ended and rating questions to assess committees are shown in Exhibit 5.11.

Exhibit 5.7: CGLA Organizational Performance Dashboard: *Board Dashboard Report—FY10, 2nd Quarter*

Key Performance Indicators

KPI or Metric	Status	Qtr 3 FY09	Qtr 4 FY09	Qtr 1 FY10	Qtr 2 FY10	Benchmark
Clients Stronger in top two boxes (28 clients Q2)	▲	91%	89%	70%	83%	100%
Cases Accepted/ Intakes	▲	200/281	186/307	153/243	179/245	170/275
Case Acceptance Ratio	▲	71%	61%	63%	73%	62%
Served at Help Desk	▲	1.226	1.215	1.020	1.190	950
Provided Support Service	▽	15	13	14	11	20
Volunteer Hours	▲	2.394	3.140	3.069	2.788	2.500
Cost to Serve One Client	▲	$220	$217	$318	$241	$290
Donor Meetings (nonboard)	▲	38	34	33	42	25
New Donors	▽	28	50	150	19	25
Board Giving: YTD Benchmark	▲	$37,402	$63,392	$65,850	$75,200	$44,325
India Gifts: Board Driven	▽	$0	$4,600	$15,708	$740	TBD
Board Attendance (Meetings/Comm)	=	71%	85%	70%	74%	75%
Media Hits	▲	?	5	3	3	2

▲ Upward Trend   ▽ Downward Trend

Impact on Lives

Recently our client "Janice" was served with an eviction action from public housing because of her teenage son's arrest for burglary. Janice is 41 years old and is raising an 8-year-old daughter and a 13-year-old son while also caring for her mother, who has Alzheimers. In the burglary case, a group of teens are accused of taking video games and, unfortunately, our client's son is friends with these kids. The stolen games were found in the home of one of his friends, but they were discovered in a bag that belonged to our client. We accepted the juvenile case in an effort to protect Janice's son's future while also strengthening the eviction defense in Housing Court. We were uniquely positioned to comprehensively address the family's problems because we are the only civil legal aid organization with a Criminal Defense practice, as well. Whatever involvement Janice's 13-year-old son had in the theft of these games, to evict an entire family for this offense is very harsh. The coordination between our Housing Program and our Criminal Defense Program positions us to comprehensively meet the family's needs.

Exhibit 5.7: CGLA Organizational Performance Dashboard (*Continued*)

Other Important Metrics

Volunteers thanked over phone	140	■
Volunteers thanked with personel note	290	■
CSS Appeal 2010, raised in first 10 days	$4,500	■
Spring Appeal 2009, raised in first 10 days	$3,200	■
New $5,000–Found/Corps/church, FY10	5	■
Total raised from sliding scale clients	$4,080	☐

Alerts: This Quarter

Case management system target completion in May	■
Lead benefit sponsorship gift from Anon. Corporation—$25K	■
Invitation to give begins at Expungement Help Desk	■
CGLA featured on home page of Chicago Community Trust website	■
Funder: "CGLA has more $1,000 + donors than any other IL legal aid"	■
Chris C facilitates record Girl Scout cookie year, CGLA gains 45 lbs.	☐

■ Upward Trend   ■ No Change   ☐ Downward Trend

Progress on Strat Plan

Northwestern Student Group completes report on opportunities for expansion
Donors green light East Garfield Park satellite with Breakthrough Urban Min.
Talks with Anon. Agency about satellite focused on Latino community
Legal Director attends three-day training for legal aid supervisors
Donor makes possible a very special Staff Retreat in January
Employment Opportunity Dialogue with biz leaders planned for April

Rev Sources FY10

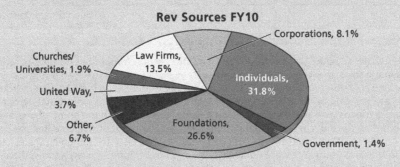

Corporations, 8.1%
Churches/Universities, 1.9%
Law Firms, 13.5%
Individuals, 31.8%
United Way, 3.7%
Other, 6.7%
Foundations, 26.6%
Government, 1.4%

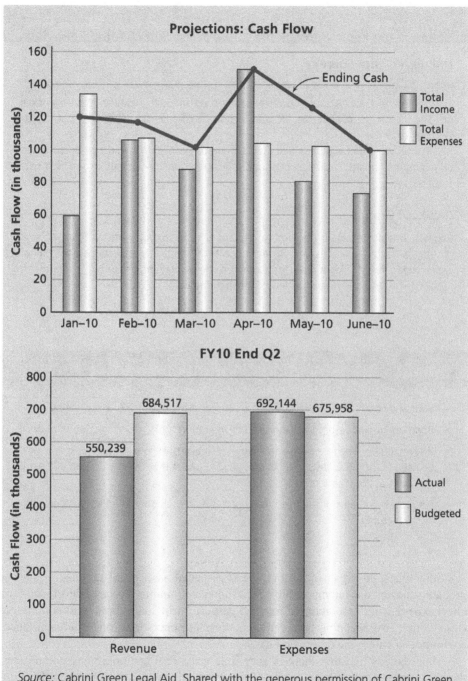

Projections: Cash Flow

Cash Flow (in thousands)

Total Income
Total Expenses

Ending Cash

Jan–10   Feb–10   Mar–10   Apr–10   May–10   June–10

FY10 End Q2

Cash Flow (in thousands)

	Revenue	Expenses
Actual	550,239	692,144
Budgeted	684,517	675,958

Source: Cabrini Green Legal Aid. Shared with the generous permission of Cabrini Green Legal Aid.

Exhibit 5.8: Advance Surveys and Breakout Groups

Online Advance Surveys

Poll board members in advance of the meeting rather than take time at the meeting.

For example, CGLA could have asked board members to answer: "What went particularly well at the annual event?" and "What could have gone better?" prior to the October 2009 meeting.

Thoughts could have been summarized and presented, followed by the committee engaging the board in a dialogue about making the next event an even greater success.

Breakout Groups

Some boards like to multiply air time and board member engagement by assigning small groups to discuss critical issues. Because the time allotted is apportioned to multiple issues, this process allows fuller engagement, helps prevent groupthink, strengthens social capital, and builds trust while conserving time.

Exhibit 5.9: Pre-Meeting Clarification Protocol

- Staff and committee reports are sent electronically in advance of the meeting.

- Board member questions are e-mailed to the report author for direct answer back.

- If several board members have the same or similar questions, those questions may be used to form the basis of a bulleted "Q&A" sheet that can be given to all board members at the meeting.

- Particularly complex or nuanced questions and answers should be addressed orally at the meeting.

Sometimes, an organization may need a special assessment targeted to surface problems the board is facing. Exhibit 5.12 shows a committee survey I developed for a client experiencing a modicum of role and purpose "drift" with some of its committees (for example, overstepping boundaries, getting into operations, and confusion about committee fit within the organization).

Many boards find that there is very little cross-fertilization among committees; therefore, more value can be extracted from committee assessments when the comparative data are mined and explored to discern why some committees score better than others and to determine the reasons, so that good practices might be shared.

Exhibit 5.10: Board Retreat/Meeting Evaluation:
Sample Assessment Form

	1	2	3	4	5
The issues covered were	Not Very Important ☐	☐	☐	☐	Very Important ☐
The meeting goals were	Unclear or Nonexistent ☐	☐	☐	☐	Clear; Well Stated ☐
The discussion was	Unfocused ☐	☐	☐	☐	Focused ☐
The materials were	Confusing ☐	☐	☐	☐	Informative ☐
The materials were sent	Too Late to Ensure Preparation ☐	☐	☐	☐	In Plenty of Time to Prepare ☐
The meeting structure allowed	Limited Participation ☐	☐	☐	☐	Full Participation ☐
The meeting was	Uninteresting ☐	☐	☐	☐	Engaging ☐
Opportunities to participate were	Limited ☐	☐	☐	☐	Ample ☐
The meeting was	Poorly Run ☐	☐	☐	☐	Well Run ☐
We accomplished	Very Little ☐	☐	☐	☐	A Great Deal ☐
Our time was	Poorly Utilized ☐	☐	☐	☐	Well Spent ☐

Source: Adapted from: Chait, Holland, and Taylor, 1996, 30.

Meeting and retreat written assessment might also include open-ended questions such as:

- What was most valuable and why?
- What was least valuable and why?
- What did you like most about the format?
- What did you like least about the format?
- What is the most important thing you learned?
- What were you hoping to learn, but didn't?

Ask two or three board members to stay after for a few minutes to discuss their assessment with the chairs of the board and the governance committee, or the retreat planning committee.

Open the floor to verbal feedback toward the end of a retreat or meeting by asking:

- What went especially well?
- What didn't go so well?
- What did we learn as a board?
- What did you learn as an individual?
- How did we perform as a team? (See Board Team Assessment Survey, Exhibit 4.9.)

At the start of the meeting, randomly assign one or two "on-the-balcony" (see Chapter Three) board members whose job it is to watch and critique the board's performance during the last portion of the meeting as they reflect on "the view from the balcony."

Exhibit 5.11: Sample Committee Assessment Questions

- How would you summarize the central purpose of this committee?
- What was the most strategically significant work this committee did in the past year?
- What is the most strategically significant work this committee should do in the year ahead?
- What would be lost to the organization if this committee did not function for two years?
- What have you most enjoyed about serving on this committee?

- What have you least enjoyed about serving on this committee?
- What could the chair of this committee do to make the committee more effective?
- What is the most important thing you have learned from serving on this committee?

Please check the appropriate box for each question. 1 = Poor; 5 = Excellent

	1	2	3	4	5
Clarity of committee's purpose.					
Importance of committee's purpose.					
Significance of agenda items.					
Opportunities to propose agenda items.					
Timeliness of information.					
Usefulness of information.					
Opportunities for candid give-and-take.					
Opportunities to influence decision making.					
Benchmarks for areas within committee's purview.					
Overall assessment of committee's performance.					

Source: Richard Chait, 2006.

Exhibit 5.12: Sample Committee Assessment Tailored to a Specific Need

Please state your level of agreement or disagreement with each of the following statements:

COMMITTEE NAME:_____	Strongly agree	Agree	Disagree	Strongly disagree
This committee's members understand the central purpose of this committee.				
This committee's agendas generally reflect committee-appropriate subject matter.				
The committee's agendas allow enough time for critical dialogue on important matters.				

Exhibit 5.12: Sample Committee Assessment Tailored to a Specific Need (*Continued*)

COMMITTEE NAME:_____	Strongly agree	Agree	Disagree	Strongly disagree
The goals of any given committee meeting are generally clear.				
Meaningful dialogue typifies this committee's meetings.				
The committee understands its role vis-à-vis the full board.				
The committee understands its role vis-à-vis the administration.				
The committee's members understand their role on this committee.				
Committee members are well prepared.				
The committee receives in advance information relevant to the issues at hand.				
The committee receives information in a timely fashion.				
This committee receives the right amount of information for committee meetings to be effective.				
This committee appropriately engages faculty and/or staff.				

Executive Committees

Used effectively, executive committees (EC), typically composed of the board's officers and committee chairs, can be helpful for large, geographically dispersed boards that do not meet very often. However, boards must be cautious to ensure that the EC does not usurp the power of the rest of the board who may justifiably feel as though all the decisions are made at the EC level and the full board is just a rubber-stamp.

It is easy to discern when the EC has the power. They meet right before the board meeting, essentially as a dress rehearsal. They take recommendations to the board that are presented, more or less, as a fait accompli. There is not much dialogue at meetings and those not on the EC tend to disengage. Rumblings may be heard about an elite or "inner circle" who make the real decisions. A board chair commented on this practice, "We have a large board of 40, so we have an EC; our standard practice was for its members to meet two weeks before the full board meeting to do a 'dry run.' This created the perception that the EC was the 'real' board." A CEO interviewed for this book said, "Prior to my arrival, the EC of the board was involved in day-to-day management and the board only met quarterly for two hours. We rewrote the bylaws and now the EC only meets as needed and the full board meets quarterly for a full day and sometimes a day and a half. These changes have helped the board focus on what matters—strategy, not operations."

I agree with Mark Light (2004) who wrote that "The only legitimate reason to create and use an EC is to help the full board do its job—to make sure that the organization does what it is supposed to do, accomplishing its mission" (xiv). The most popular roles for the EC are to: (1) act for the board in between meetings in the case of an emergency; (2) coordinate the full board's review of the CEO's performance and compensation; (3) serve as a smaller sounding board for the CEO; (4) focus the board's work, set goals, and development agenda; and (5) coordinate the work of the full board (Light 2004, 4).

If your board does not have an EC, but is considering one, some good questions to ask are: What problems are we experiencing that we think having an EC will help solve? What problems might having one create? Do we feel we are missing some opportunities because we don't have an EC? Are there other ways to seize those opportunities? If we establish an EC, what will be most different about how we govern? If we create an EC, what steps will we take to ensure that the full board remains fully engaged?

Some good practices concerning the role and functioning of an EC are to: (1) have the full board decide if an EC is needed, what its role should be, and who should be on it; (2) be clear about the authority granted to the EC along with limitations, as stated in bylaws; (3) utilize the EC judiciously to help ensure that it doesn't inadvertently overstep; (4) hold meetings of the EC separately from board meetings so that they do not become dress rehearsals; and (5) communicate what happens at EC meetings with the full board (Light 2004, 28).

The next example showcases how a school reframed the work of its executive committee which led to changes to board agendas that have engaged the board in critical thinking about important issues.

Dashboards

The Cabrini Green Legal Aid example (earlier in this chapter) demonstrated how one nonprofit redirected the focus of the CEO's report by using a "dashboard" to keep board members focused on critical factors at meetings. Like the dashboard on a car, that tells the driver "at-a-glance" three critical pieces of information—speed, temperature, and fuel amount—an institution's dashboard should show critical success factors or categories (the essential areas of performance). Unlike a car's dashboard that shows

Example 12: Greenhill School Board

In 2001, the Greenhill School board was composed of more than sixty trustees and its executive committee (EC) had sixteen members. The overwhelming majority of the trustees were current parents.

The board chair noted that, "With our board size and structure the 'real' work of the board was undertaken primarily by the EC and the full board met to 'rubber stamp' decisions."

The head of school commented, "The EC meetings were held two weeks before the regular board meeting as, essentially, a dry run through the agenda. That's not a bad thing if there are contentious issues because you can begin to work things out with the smaller group, but many of the full board often felt left out. And, by the time the full board met, some members were hearing the same things for the third time—at committee, at EC, and then at the board meeting."

A bylaw revision in 2007 set the maximum board size at forty-eight, and recent practice has been a board size of around forty, with no change in the executive committee structure. In 2011, a decision was made to limit EC representation to committee chairs, the three officers, and the head of school, so now there are ten.

In addition to shrinking its size, the board decided to change the focus of the EC; it now meets as needed and outside the regular cycle of board meetings to provide a critical sounding board for the school head. "The EC is a smaller group of trusted advisors with whom I can bounce ideas around a bit and talk about what's keeping me awake at night. There is an extra layer of trust because the group is small and people understand how crucial these meetings are; they protect the confidentiality of discussions. These changes sent a clear message to the board—that the EC is *not* where decisions are made; we need a fully engaged board for discussions and decisions."

Changes to the EC's focus and the need for a fully engaged board required changes to the agendas and processes at full board meetings. Now, every meeting has a block of time set for the board to meet in small groups (where everyone participates fully) to think critically about a topic central to the school's strategy and mission.

At one meeting the board was asked, "What questions should we be asking and addressing about diversity and outreach as related to admissions?" and at another meeting, the board was asked to write "elevator speeches" about the school's mission. The topics are challenging, compelling, and engaging, and the outcomes of the thinking are helpful to school leadership. "Since we've changed board process and agendas, attendance is up at meetings and everyone participates," said the head of school.

Although these changes have been good for governance, the Committee on Trusteeship is taking a still closer examination of board size, function, and composition. Said the board chair, "We are considering further reductions in board size. At forty the board functions well, but we feel having still fewer people around the table will help the board function at a higher level. We are searching for the right balance between diverse representation on the board, perhaps adding more alumni, and inclusiveness and full engagement of trustees."

No matter what happens next, one thing is for sure, the Greenhill School's board has found new meaning in its work and the school is enriched because of it.

the current situation, organizational dashboards also reflect past (and in some cases, projected) performance. Organizational dashboard indicators should be: (1) easy to understand; (2) relevant to the user; (3) strategic; (4) quantitative; (5) up to date with current information; and (6) not used in isolation (Geronimo Terkla 2011, p 12).

The use of a dashboard is not only a good way to keep the board's focus on what matters, but also a good means of holding management and the board accountable for important institutional performance indicators. Whatever indicators are within acceptable parameters need not be discussed at meetings, but those that are not provide fodder for board dialogue. Dashboards serve at least one other critical function: the very process of creating one, with the staff, allows the board to discern what matters, and is thus a very important collaborative learning experience. The process of selecting dashboard indicators "can reveal the institution's priorities, values, and sore spots" (Association of Governing Boards 2011, 13)—an excellent triple-helix and sensemaking opportunity. Engaging the board in periodic conversations about the relevance of dashboard indicators, gauges, and benchmarks elicits critical and generative thinking and helps build the board as a team. For more on dashboards, see "The Nonprofit Dashboard: A Tool for Tracking Progress" (Butler 2007).

The next example is about how an independent school designed and implemented a dashboard of *quantitative* key performance indicators—not an easy task in an environment where *qualitative* factors like "student experience" and "campus climate" are often, and should be, the focus, but where other measures like financial liquidity, endowment return, and discount rates also matter.

Example 13: St. Paul's School Board

When the board of trustees began developing a dashboard to follow quantitative key school performance indicators for its own use, the rector (headmaster) saw an opportunity to develop a parallel process with indicators for the school's operations.

Educational institutions often rely on subjective measures and anecdotes to assess their effectiveness. "Having a dashboard at a school, especially on the operations side, can be tricky," the board president (chair) commented, "because educators are predisposed to thinking of the softer side of educating young people and not necessarily about financial liquidity or more importantly objective measures of student and faculty performance."

To help organize and simplify such a complex process, both the operations and board dashboards were broken into two phases, considering first those indicators that change during the school year (for example, making sure the annual fund is on target; monitoring the operating budget, health center visits, and energy usage) and second, those that change just once a year (for example, number of applicants, selectivity, yield, college placement results, SAT scores, and faculty turnover).

For both phases, in order to maintain focus and ensure that all important aspects were covered, the board's standing committees met. The Buildings and Grounds

(continued)

Committee, for example, noted the need for indicators to track capital projects, electricity, and energy consumption. The Finance Committee wanted indicators for tracking operating and capital expenses, as well as the budget targets. The Education and Student Life Committee considered such issues as admissions, college placement, grade distribution, SSAT versus SAT scores, health center visits, and discipline cases. The Development Committee was interested in campaign progress, the annual fund progress, and the percentage participation of alumni and parents, while the Investment Committee focused on the endowment's market value and key liquidity and diversification metrics.

"We decided it was best that the board dashboard fit on one page to maintain focus on the most important issues," the board president noted. "We ranked all the proposed dashboard items with a simple vote of the entire board; the items with the most votes made the final cut. In the end, each committee had a larger individualized dashboard, and the entire board had a one-page consolidated dashboard. Everyone was pleased. Having a dashboard has led to tighter focus on critical issues during discussions at committee and full board meetings."

"With a large endowment, it can be easy to fall into the trap of complacency," the board president said. "While we did not have a cash crisis in 2008 like many other endowment-driven schools, the board wanted to ensure that we were fiscally responsible; this in part means that we keep expenses under control."

"When I joined the board in 2004," he continued, "55 percent of our operating budget was tied to the endowment. We put that on the dashboard and focused on reducing it over time. The board wasn't in the business of telling the administration how it should do this, only that it felt the percentage was too high given the potential volatility of our endowment. By focusing on this metric, we had reduced the percentage to 33 percent by the time the 2008 recession hit. If you combine that with a maximum endowment draw of five percent, then you have a window in which the institution can operate. We didn't frame this as clamping down on expenses, but instead on being a fiscally responsible school with a large endowment. With a dashboard, everyone knows the rules and key metrics. The dashboard shapes behavior. It helps frame discussions."

Some board members express concern that the use of dashboards can tilt the focus of the board's attention too far in the direction of that which can be easily quantified and neatly displayed on one page, causing the board to miss what really matters—in an educational context—quality.

At most colleges and universities, there are quantitative measures of educational quality including: faculty diversity (for example, percentage of women and minorities); student graduation and retention rates; students in postbaccalaureate educational programs and postbaccalaureate employment; percentage of students engaged in research; the number of students completing senior honors theses; undergraduate satisfaction with advising and career services; the number of major fellowships received by undergraduates (for example, Rhodes, Marshall, Fulbright, Truman). Tufts University also tracks overall student satisfaction measured by its senior survey (Association of Governing Boards 2011, 13). Former Tufts president Larry Bacow noted something else that is especially important to keep in mind about dashboards—the interaction between individual metrics; Bacow said, "For example, several years ago, we consciously decided to reduce reliance on early decision admissions. We knew this would have an adverse affect on our yield and our selectivity. However, we have been able to demonstrate to the board how the quality of the entering class, as measured by average class rank and average SAT scores, has increased as a result of trading off yield and selectivity for quality" (Association of Governing Boards 2011, 13).

Because the board is responsible for providing independent oversight of the organization's performance and the CEO who leads it (see Example 14), dashboards, benchmarks, and scorecards are helpful tools. The Baylor Health Care System example tells the story of the board taking the lead on linking CEO compensation to the four key performance indicators in its strategic plan.

Example 14: Baylor Health Care System Board

Baylor Health Care System (a "Dallas Top 25 Employer" in 2009, 2010, and 2011) instituted a pay-for-performance incentive compensation program approximately fifteen years ago and has been making steady progress ever since.

The chair of the Compensation and Governance Committee (CGC) remarked, "The board wanted a large portion of executive compensation to be at risk and based on executive performance against the strategic plan which would be determined by a performance evaluation program for the executives."

The compensation program had only one goal the first year—to meet the financial performance of the previous year—with a stretch goal to better it. The goal was exceeded resulting in a payout the first year.

The CGC chair commented, "In the second year, a performance goal based on customer satisfaction was added to get focus on this important issue—taking care of our customers—the patients. We set stretch goals for financial performance and customer satisfaction, and again reached the goals, resulting in an incentive payout. Next, we added a quality goal and quickly established a leadership position in delivering quality care in our industry. The last goal added was employee retention which has helped executives focus on training and keeping good employees."

On July 1, 2005, Baylor added a Long-Term Incentive Plan for the top executives (limited to key strategic level decision makers). The CGC chair noted, "Rather than us setting the goals, we compared our performance in the four areas with our hospital peer group. The pay-for-performance compensation plan for executives has been extremely successful. We have continued to improve performance in all four areas and have

(continued)

increased pay accordingly. Our intent is to perform and pay at the 75th percentile, or better, compared to our peer group and by and large, we have been accomplishing that. This compensation plan has been extremely successful and has high credibility. It has helped the executives focus on the strategic goals for the system and move the pay closer to the 75th percentile in our industry. The payout has varied from zero (when no goals were met) to as much as 150 percent when maximum goals were met."

Last year, Baylor implemented a Stretch Incentive Plan (for employees not included in the executive plan) based on system financial, patient satisfaction and individual performance. However, payout was predicated on Baylor reaching its financial goal, which it did not, so no payment was made. This year, the Stretch Incentive Plan is based on system financial and hospital specific patient satisfaction performance. If these goals are reached, each employee's payout will be adjusted based on his or her performance review score.

According to the CGC chair, "Our patients, employees and other constituents have all benefited from this pay-for-performance compensation plan. Having the four areas of the strategic plan has helped keep the board and the executive staff focused on what matters most and having the pay-for-performance plans in place has helped everyone do a better job ensuring a successful hospital. We've been very careful, as a board working with the CEO and senior management, to be vigilant about ensuring that the compensation system is having a positive impact on the people and the hospital. We stand behind it and are accountable for it."

"The board has been proactive in establishing a compensation program that is very balanced and incentivizes the executive team to focus on the appropriate strategies to move the organization forward," said CEO Joel Allison. "Under the CGC chair, and with the board's leadership, our executives are fairly compensated based on performance using a balanced scorecard approach and placing a significant portion of our pay at risk. I truly believe this is a best practice for compensation in the health care arena. It is easily understood and can be effectively communicated."

Source: Printed with permission from Joel Allison.

Executive Sessions. Reflective practitioners (Schön 1983)—commonly referred to in the health care and teaching professions—reflect *in* action (while doing something) and *on* action (after something is done), in order to engage in continuous learning. In the boardroom, reflecting *in* action might mean pausing after a conversation, prior to making a decision, to ensure that: (1) there were no unanswered questions; (2) there was no unheard dissent; (3) there were no unspoken comments; and (4) no one knows something that all members should know but do not.

Without the CEO. Executive sessions without the CEO can provide a safe place for boards to practice the art of reflection for a several reasons; such sessions: (1) lower the

member and a student sitting at the table. Now, the independent trustees can meet and really open up. I can say the things I need to without being constrained. We've had to educate the community, especially the faculty about this—that this is a good practice elsewhere. Our board chair has been instrumental in leading these changes and helping everyone understand how important they are to our success."

Changes to agendas have also come out of this process. "Agendas now designate items as 'action' or 'discussion.' We now have a culture where discussion is expected and that discussion does not always lead immediately to a decision," said the president.

The chair noted, "One thing that has really helped us with this transition to doing business differently is our Web portal. The full meeting book is there—all the PowerPoints and reports—one week in advance of meetings. The expectation is that everyone does their homework and comes to meetings prepared for the conversations that need to take place. The portal allows everyone access to everything, not just the current board book, but all the policies, bylaws, past reports, and data, so that if people have questions, they can look it up themselves online, rather than digging through paper files somewhere. Board members are better informed so that can better discuss the issues. The president and I talk about upcoming agendas and build in time for discussions, so we don't rush anything."

The president echoed the value of having everything on the portal: "This has helped at committee meetings, too, because people aren't hunting around for things. The board chair was decisive in putting the portal up so we are now truly paperless and we won't go back to the old way—ever." The president uses the portal and the agendas to state the discussion topics and any challenges the college is facing. Reflecting on the changes the president and chair agreed that group dynamics and deliberations have improved and the board is adding still greater value to the college.

CHAPTER FIVE HIGHLIGHTS

- **There are three overarching "genetic markers" of a "governance-as-leadership-friendly" culture.**
  - The board plays a central role in discerning and sensemaking.
  - The board and management collaborate effectively.
  - The board promotes diligence through engagement.

- **Effective discernment means that boards problem find before they problem solve.** Good governance starts with figuring out what matters most and deciding how to look at issues.

- **Good problem finders (and problem framers), understand their key stakeholders.** Nonprofits are well served to situate their boards at the internal and external boundaries of the organization so that they can see and hear what constituents think.

- **Once organizations have a good fix on what matters most, the board governs well when it stays focused on those issues.** The best boards do not allow themselves to get sidetracked by inconsequential issues or seduced by operational details.

- **An effective board spends time learning and sensemaking.** The board allows time at every meeting to talk candidly with management about what is going on, how various constituents view issues, and discussing what the organization and board has learned. The board and management spend time deciding together what needs to be decided.

- **Diligence through engagement is evidenced by collegiality, dissent, robust dialogue driven by questions, not answers, and sanctions for those who violate stated norms.** The governance-as-leadership culture utilizes multiple forms of board capital; in addition to financial, there is intellectual, reputational, political, and social.

- **There are several tools to support the governance as leadership model.** The tools are: effective agendas that draw out board member intellectual capital; evaluation of meetings and committees; dashboards of key performance indicators to help the board stay focused on what matters most; the strategic use of executive committees as a sounding board for the CEO; and the strategic use of executive sessions to provide time and space for safe and candid discussion about the board's performance.

CHAPTER

6

WHAT GOVERNANCE AS LEADERSHIP REQUIRES OF LEADERS

The challenge is to be a light, not a judge; to be a model, not a critic.
—Stephen R. Covey (1991, 25)

Some nonprofit boards have made the leap from good to great, a select few from great to remarkable, and many are well on their way. Wherever boards are on their journey to better governance, they have had to adapt—and will continue to need to do so. Because governance is not static—organizational contexts and markets change, the economy fluctuates, board members and staff members come and go—leaders must be open to listening to what others think, especially when it differs from what they think, and adapting as necessary. In adaptive organizations, the elephants in the room are named; responsibility for the organization's future is shared; independent judgment is expected; leadership capacity is developed; and reflection and continuous learning are institutionalized (Heifetz, Grashow, and Linsky 2009, 101).

Building, nurturing, and sustaining consequential governance where boards discern, deliberate, and decide matters of organizational import requires effective leadership of the board and of the organization—most especially in the form of board chair and chief executive.

LEADERSHIP

Adaptive work was mentioned briefly in Chapter One in the context of why three modes of thinking—fiduciary, strategic, and generative—produce better governance; and again in Chapter Three about the importance of diagnosis in adaptive leadership. "If we define problems by the disparity between values and circumstances, then an adaptive challenge is a particular kind of problem where the gap cannot be closed by the application of current technical know-how or routine behavior. To make progress, not only must invention and action change circumstances to align with reality, but the values themselves may have to change. Leadership will consist not of answers or assured visions, but of taking actions to clarify values" (Heifetz 1994, 35).

Adaptive leaders resist the temptation to seek authoritative and absolute right answers; in complex social systems, problems lack clarity because various stakeholders will have divergent opinions about the nature of the problem and its solutions, and one faction's fix is another faction's adaptive challenge (Heifetz 1994, 86). In fact, the "most common failure in leadership is produced by treating adaptive challenges as if they were technical problems. While technical problems may be very complex and critically important . . . they have known solutions that can be implemented with current know-how. They can be resolved through the application of authoritative expertise and through the organization's current structures, procedures, and ways of doing things. Adaptive challenges can only be addressed through changes in people's priorities, beliefs, habits, and loyalties" (Heifetz et al. 2009, 19).

Adaptive and Technical Work

Heifetz (1994) used the practice of medicine as a metaphor to help distinguish between technical (Type I) and adaptive work (Types II and III). With Type I work, someone can fix the problem, as is the case when the problem and diagnosis are clear, the patient's expectations are realistic, and the doctor can provide a solution with surgery or medication so that the patient is cured. In governance, this work is often fiduciary in nature. With Type II work, the problem is definable but there is no clear-cut solution, as is often the case with heart disease. The patient's health can be reasonably restored if he or she takes responsibility by making lifestyle adjustments. All of the physician's technical solutions will not work if the patient does not implement them. There are also Type III situations where problem definition is not clear-cut and technical fixes are unavailable. "The situation calls for leadership that induces learning when even the doctor does not have a solution in mind. Learning is required both to define problems and implement solutions" (Heifetz 1994, 75), as is the case with a chronic illness like cancer. This is akin to generative governance where problem finding, sensemaking, and framing come into play.

Adaptive Leadership

Using the concept of "thriving" from evolutionary biology, Heifetz et al. (2009) remind us that successful adaptation has three characteristics: (1) it preserves the DNA essential for the species' continued survival; (2) it discards (reregulates or rearranges) the DNA that no longer serves the species' needs; and (3) it creates DNA arrangements that give the species the ability to flourish in new ways and in more challenging environments. The suggestions, then, for adaptive leadership are these (Heifetz et al. 2009):

1. Adaptive leadership is about change that enables the capacity to thrive (14) which requires leaders who can "orchestrate multiple stakeholder priorities to define thriving and then realize it" (15).

2. Successful adaptive leadership changes build in the past rather than jettison it (15). "A challenge for adaptive leadership is to engage people in distinguishing what is essential to preserve from their organization's heritage and what is expendable. Successful adaptations are both conservative and progressive. The most effective leadership anchors change in the values, competencies, and strategic orientations that should endure in the organization" (15).

3. Organizational adaptation occurs through experimentation (15).

4. Adaptation relies on diversity (15).

5. New adaptations significantly displace, reregulate, and rearrange some old DNA (16).

6. Adaptation takes time (16).

Each of these has direct application to the boardroom and governance excellence as described throughout this book.

1. By situating board members at the internal and external boundaries of the organization, having board members role-play the views of various constituents when discussing alternative courses of action, by practicing predecisional accountability, and by using the "learning in action" technique, boards are well positioned to help organizations thrive.

2. Engaging in retrospection, necessary for effective generative thinking, helps ensure that boards appreciate the past. It is important to periodically ask the board, What about our organization must never change? and What organizational core values must be preserved at all costs? Have the board fill in these blanks: "Our organization will never [blank]" and "Our organization will always [blank]."

3. The best boards experiment, realizing that what works for one nonprofit may not work for another and also that institutionalizing change is incremental. Take baby steps; see what works and what does not.

4. A diverse board is critical to ensuring a multiplicity of views and experiences (discussed in Chapters Three, Four, and Six).

5. Board member term limits, succession plans, new processes and structures are critical to thriving.

6. Rome wasn't built in a day and neither are great boards. This work takes time, constant diligence, focus, and leadership.

The Paradoxes of Adaptive Leaders

In a white paper by Susan DeGenring (2005), three important paradoxes of adaptive leadership are described:

- Applying the technical knowledge for which the leader was hired will not achieve sustainable change.

- In order to be effective, the leader must simultaneously be "in the action" and "removed from the action" ("on the balcony," in Heifetz's terms [1994, 252]).

- The humility and vulnerability of admitting one doesn't have all the answers can be the strength that galvanizes people with the problem to find a breakthrough solution to the problem. In other words, not having the answer *is* the answer, after all.

A CEO interviewed for this book described some of this tension by saying, "Good governance is good leadership; it's the process by which you lead well. To me, there has to be a balance between being a participant in generative thinking but realizing that, at the end of the day, my well-being depends on the board's being confident in me. I am a partner and a teammate but also an employee."

Boards as Viewed by Executives

The objectives of and corresponding actions taken by CEOs with respect to their boards is largely a function of how executives view their boards ranging from nuisance or threat to thought leaders (see "CEO Ambivalence" Chapter Two). When the CEO views the board as nuisance or threat, damage control becomes the objective, requiring the CEO to "handle" the board. At the other end of the spectrum, the CEO sees board members as thought leaders from whom ideas and insights flow, leading the CEO to "engage" the board (see Table 6.1). CEOs who subscribe to the principles of governance as leadership see their boards as thought leaders to be fully engaged, not merely handled.

TABLE 6.1   *CEO Perceptions, Objectives, and Actions with Respect to Boards.*

Perception	Objective	Action
Nuisance or threat	Damage control	Handle
ATM	Resources	Court
Fiduciaries	Oversight/Legitimacy	Inform
Consultants	Technical expertise	Tap
Advisers	Professional opinion	Confer

Source: Richard Chait 2009.

The Effective CEO in General

There is no doubt that effective governance begins and ends with the CEO. Without the CEO's support, any board will have difficulty partnering in leadership because almost any action the board wants to take can be rebuffed as micromanaging or overstepping into management's domain. Of four factors that build collective board team strength, Demb and Neubauer (1992) place the personality and style of the CEO first (133) followed by having: a climate of openness; the right people on the board; and a clear and common purpose (discussed in previous chapters). Effective CEOs:

- *Ensure that nothing is undiscussable in the boardroom.* Citing the scandals at Penn State, Olympus, and MF Global Holdings, among others, the December 20, 2011, issue of *Knowledge @ Wharton*, showcased the problems faced by CEOs who bury bad news or consider certain incidents as taboo. "When an issue is undiscussable, it cannot be managed rationally," said consultant to numerous large corporations, Don Russmore. While that is true, "fear can blind us," write Philip Tetlock and Paul Schoemaker, research director of Wharton's Mack Center for Technological Innovation, in a forthcoming article (Tetlock and Schoemaker in press).

- *Do not think they have all the right answers or even all the right questions.* Nothing undermines a board like a CEO who makes it clear that he or she merely tolerates board members. Habit number three of "spectacularly unsuccessful executives" is they think they have all the answers. "Leaders who are invariably crisp and decisive tend to settle issues so quickly that they have no opportunity to grasp the ramifications. Worse, because these leaders need to feel they have all the answers, they aren't open to learning new ones. . . . Leaders who have all the answers shut out other points of view (Finkelstein 2004, 2–3). A CEO interviewed for this book said, "I think an effective president is willing to let his or her board see that he or she is fallible and doesn't have all of the answers. It's very supportive to have the board gather to engage on really difficult questions and scratch their heads along with you."

- *Invite dissent.* Habit number four of unsuccessful CEOs is they ruthlessly eliminate anyone who isn't completely behind them. "Anyone who doesn't rally to the cause is undermining the [CEO's] vision . . . [and should] get with the plan or leave" (Finkelstein 2004, 3). Of course, as we know this is completely counterproductive and contrary to effective group decision making, group learning, team building, and adaptive leadership. "By eliminating all dissenting and contrasting viewpoints, destructive CEOs cut themselves off from their best chance of seeing and correcting problems as they arise" (Finkelstein 2004, 3). "CEOs who don't welcome dissent try to pack the court, and the danger of that action is particularly clear right now," wrote Sonnenfeld (2002, 111), citing scandals at Enron, Arthur Andersen, and Tyco. Boards are well advised to understand the difference between dissent and disloyalty—a distinction that cannot be legislated through rules and guidelines; "it has to be something that leaders believe in and model" (111).

- *Share information, power, and leadership opportunities.* High-impact boards are led by CEOs who share power (Crutchfield and McLeod Grant 2008)—"neither one is really on top or has ultimate control of the organization" (173). "The board balances power with that the executive director and senior staff, or works in partnership with them, rather than dominating" (174).

- *Are not completely wedded to the past or too far ahead of the organization.* They understand history, context, and culture. This is part and parcel of practicing adaptive leadership.

The Effective Governance-as-Leadership CEO

All of these abilities and actions of effective CEO leadership apply in the context of governance as leadership, but there are several other things nonprofit leaders should keep in mind in their central role of guiding the board to better governance.

The "First Law of Generative Governance" is that the opportunity to influence generative work declines over time (Chait et al. 2005), depicted as the "generative curve" in Figure 6.1. The authors' framework suggests a companion hypothesis: "Trustee involvement is lowest where generative opportunity is greatest, and trustee involvement increases as generative opportunity declines" (Chait et al. 2005, 102)—a classic "x-ray of micromanagement." In this view, board members micromanage because they are invited to do so by being presented with low curve, downstream, technical—in some cases, "no brainer"—topics instead of high curve, upstream, adaptive issues where sensemaking, critical thinking, and framing are required.

Another way to think about the generative curve was brought to my attention in conversations with William Ryan and Richard Chait: it can be tempting for CEOs to

FIGURE 6.1 *Boards and Generative Opportunity*

Hypothesis on boards and generative work: Trustee involvement is lowest where generative opportunity is greatest, and trustee involvement increases as generative opportunity declines.

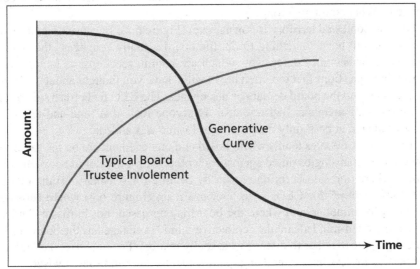

Source: Chait, Ryan, and Taylor 2005, 103. Reprinted with permission of John Wiley and Sons, Inc.

FIGURE 6.2 *Contested Territory: In Theory*

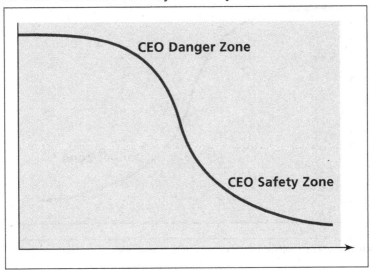

Source: Printed with permission from Richard Chait and William Ryan.

see the upstream part of the generative curve as a "Danger Zone" and the lower part of the curve as the "Safety Zone" (Figure 6.2). Why? Because those Type I, downstream, fiduciary issues are bounded, narrowly defined, and technical; the stakes are relatively low. The board "discussion" can be tightly scripted and staged by the staff; a preferred, clear course of action can be presented. In these situations, the board is "handled," not "engaged." What could go wrong?

The real contested territory is downstream (Figure 6.3). Because of their technical expertise, and to have something to do, the board actually "engages" the issue. The staff bristles or becomes defensive—which are natural reactions, as board members ask oversight questions that too often begin with "have you thought about . . . ?" A tug-of-war ensues and the board demurs or disengages. The CEO feels frustrated or under-cut and the staff members feel resentful. Everyone feels that time and energy have been wasted and, at best, only marginal board value was added.

Again, think doubles tennis where board and management are on the same side of the net, rather than singles pitted against each other with a divider in between demark-ing turf, where one side is trying to win by beating (or outsmarting) the other. The actual "safety zone" for CEOs is to look upstream (Figure 6.4) where substance is substituted for minutiae and where the board is engrossed, not intrusive. The senior staff is more open-minded and the "collective mind" is engaged as the board and man-agement grapple together to discern what really matters. Personal agendas and techni-cal expertise are less important than organizational values and shared wisdom.

FIGURE 6.3   *Contested Territory: In Reality*

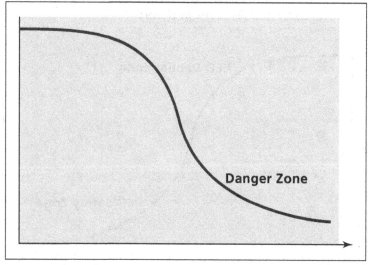

Source: Printed with permission from Richard Chait and William Ryan.

FIGURE 6.4   *Common Ground*

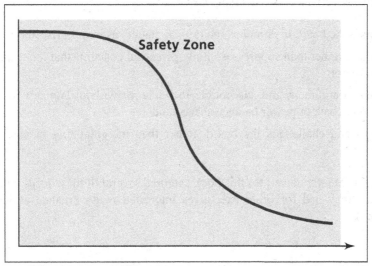

Source: Printed with permission from Richard Chait and William Ryan.

Therefore, governance-as-leadership CEOs are well advised to:

- Invite the board in early by bringing top-of-curve challenges to frame, rather than mid-curve or downstream proposals to approve.

- Emphasize the criticality of sensemaking prior to decision making.

- Highlight rather than downplay the really difficult, ambiguous issues and questions.

- Work inside the boardroom to engage the board collectively, rather than outside the board, engaging allies unilaterally.

- Rather than seeking downstream "buy-in" to prepackaged issues, decide *with* the board what to "buy."

- Discuss and deliberate rather than persuade and prevail.

"The challenges that governance as leadership pose for executives are more about sharing, not assuming greater responsibility" (Chait et al. 2005, 180). To the extent that the CEO views him- or herself as a heroic leader with all the right answers, rather than an adaptive leader with better questions—and the board expects the same—the organization will not be as well led and attempts to govern differently will not succeed. Governance as leadership requires that CEOs truly share generative work with boards; the capacity to do so "ranks among the executive's major contributions" (180). The effective governance-as-leadership CEO:

- Immerses the board in complex and critical matters as issues arise and unfold;
- Describes, rather than suppresses, dimly perceived concerns that incite an instinctive wariness;
- Is open to argument and susceptible to influence without concern for wins or losses on debate or power balance sheets; and
- Engages and challenges the board, rather than marginalizing or shielding the board.

Three CEOs interviewed for this book captured several of these ideas when asked what advice they had for other executives interested in governance as leadership (Exhibit 6.1).

Exhibit 6.1: CEO Advice

It helps to meet the board on their level and not try to move too fast. This [governance-as-leadership] framework allows a chief executive to invite the board into conversations that are really helpful. Process can truly affect the outcome of a decision, so the CEO needs to give thought to engaging the board in the most meaningful ways. I now realize that governance doesn't just happen; you create it. As CEO, you have the ability to make it better or worse. My best advice for putting these ideas into practice is to find key, persuasive board members who agree on the need and agree on the needed skill set necessary to take governance to a higher place. This isn't something a CEO can impose on a board. It would be impossible to do if you thought it was important but the rest of the board did not. I can't imagine coming in and knowing that we needed to improve governance and not having strong allies to move it forward.

• • •

Governance is not initiated by any one person, but the leadership should model accessibility and openness. People should feel free to share their opinions whether they are pro or con; that is really key to the success of a good board. The best thing a CEO can do to fully engage the board is to be accessible and to engage the board in ways where they can think about the institution and its existence; that's why they are there. They are there because of love and commitment and the

CEO can facilitate true engagement with and among board members at every event, not just board meetings.

• • •

The CEO needs to bring as much clarity to the governance improvement process as possible so that people have a good, shared understanding of what you are trying to do and why. You have to explain it well and then challenge board members to move beyond the fiduciary work and to not fall back into it. The CEO can gently remind board members of the level of thinking he or she is after and how board members are well suited and situated to do that. As CEO, you also have to be aware of your own comfort level with taking questions, not answers, to the board because we're no different from board members that way. Because this feels new, it is unsettling. You have to guide gently, trust the process, and not revert back into old habits or your own default leadership mode.

Leading differently is not easy; it is important to keep in mind comments about trust and CEO vulnerability (see Exhibit 4.1). To be most effective, the CEO needs a board chair true partner. As executives reflected on implementing governance as leadership, they also spoke about the pivotal role of the board chair, the subject to which we now turn.

The Effective Board Chair in General

After the CEO, the chair of the board is the most influential person shaping the board's effectiveness. It is extremely difficult for boards to overcome the problems of weak, poor, or overly controlling leadership on the part of the chair. Effective board chairs:

- Shape board meeting agendas with the CEO, including ensuring that meeting goals are stated and met.

- Carefully manage air time at meetings. It is the chair's job to ensure that everyone has an opportunity to weigh in and that no one dominates or bullies.

- Draw out multiple views, the voices of various constituents, dissent, and seek consensus when the time is right.

- Participate and lead without overpowering or staying silent.

- Summarize what happens at board meetings, tie up loose ends, and state what needs to happen next.

The Effective Governance-as-Leadership Board Chair

If governance as leadership is orchestral, the board chair is the conductor. The chair is responsible for guiding the board in its critical thinking, developing and supporting the board as a team, and nurturing the requisite culture where governance as leadership can thrive. The effective chair:

- Sets the tone for the board's deliberations and models the behavior expected of board members.
- Enforces the board's norms by publicly commending noteworthy and productive board member contributions and sanctioning those who violate them.
- Engages board members appropriately and manages the board's work.
- Guides the board's sensemaking and learning.
- Seeks feedback from the board about his or her performance.
- Invites senior management to evaluate the board.
- Serves as intermediary between the board and the CEO.
- Serves as close confidante and counselor to the CEO.

Because governance as leadership requires diligence and playfulness, the ability to be intentional but also spontaneous, and comfort with ambiguity, more is demanded of the board chair than is of chairs of traditional boards, who preside rather than guide. The best chairs take the work seriously, but not themselves. Said one board chair, "The biggest enemy of effective chairmanship is ego; it's deadly for the organization. When the chair has a big ego, other board members tend to also let their own run unchecked and things get out of control as the boardroom becomes a battle for airtime and superiority. If one-upsmanship becomes the norm you can forget about good governance."

Those interviewed for this book—chairs and CEOs alike—noted the criticality of having a strong board chair. One CEO stated that improving governance would have been *impossible* without his chair:

> I didn't have a mandate to change the board; it had already begun this process when I got here. I think it all starts with the modeling of the chair and the board officers; everyone can see how seriously they take this job. They have learned that governance is fairly complicated; they have a sense of the complexity at hand. The board members are temporary stewards of an institution that is fairly old; they have a sense of humility and awe of the task at hand. The leadership of the chair is critical in ensuring that all board members conduct themselves in a way that upholds the public's trust in them.

Another CEO remarked, "My advice for improving the board's effectiveness is to make sure you have the right board chair. Change needs to be driven by the chair, not mandated by the CEO. There is no substitute for having a highly qualified person as chair, leading the board to excellence." But, noted one chair, "You can't mandate change on a board, not even as chair. The retreat opened the boards' eyes to possibilities as we did the foundational work there. After that, the ball is in our court to try out these new ideas and techniques together and with the CEO." Another chair commented on his role as master of ceremonies; "The role of the chair is to create the culture to improve decision making; it is not to generate new ideas for action."

The Dynamic Duo: CEO and Chair

"Most governance experts agree that the relationship between the board chair and the chief executive officer is critical to board effectiveness and important to organizational success. Yet board chairs and CEOs readily admit they don't spend enough time together developing and strengthening that relationship" (Totten and Orlikoff 2007, 1).

The CEO has a predominant influence on the board chair's success, and vice versa. Together, they motivate or enervate the board; propose or impose the agenda; promote a culture of inquiry or one of passivity. They can facilitate or dominate deliberations; orchestrate or isolate board members; reinforce or undermine group norms; and model openness or defensiveness (interview with Richard Chait, in Totten and Orlikoff 2007). The CEO and chair together are also team builders; they work together to recruit board members who are team players and ensure that a code of conduct is written and adhered to. The CEO-chair duo plays an important role in facilitating connections among board members and between board members and staff members.

Ideally, the CEO and board chair get along well and work closely to ensure that the board is composed of the right people doing really important work. They should epitomize the elements of a high-performing team through trust, mutual respect, and honest dialogue. The comments showcased in the next exhibits (6.2 and 6.3) reflect the critical chief executive-board chair dynamic.

Exhibit 6.2: CEOs and Board Chairs Reflect on Their Relationship and Leadership

CEOs

There have been substantive improvements to how we operate and what we do in board meetings. I attribute so much of the positive changes to the board chair's leadership. She has been great—her willingness to commit to this and the time she takes to do it. She calls one third of members after every meeting to seek their feedback. A president has certain limitations to move the board in its own growth; she needs a strong board chair. I said to her, "I have learned what I want from a board chair . . . it's about strong leadership" . . . but effectiveness is also about the how the chair and CEO think about the world together. She'll ask me, "What is

> ## Exhibit 6.2: CEOs and Board Chairs Reflect on Their Relationship and Leadership (*Continued*)
>
> your thinking about this?" We talk weekly and go through our list of things. There are difficulties we work through, sure, but you can only do that . . . get through the tough stuff . . . with honesty and candor and a really solid relationship. If she wasn't calling me, I would be calling her; she helps me keep my finger on the pulse of the board.
>
> Another CEO commented that her board chair has provided "phenomenal leadership." "We have an extremely positive relationship and the board sees that. We pick up the phone and touch base; we conduct post-mortems after meetings. He has been an advocate for changing the way we do business and I have made board engagement a priority; it's one of my stated goals for which I am held accountable."
>
> ### Chairs
>
> A board chair noted that her relationship with the CEO is now more collaborative. "We talk about things in a deeper way, asking, 'What does all this mean? How well is the board supporting the work of the organization?' There's more mutual accountability instead of having everything in the CEO's lap, and there's a much stronger relationship because of that. Having the commitment from the CEO and the chair is essential in moving the process forward—to achieving better governance. Again, the foundational work is really appropriate so that you're walking with people up the hill as opposed to pushing them from behind."
>
> Another chair said that it takes a determined CEO and board chair to bring about change. "I recognize that we have a really talented CEO and we are all rowing in the right direction. We don't have that problematic, 'But we've always done it this way' mentality. We're willing to experiment. The CEO and I are totally in sync on this, but it does take practice working diligently with the entire board. It can't just be the two of us way out in front dragging everyone along. You have to aspire to a higher level of governance; it's not an on and off switch. It takes time and effort."
>
> "My board chair has a very different style from me. I think of us as dance partners who stepped on each other's toes in the beginning. Now we move together much more fluidly with intuitive understanding. He and I are both completely in agreement about raising the governance bar, and I think that is instrumental in galvanizing change."

As the last quotation demonstrates, the relationship between CEO and board chair is personal, not always perfect, and requires vigilant attention. New CEO-chair relationships benefit from clarifying how to communicate with each other most effectively—discussing a preferred style and medium as well as mutual expectations, concerns, and leadership styles.

Longer-standing CEO-chair partners might want to ask themselves the following questions about their relationship and the board:

1. Can you give me an example of where I was especially helpful and one where I could have been more helpful?

2. I think the greatest challenge to working with me is _____. Do you agree?

3. When you say _____, I hear _____. Is that what you mean?

4. What can I do to improve our working relationship?

5. What keeps you awake at night? How can I help?

6. What steps can we take together to improve governance? Do we perceive or anticipate any obstacles? How might we overcome them?

7. What steps might each of us take to build the board as a team? Do we perceive or anticipate any obstacles? How might we overcome them?

8. Reflecting on steps we have taken to improve governance, or to build the board as a team, what worked well? What did not work, or backfired?

Whatever questions you use, the idea is to communicate openly and honestly and keep the focus on the mutuality of the relationship.

In our "Partners in Leadership" workshop, Richard Chait and I offered several additional ideas for CEOs and chairs (see Exhibit 6.3).

Exhibit 6.3: Tips for Building the CEO-Chair Relationship

- Meet regularly outside of regular board meetings to have candid, meaningful discussions about your relationship and about issues facing the organization to ensure no surprises for either partner.

- Keep track of key concerns about your relationship and about the board, set goals, and develop an action plan to work on them.

- Seek clarity about each other's point of view by asking questions and being open to learning; sense-make together.

- Be realistic about what you can accomplish and discuss more than one avenue to success on any given issue (for example, could something be best addressed by the chair of the governance committee or by the executive committee?).

- Establish a process for measuring progress and set markers for success.

- Avoid becoming a "two-person" board; avoid creating a dynamic in which the CEO and board chair so dominate the governance process that no one else has input or impact.

Most important, decide what works best for the two people involved, for the organization, and for the board. Some CEOs and chairs touch base once a week; others find that once a month works well. Some pairs meet in person; others by phone. Venue and method matter less than process and content. As in any effective partnership, honesty and commitment to betterment will serve you well.

As Einstein observed, "We can't solve problems by using the same kind of thinking we used when we created them." Though that is certainly true, old habits die hard, and sustaining governance excellence demands that organizations keep pressing forward and not allow reverting to old behaviors, however comfortable. A CEO noted, "You have to explain all this really well and it helps to have an expert come talk to the board. You have to challenge people to move beyond the fiduciary mode, to get out of their comfort zone a bit. Clarity of expectations is crucial and keeping an eye on the outcome of better governance. When you're dealing with big thoughts and issues, people have to put themselves out there. This process has opened up opportunities for me to throw options out there, but safely, and this has invited better thinking and better solutions to challenging problems."

Getting to excellence and sustaining it take hard work, but the payoff is tremendous. One CEO said, "I've become pretty clear that great governance can raise the bar for an organization by providing courage, insight, wisdom, connections, and resources that could never be generated in house. You can be a really good organization without a great board but you won't go to that greatness level without a great board. Bad governance can be distracting and enervating; even mediocre board performance is a detriment. A nonprofit will never advance without a great board, and that takes great leadership and a true partnership."

CHAPTER SIX HIGHLIGHTS

- **Governance as leadership requires that boards spend more time on adaptive challenges than on technical problems.** As noted in Chapter One, all three governance modes (Type I, fiduciary; Type II, strategic; and Type III, generative) are important; the point here is that with Type I work, someone can fix the problem. This is in contrast with Type III situations, where problems still need to be defined and issues framed.

- **Chief executives are well served to think about how they view their boards and what actions that suggests.** In the governance-as-leadership framework, CEOs view their boards as thought leaders from whom they seek professional ideas and insights. Doing so requires leaders to engage board members at meetings.

- **The "First Law of Generative Governance" is that the opportunity to influence generative work declines over time.** Chief executives do well to invite the board in early in the thinking stages—that is, upstream on the generative curve; emphasize sensemaking before decision making; highlight ambiguous issues and challenges; engage board members collectively; and encourage the board to thoughtfully deliberate critical issues in the boardroom.

- **As partners in leadership, the chief executive and board chair are critical to successful governance.** The CEO and chair play pivotal roles in leading the board to better governance. They are well served by paying close attention to their own interpersonal relationship by spending time getting to know each other, coming to understand each other's style, and troubleshooting issues that will come before the board.

CHAPTER

7

MEASURING AND SUSTAINING GOVERNANCE AS LEADERSHIP

The better the board understands governance, the better governed the organization will be. This is not a vicious circle; it is the cycle of successful governance.

—Chait, Ryan, and Taylor, 2005

Sustaining governance excellence requires that the board measure its performance, make sense of it through focused discussions, learn from what it does well and less well, and take deliberate actions to improve. In earlier chapters, I have addressed the evaluation of individual board member performance and the board as a team (Chapter Four), as well as meetings and committees (Chapter Five). This chapter is about ways to measure the board's performance overall, the steps boards can take to improve governance, and what a board might do to sustain a culture of excellence through vigilance and ongoing learning. For some boards, that means periodically bringing in a consultant, or engaging a board coach.

MEASURING BOARD PERFORMANCE

Board performance can be evaluated in a several meaningful ways, including interviews, outsider observation and feedback, reflective practice, and board self-assessment surveys.

Interviews

Personal interviews with board and senior staff members can provide rich data about the board's performance. Interviews are especially useful when: (1) group dynamics are poor and there are factions or mistrust; (2) governance is particularly complex because of external factors (for example, the industry, political environment); or (3) there is some sense that the board is underperforming but leaders are not quite sure why. Interviews may also be appropriate to help discern what questions to ask in a written board self-assessment survey, or as follow-up to probe answers provided in a written survey. Interviews provide especially rich data because the interviewer can probe respondents' answers to develop deeper understanding and nuance than survey questions allow. A good practice is to send the interview protocol (see sample questions in Exhibit 7.1) to respondents in advance so that they have time to think about the questions.

Some organizations feel it is important to interview all board members and key staff members, whereas for others this would be difficult, overly costly, and time-consuming (with a very large board), or unnecessary because longer interviews with a representative cross-section of board members (by length of service, demographic characteristics, committee assignments, and leadership or nonleadership roles) provides rich information that would become redundant at a certain point, as interviews yield less and less new information.

To learn the organization's mental models about governance, ask board and staff members: "What would be the gravest consequence to the organization if the board and its committees ceased operations for the next two years?" (this is the "no board scenario" described by Chait, Ryan, and Taylor 2005, 18). Most commonly, and symptomatic of Type I boards, the answers have to do with fiduciary matters such as no budget, loss of fundraising capacity, regulatory exposure, less legitimacy, absence of accountability, and loss of technical advice. Sometimes respondents say that strategic acumen would be lost, and organizational direction would suffer, signaling a Type II board. Few respondents mention that mission drift or compromised values would occur as a result, providing fodder for conversations about why that might be and what might be done differently to engage board members at a generative level.

To discern how board and staff members view the board's culture, ask, What three adjectives best describe the personality or culture of the board today? Responses can be categorized as positive (for example, dedicated, engaged, collegial, strategic, thoughtful), negative (for example, complacent, clannish, cliquish, disengaged, unfocused), or neutral (for example, civil, strong personalities, evolving). It is instructive to examine the ratio of positive to negative responses, the adjectives themselves and what they say about the board's operative norms, and what they imply for the quality of governance.

As follow-up to a survey, interview questions might probe specific results. For example, if the survey revealed that the board does not play a significant role in shaping its agendas and discussions, ask: Why is that? Do you see this as a significant issue? Why or why not? In your judgment, what should be atop the board's agendas this year? Who should decide?

Exhibit 7.1: Sample Interview Questions

For Board Members

- How long have you been a board member? Why did you agree to serve?
- What do you find most fulfilling about serving on this board?
- What do you find most frustrating about serving on this board?
- What are the two most important issues currently facing the organization?
- What are the two most important governance issues facing the board?
- If you could change one thing about the working relationship between the organization's senior staff and the board, what would it be? (Or the relationship between the CEO and the board?)
- What could the chair do to increase the board's effectiveness? What could the CEO do?
- What could the board do to increase the CEO's effectiveness?
- What is the single best piece of advice you would offer a new board member about how to be valuable to the organization?
- Would you favor individual performance reviews for board members? If so, by what process?
- Are there any serious points of contention within the board?
- Do you think there are substantial and significant disagreements within the board about the organization's strategic vision or current leadership? If so, please explain.
- What will be this board's legacy—its crowning achievement for which future boards will be most grateful?

For Senior Staff Members

- How has the board been most helpful to you? (Or tell a story about the board at its best.)
- How has the board been least helpful? (Or tell a story about when the board fell short.)
- How have the committee(s) with which you work been most helpful? Cite a specific example.

Exhibit 7.1: Sample Interview Questions (*Continued*)

- How do you decide what issues to bring before the board?

- What is the most important decision the board has made in the last two years? What is your assessment of the quality of that decision?

- Have discussions with the board or a board committee modified your thinking on an important issue in the last year or two? If so, cite a specific example. If not, why is that?

- Without citing names, think of individual board members whom you regard as problematic. What makes them particularly troublesome? What, if anything, do they have in common?

- Without citing names, think of individual board members whom you regard as especially helpful. What makes them particularly valuable? What, if anything, do they have in common?

For Board Members and Senior Staff Members

- What is the most important contribution this board has made in recent years?

- What should the board be worrying about, or at least thinking about?

- What are the three most important issues that should occupy the lion's share of the board's time for the foreseeable future?

- What would be the most valuable outcome of this initiative to review the board's effectiveness?

- How would you describe the board's role in general? How do you personally reach a judgment about how well the board is fulfilling its responsibilities?

- If you were to give the board an overall letter grade of A–F, what would it be?

- If you could take one step to improve that grade, what would it be?

- Taking everything into account, what is your single greatest concern about the board's performance?

- What should be the board's role in strategy?

- On what issues, and how, does the board add the most value? Least value?

For all questions asked of board members and staff members, it is instructive to see whether the two groups view things differently and then to discuss why that might be.

Outsider Observation and Feedback

Another way to assess the board's performance is to have an outside consultant or coach observe the board in action and provide feedback about that observation for discussion with the board. An outsider brings a broader frame of reference due to wider experience. He or she will often discern key dimensions of culture that insiders cannot see or do not notice because the board's practices have become routine and habitual; and its behaviors are taken for granted, and therefore, beneath the radar screen.

An outsider will bring a fresh perspective to comment on the following:

- Venue and logistics
  - Setting conducive to dialogue
  - Line of sight
  - Name cards
  - Ratio of board members to staff or guests
  - Timely start
- Board materials
  - Quality
  - Quantity
  - Differentiation of materials by significance
  - Dashboard
  - Discussion questions in advance
  - Organization of materials
- Use of time
  - Allocation by agenda item
  - Air time
  - Who participates and how
  - Number and quality of reports

More important, a skilled outside observer will also be able to comment on the following:

- The quality of the discourse
  - Questions raised by the presenter for board members
  - Questions from board members
  - The nature of the questions—informational, clarification, challenges to proposals and assumptions, dissent, reframes
- Substance
  - Items explicitly tied to work plan or strategic plan
  - Any explicit or observable themes versus a laundry list of unrelated matters

- Where on the generative curve the board enters and moves the discussion
- Whether all three modes are in play
- What is assumed
- Whether values are explicitly implicated or discussed
- Fiduciary, strategic, and generative questions not asked or if asked, not taken up
- Meeting synthesized
- Conflict or consensus articulated
- Next steps stated
- Relationships or culture
  - High-performing team values—respect, trust, collegiality, camaraderie—made visible
  - Sidebar conversations
  - Cell phones or PDAs in use
  - Interruptions
  - Disruptions
  - Participation patterns
  - Board member engagement

When I am asked to observe board or committee meetings, I also like to review relevant documents (for example, bylaws, the past two or three meeting agendas and minutes, committee structure, and committee agendas and minutes) to see what can be discerned by putting these various elements together. A follow-up visit is also instructive to see what has changed over time. Observation and feedback in real time falls within a coaching model (covered later in this chapter).

Reflective Practice

This section discusses several ways that CEOs and board members can be reflective practitioners (Chapter Five) and retrospective sensemakers about governance.

Evidence of Trimodal and Generative Governance. Board members and executives can reflect on how the board has done working in three modes and at the generative level (Chait et al. 2005) by:

- Comparing recent and past agendas to discern evidence of more generative work.
- Reviewing the past year to determine where and when board members worked at the organization's internal or external boundaries.

- Surveying board members on whether the climate for robust discussion has improved or deteriorated.
- With input from the senior staff, discussing these questions:
  - Have we clarified (or muddled) organizational values and beliefs?
  - Have we clarified (or muddled) the organization's vision?
  - Have we discovered new ends as we have modified means?
  - Have we reframed important problems?
  - What do we know now about governing that we did not know before?
  - What did we once know about the organization that is no longer true?
  - What did we once know to not be true about the organization that now is?
  - Where did we miss the landmarks of generative issues and why? (Chait et al. 2005, 130–131)
  - Can we cite occasions when we worked in each of the three modes?
  - Did we take a "triple-helix" (or even double-helix) approach to any issue? (Chait et al. 2005, 173)
- Asking the following questions:
  - Is there evidence that we are a Type I, II, or III *board* rather than a board that moves deftly between Type I, II, and III *work*?
  - What important assets of the issues we addressed might have been illuminated if we had governed in a different or additional mode?
  - How were the issues before us framed, and by whom?
  - Did we overlook better, deeper questions because we bypassed the generative mode? (Chait et al. 2005, 173–174)

Discussions After Experimenting with Trimodal Thinking. Examples 1–3 (Chapter Two) showcased the output of three boards as they "practiced" generating questions in the three modes. Importantly, after those sessions, the boards made sense of the experience by discussing:

- What challenges did the exercise present? What were the benefits?
- Were some modes easier to think in, and generate questions about, than others?
- What approach did the group take to the assignment?
- Did the group try to answer questions along the way? If so, why is that?
- What underlying assumptions—individual or group—were revealed by this process?

Examining Past Decisions.   As hindsight is 20/20, it is always a good idea to have boards think about what they discern looking in the rearview mirror. This can be accomplished by examining successful and unsuccessful decisions the board made. For example, a hospital board split into three groups, each assigned to discuss a different successful strategy implemented in the past year by asking themselves: What was the end to which the strategy was the means? What role did the board play? What role might the board have played? Why did the strategy succeed?

Then, in three groups, board members asked those same questions about one failed strategy. The dialogue that ensued following these breakout groups was fascinating as the board became increasingly aware of: to what it attributed success and failure; their own role, as a collective, for both good and bad decisions; and how it could be more effective going forward. An intriguing outcome of this process was that, for the failed strategy, the three groups each had a different perception of the end to which the strategy was the means; this suggests that spending time framing is a critical first step, asking, What are we trying to achieve? How do we define the problem? The board also learned that it could have done a much better job questioning conflicting data, playing devil's advocate, and discussing management's assumptions first in executive session without the CEO, and then with the CEO to see what would have been revealed. The board also learned that the successful strategies were not so much a function of anything the board did; instead, timing, luck, savvy management, and outside forces played more critical roles than did the board.

In another example, a nonprofit board examined the organization's entrance into four new markets over the past couple of years—two successful and two not. In advance of the retreat, board members were asked to answer these questions online for analysis and synthesis at the meeting: What have we learned from these experiences, as an organization? What have we learned as a board? The dialogue at the meeting revealed the board's need to ensure: (1) due diligence, including exposing underlying assumptions about strategies new products, services, or markets and discussing what is nonnegotiable (for example, mission fit, core values); and (2) that they spend sufficient time on business planning, market analysis, scenario building, feasibility, and risk assessment. The board also discussed its role vis-à-vis management in ensuring effective leadership and governance. It is important to note that although not all board members were on the board when these decisions were made, they were still able to engage the issues based on what they had heard and during the discussion at the meeting; in fact, having not been responsible or involved, they were not defensive and were able to bring fresh eyes to the situation. In addition, they were quite helpful talking through what the board wanted to do going forward to ensure better decisions.

Thinking Forward.   In its sensemaking role, boards also consider the past in order to think about the future. At a board retreat, a foundation reflected on its governance practices, self-assessment, and the success the organization had achieved in recent years. Rather than resting on its laurels, the board asked: Will the board behaviors that produced our current level of success be the same ones that will take us to the next level? This required that the board consider these questions:

1. What are the most compelling signs of the success of our organization to date?

2. What best explains our success to date?

3. What will be the most compelling signs of success in ten years?

4. What will best explain our success ten years from now?

5. What is different about the signs now and ten years from now? The explanations?

6. What governance/board issues could impede our progress?

Another board's self-assessment revealed three critical governance issues that needed to be addressed. The board met in groups; each considered one issue and answered the following questions:

1. What would signal progress on the issue?

2. What would be the surest signs of success?

3. What could stop us or hinder our progress?

4. What would help propel or enable our progress?

5. Who might do what next to ensure progress?

In a variation of this process, after examining its self-assessment, another board formed small groups to discuss: What should the board STOP doing, START doing, and KEEP doing?

Board Self-Assessment Surveys

There are numerous board self-assessment surveys on the market. They typically address the following areas: board member views of the board's effectiveness in fulfilling its basic roles and responsibilities (for example, mission, fundraising, program oversight, financial oversight, CEO oversight, and strategic planning); board size and composition; board structure; and meetings.

Global Assessment on Key Dimensions of Board Performance. Richard Chait, William Ryan, and I have designed a board self-assessment tool that supports the governance-as-leadership framework. It measures the board's performance as fiduciaries, strategists, and sensemakers; board member understanding of organizational context; organization and operations; discussion and deliberations; composition; and board members' feelings about their personal experience. Exhibit 7.2 shows a sample of questions in each category.

Exhibit 7.2: Sample Questions—Board Performance Profile

Fiduciary Responsibilities/Oversight

- The board ensures that resources are allocated effectively.
- The board carefully monitors organizational performance.
- The board ensures prudent risk management.
- The board ensures systematic review of the CEO's performance.
- The CEO's compensation is carefully considered and determined.
- The board surfaces and discusses assumptions behind proposed budgets.
- The board surfaces and discusses choices implicit in proposed budgets.

Strategy/Foresight

- The board has a shared sense of the organization's strategy.
- The board ensures the capital budget reflects strategic priorities.
- The board ensures the operating budget reflects strategic priorities.
- The board ensures the strategic plan is realistic.
- The board generates some ideas key to organizational strategy.
- The board discusses why strategies have succeeded or failed.
- The board discusses the assumptions behind proposed strategies.

Discernment/Insight (Generative)

- The board often helps spot problems and opportunities.
- The board has a strong say in deciding what we discuss.
- The board often proposes issues for management to consider.
- Before considering what to do, the board usually asks whether the matter has been thoughtfully defined.
- Before deciding major issues, the board learns what key constituencies think.
- Now and then, we ask ourselves, "What lessons have we learned as a board?"
- Now and then, we ask ourselves, "What lessons have we learned as an organization?"

Context

- The board understands the external forces that most affect [our sector] as a whole.
- The board understands the specific internal challenges the organization faces.

- The board agrees on what matters most to the organization's long-term success.
- The CEO has made clear what he or she most needs from the board.

Organization and Operations
- The board receives information relevant to the issues at hand.
- The board receives information in a timely fashion.
- The board receives the right amount of information.
- The board has an effective orientation for new board members.
- The board has the right committees for the work we need to do.
- The board uses task forces or ad hoc groups effectively.
- The executive committee does not usurp the board's role.

Meetings: Discussions, Deliberations, Group Dynamics
- The goals of any given board meeting are generally clear.
- Board meetings are not a race against time; we take the time we need.
- Meaningful dialogue typifies our board meetings.
- Board meetings balance staff presentation and board discussion.
- Most board meetings are not dominated by the same one or few board members.
- Board meetings involve a lot of give-and-take with management.
- Board meetings involve a lot of give-and-take among board members.
- The board's thinking is not swayed by the same one or few board members.
- The board's dialogue is respectful even when people disagree.
- No single or few board members wield most of the power most of the time.

Composition
- The board has sufficient generational diversity for smooth transfer of responsibility over time.
- The board has sufficient racial/ethnic diversity.
- The board has sufficient gender diversity.
- The board has sufficient geographic diversity.
- The board has a good mix of minds/ways of thinking.
- The board has the talent we need to do our job well.
- On the whole, the board has the highest caliber board members.

Exhibit 7.2: Sample Questions—Board Performance Profile (*Continued*)

Personal Experience

- I find serving on this board to be worth my time.
- I find serving on this board to be personally fulfilling.
- I would recommend serving on this board to someone I highly respect.
- When I speak I feel that the CEO is listening closely.
- When I speak I feel that other board members are listening closely.

Respondents state their level of agreement or disagreement with each statement.

Source: Chait, Ryan, and Trower.

Exhibit 7.3: Sample Questions—How Well Informed Is the Board?

Scale: 3 = Very well informed; 2 = Well informed; 1 = Somewhat informed; 0 = Uninformed

As a board member, how informed ARE YOU about the following topics?

- The board's role in strategic planning
- The board's role in board meeting agenda development
- Annual operating budget
- Annual capital budget
- The assumptions behind annual budgets
- Investment performance
- Operating risks
- The organization's key performance measures/benchmarks
- The CEO's performance
- The board's performance
- The performance of board committees

As a board member, how informed SHOULD YOU BE about the following topics?

- The board's role in strategic planning
- The board's role in board meeting agenda development
- Annual operating budget

- Annual capital budget
- The assumptions behind annual budgets
- Investment performance
- Operating risks
- The organization's key performance measures/benchmarks
- The CEO's performance
- The board's performance
- The performance of board committees

Note: For data display, see Figure 7.1.

FIGURE 7.1 *Information Gap Display Between What the Board "Should Be" and "Is" Informed About*

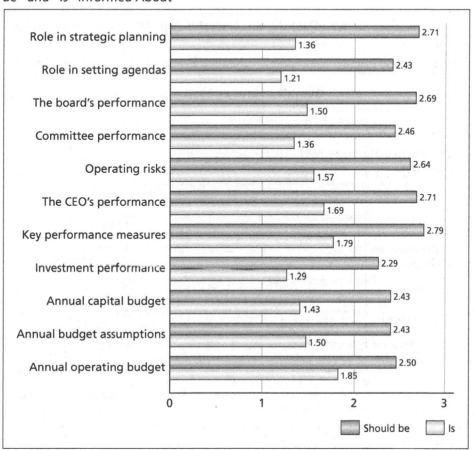

Assessing How Well Informed the Board Is and Should Be.   Oftentimes, boards are aware of specific areas about which they want additional questions; one commonly requested topic area concerns the information provided to the board. Sample questions about how informed board members are, and feel they should be, are provided in Exhibit 7.3. This survey also allowed board members to comment, in open-ended fashion, on the quality, timeliness, volume, and utility of the information provided to the board.

Another way to gather more information about a specific area of interest is to include an open-ended response box for board members who disagree with a rating question. For example, suppose board members are asked to state their level of agreement or disagreement with this statement: "The frequency of board meetings is right for the work we need to do." This can be followed by the statement, "If you disagree or strongly disagree, what number of meetings would be preferable?" and respondents can enter a specific number. Similarly, when asked "The length of board meetings is right for the work we need to do," those who disagree can answer, "What should be the length of board meetings?"

FIGURE 7.2 *Sample Data Display: Lowest to Highest Composite Scores by Theme*

Scale: 5 = Strongly Agree; 4 = Agree; 3 = Neutral; 2 = Disagree; 1 = Strongly Disagree

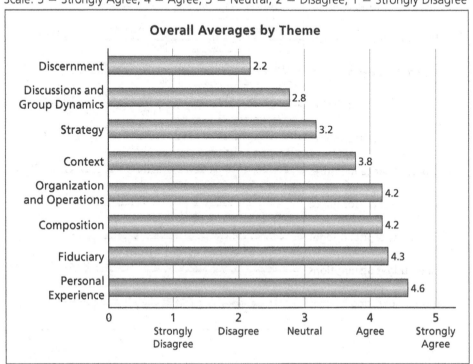

Exhibit 7.4: Sample Data Display—Highest and Lowest Ratings

Highest Ratings

Item	Average Rating	Theme
I find serving on the board to be very fulfilling.	3.89	Personal Experience
When I speak, I feel the CEO is listening closely.	3.78	Personal Experience
I have a good working relationship with the CEO.	3.78	Personal Experience
The board encourages the CEO to speak her mind.	3.67	Discussion and Meetings
The board ensures external audits are thoughtfully reviewed.	3.56	Fiduciary Oversight

Scale: 4 = Strongly agree; 3 = Agree; 2 = Disagree; 1 = Strongly disagree

Lowest Ratings

Item	Average Rating	Theme
The board receives the right amount of information at the right time.	2.44	Organization and Operations
The board discusses why strategies have succeeded or failed.	2.38	Strategy
Before deciding major issues, the board learns what key constituencies think.	2.22	Discernment
Now and then, we ask ourselves, What lessons have we learned as a board?	2.22	Discernment
Now and then, we ask ourselves, What lessons have we learned as an organization?	2.11	Discernment

Scale: 4 = Strongly agree; 3 = Agree; 2 = Disagree; 1 = Strongly disagree

Data Analysis and Display. Without attempting to relay here the myriad of ways that board self-assessment ratings might be analyzed and displayed, a few ideas are instructive. A place to start is to examine the average ratings, by item, and across relevant survey themes. The data may be displayed in one table showing all average ratings from high to low and the theme into which they fall (Exhibit 7.4), or in a chart showing thematic averages from low to high (Figure 7.2).

FIGURE 7.3 *Sample Data Display: Single Item Score Difference by Length of Service on the Board*

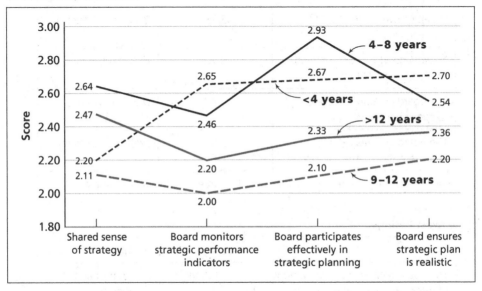

FIGURE 7.4 *Sample Data Display: Single Item Score Difference by Executive Committee Service*

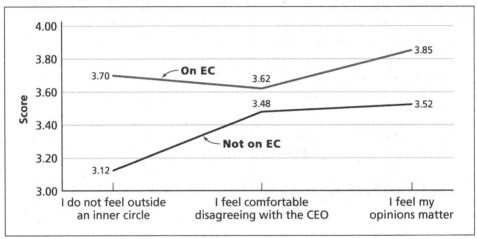

FIGURE 7.5 *Sample Data Display: Excel "Radar" Chart*

Dimensions of Effective Governance
Years of Board Service,
5-Point Scale

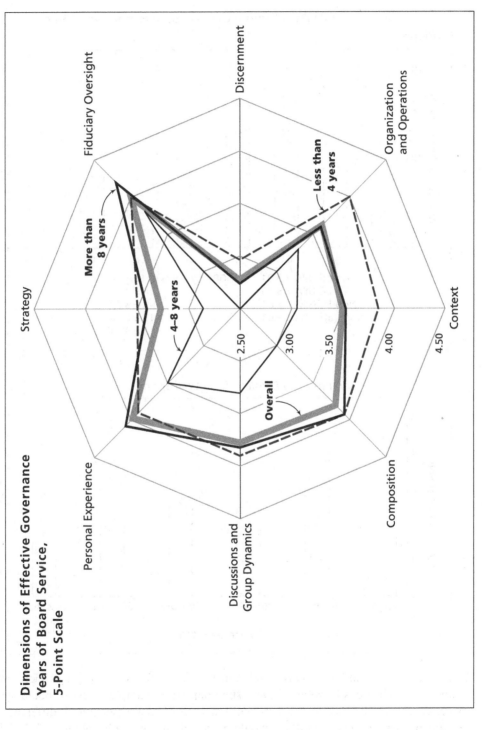

FIGURE 7.6 *Sample Data Display: Overall Board Performance Grade Distribution*

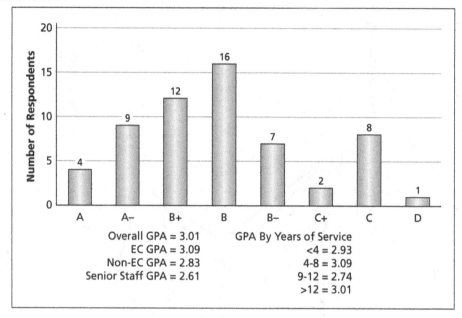

Overall GPA = 3.01   GPA By Years of Service
EC GPA = 3.09   <4 = 2.93
Non-EC GPA = 2.83   4-8 = 3.09
Senior Staff GPA = 2.61   9-12 = 2.74
>12 = 3.01

FIGURE 7.7 *Sample Data Display: Time Well Spent*

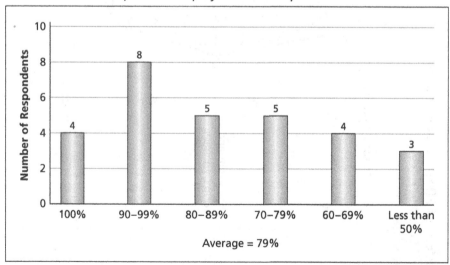

Average = 79%

I like to "eyeball" the dataset and "slice" it in several ways to see if there are important distinctions between relevant subgroups (for example, years of board service; gender; on the executive committee or not). If there are meaningful differences by any of these groups, then those should be called out for display (Figures 7.3, 7.4, and 7.5) and discussion by the board.

In Figure 7.5, note that the closer the lines are to the periphery, the more highly rated the category. For example, the highest score was recorded on "Fiduciary Oversight" by trustees with more than eight years of service. The lowest score was recorded on "Discernment" by trustees with four to eight years of service.

The greater the distance between the lines, the greater the variance in response by length of service. The largest disparities by length of service were on "Context" and "Organization and Operations" where trustees with less than four years of service responded more favorably than the other two groups.

Exhibit 7.5: Sample Data Display—Least Consensus

Items with the Least Consensus: Smallest Differences Between Agree and Disagree

	Agree (5–3)	Disagree (2–0)	Theme
Meaningful dialogue on consequential issues typifies board meetings.	17	15	Discussion and Meetings
The board monitors strategic performance indicators.	15	17	Strategy
The board has sufficient gender diversity.	14	18	Composition
Board meetings balance staff presentation with board member discussion.	18	14	Discussion and Meetings

Scale: Strongly agree = 5; Agree = 4; Slightly agree = 3; Slightly disagree = 2; Disagree = 1; Strongly disagree = 0

Most Polarized Responses: Smallest Differences at the Extremes

	Most Agree (5–4)	Most Disagree (1–0)	Theme
The board effectively participates in strategic planning.	16	16	Strategy
There should be a maximum number of years of board member service.	13	10	Composition
Most discussions involve more than a handful of the same board members.	10	9	Discussion and Meetings

Scale: Strongly agree = 5; Agree = 4; Slightly agree = 3; Slightly disagree = 2; Disagree = 1; Strongly disagree = 0

Those with four to eight years of service rate the board least favorably on all thematic areas.

Certain individual items—such as a letter grade for the board's performance and percentage of time well spent—are particularly well suited to be presented graphically. Figure 7.6 shows the number of board members who gave each letter grade, an overall grade point average (GPA), and the GPA by years of board service, EC versus non-EC, and senior staff. Exhibit 7.7 shows how board members responded to the question, "What percentage of time at board meetings, on average, is well spent?"

It may also be instructive for board members to see on which items there was the least consensus and which items were the most polarizing (Exhibit 7.5).

Postsurvey Follow-Up.   Whatever form the board's self-assessment takes, it is critical that time be spent with the board discussing the results and what they mean for governance. Too often, after the box is checked that the organization conducted a board self-assessment, survey results end up on a shelf somewhere, or a report of data highlights is given to board members in cursory fashion. These outcomes defeat the very purpose of conducting a board self-assessment—to enhance governance.

It is expeditious to send a full report of the data to board members, along with an executive summary, well in advance of the meeting at which the board will discuss the findings. Board members might be asked to think about several questions while they peruse the findings, such as:

1. What confirmed what you thought?

2. What surprised you?

3. What is reassuring?

4. What is troubling?

5. If you were writing the headline for a reputable newspaper reporting on the findings, what would it be?

The final example shows how one board reinvented itself in response to its self-assessment.

Example 16: Massachusetts General Hospital Institute of Health Professions Board

The MGH Institute of Health Professions ("the Institute") is a graduate school founded by, but independent of, Massachusetts General Hospital. As a relatively young institution, the Institute has evolved from a small collective of health professions graduate programs to a mature academic organization, with two academic schools (Nursing and

(continued)

Health & Rehabilitation Sciences), a Center for Interprofessional Studies and Innovation, and state-of-the-art facilities, technology, and operations that support its teaching, research, and service missions.

Historically, the Institute's eighteen-member Board of Trustees met more often than is typical for colleges and universities, and largely to hear reports and approve recommendations from senior administration. Board committees met at varying times, without predictability and according to trustee availability, a schedule that proved inefficient for both trustees and senior leadership. Further, the board had not previously assessed its own effectiveness against board governance standards.

In 2009, the board engaged a consultant to work with trustees to conduct a comprehensive board self-study. She led the board in a half-day retreat in which she presented the results of the self-assessment and also engaged the board in a robust discussion of governing board best practices.

Subsequently, the board modified its meeting schedule to quarterly meetings, with committees meeting in the afternoon, followed by a board dinner with a brief program featuring faculty, students, or programmatic innovations, and concluding with a full board meeting the following day. Board attendance improved, as did the efficiency of planning and managing board meetings. Most important, however, was the restructuring of the content and focus of full board meetings based on findings from the self-assessment.

The 2009 self-assessment revealed that the board was spending little time engaged in generative thinking, characterized by fully exploring and probing challenges and opportunities, considering various angles of issues to make sense of them, and determining lessons learned as a board and as an organization. Although the board had consistently and effectively focused adequate time on its fiduciary role—overseeing operations, effective use of resources, legal compliance, and fiscal responsibility—as well as its strategic role of setting goals and priorities, and monitoring performance against them, little meeting time had been devoted previously to discernment, the hallmark of generative governance.

Consequently, the board chose to make a significant shift in the structure of its meetings. Previously, all but the standard executive session toward the end of the meeting was open to administrative and faculty leaders, which had the unintended effect of dampening trustees' willingness to surface difficult issues, express diverse opinions, raise questions, and critically examine both opportunities and challenges out of concern that they would be misinterpreted or misunderstood.

At the same time, In the interest of both historical practice and transparency, the board did not wish to fully close its meetings. As a result, the board decided to preserve a portion of each meeting as open, focused primarily on strategic and fiduciary matters, while also devoting at least half of each full board meeting for trustees only to focus on issues related to the board's generative or discernment mode, and has done so for the past two years, with great success.

The effectiveness of the board's growing focus on the generative, or discernment, mode of its work is evident when comparing the self-assessment scores from 2009 with

(continued)

those from its replicated self-assessment in 2011. In 2009, scores ranged from a low of 1.91 to a high of 4.69 (on a scale of 1 to 5), with a mean of 3.26 and mode of 3.62; only 24 items were rated 4.0 or higher. In 2011, scores ranged from a low of 2.64 to a high of 4.86, with a mean of 3.96 and mode of 4.00; 40 items were rated 4.0 or higher. Perhaps most significant were the dramatic increases from 2009 to 2011 on items related to discernment, as the following examples illustrate:

MGHIHP Board Self-Assessment Scores on Select Items

Self-Assessment Survey Item	2009 Average Rating	2011 Average Rating
Before considering what to do, the board usually asks itself whether the matter has been thoughtfully defined.	2.69	3.43
The board has a strong say in deciding what we discuss.	2.85	3.57
As a board, we regularly talk about how we see things and what they mean.	2.92	3.43
The board often views issues from different angles before reaching a decision.	3.23	3.86
The board often discusses the organization's values and identity.	3.54	4.36

Over the past two years, the board has dedicated time to its generative mode on such critical issues as the size and pace of institutional growth, the role of and fiscal support for research in the Institute's mission, diversity as a strategic priority, and the potential impact of key trends in higher education and health care on the Institute's future. The board chair commented, "The increased amount of time that the board has spent in closed session discussing the important issues for the Institute's future has resulted in greater clarity about the board's role and better advice to the Institute's leadership. It also has brought the board closer together and enhanced board members' satisfaction."

Source: Written by Janis P. Bellack, CEO, MGH Institute of Health Professions. Printed with permission from Janis P. Bellack.

Governance Dashboard

Although many nonprofits have developed dashboards of organizational performance (see Chapter Five), few have created a dashboard for board performance. Given that the board should be a model of what it expects from the rest of the organization, it makes sense for boards to create such a dashboard.

FIGURE 7.8 *Board Performance Dashboard*

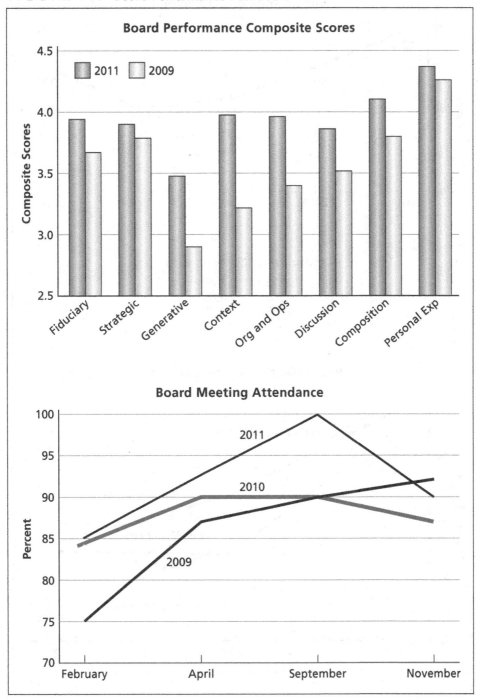

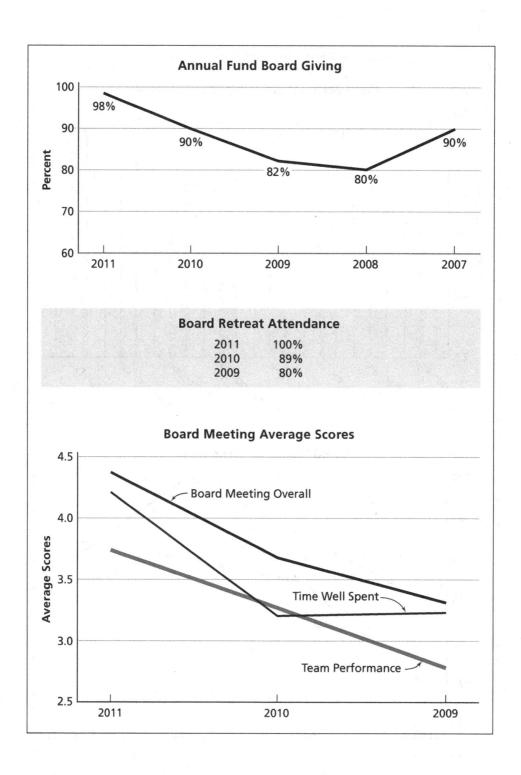

A one-page set of quantitative key performance indicators for the board might include: meeting attendance; retreat attendance; percent giving to the annual fund; scores on major self-assessment survey themes; and the overall assessments of the board as a team and of the past years' meetings (see Figure 7.8 for a sample board dashboard, set on two pages 209–210 for optimal clarity in this book).

SUSTAINING GOVERNANCE AS LEADERSHIP

Vigilance on the part of the CEO and board chair is necessary, but not sufficient, for boards to sustain governance as leadership. It also helps to have a governance committee that is focused on measuring board performance, recruiting and orienting board members who will contribute to high team performance, and providing ongoing education. Periodic board performance assessments and occasional retreats where governance is the focus also foster a culture where governance as leadership thrives. But some nonprofits find that the best way to keep the focus on high performance, sometimes for a year or two as they put the governance-as-leadership principles into practice, is to retain a coach.

Why a Coach?

Before writing about board coaches, I want to discuss coaching in the context of human behavior about which everyone is familiar—physical fitness and health. The number of people around the world, including children, who are overweight or obese is staggering. In the United States alone, it is estimated that 34 percent of adults and 17 percent of children are obese. There were an estimated 75 million "dieters" in 2009–2010. The United States spent $60.9 billion in 2010 on weight-loss products and services including diet pills, meal replacements, self-help books, commercial weight loss chains, and the like. Most dieters try to go it alone; "the typical American dieter now makes four weight loss attempts per year—the highest in 15 years"; and "80 percent want an inexpensive, low-cost, home-based plan" (PRWeb 2012).

As anyone who has tried to lose weight—and keep the weight off—knows, it takes a combination proper diet and exercise; few succeed with one or the other. Staying at a diet and exercise plan takes determination and diligence. Going it alone means holding yourself accountable, something many people find challenging, so backsliding occurs. To help prevent relapses into unhealthy behaviors, some people hire personal trainers or fitness coaches. A trainer's job begins by listening, assessing, setting goals, and writing a fitness plan. The trainer may then show the client how to use various pieces of exercise equipment. During workouts, the trainer encourages the client to work harder than s/he might if left alone. The trainer is a source of motivation and accountability. The most effective personal trainers help their clients not only with the mechanics (for example, fitness plan, nutrition, and the proper use of exercise equipment) but, perhaps more importantly, with the mindset (for example, confidence, motivation, and perseverance).

Why a Governance Coach?

First, permit me a caveat. This next section is not meant as a "hard sell" to hire a governance coach. It is meant as an expression of the simple reality that boards can experience difficulties getting started, gaining traction, getting unstuck, and persisting. Just as personal trainers can help dieters stay on track in their quest for improved health, so can ongoing consulting, or coaching, help nonprofits clear each hurdle they may face. Getting started making changes to board practices and process is the first (and sometimes quite difficult) step; Chapter Two addressed the challenges organizations face at this stage—inertia, fear of change, feelings of vulnerability, CEO ambivalence, comfort with the status quo—and offered ideas to help overcome them including surveying board members, building support, and calculating the cost of the status quo. To get traction, boards can discuss the benefits of governing differently and how the board is doing, and practice triple-helix thinking. Once new governance processes are under way, the board will confront more challenges to: critical thinking (Chapter Three); building a high-performing team (Chapter Four); and creating a supportive culture (Chapter Five). Skilled CEO and board chair leadership (Chapter Six) is required. But old habits are difficult to change (as noted in the review of change leader Kotter's work in Chapter Five). Boards will face those moments when members wonder if it isn't easier to revert back to governance as usual, thinking "it wasn't all that bad," or "we have really pressing fiduciary issues to deal with, so let's table that other stuff until there is time," or "governance as leadership takes too much work," or any other set of excuses. CEOs and chairs interviewed for this book acknowledged these issues, saying:

- We are just beginning to develop our governance muscles. We're still in the learning mode and have to work hard not to slip back into old, bad habits. You really have to work at it and practice.

- Some board members cling to the old model and try to provide direction and oversight on operational issues. Change is hard and it's not a uniform process. Some people even resent it thinking that management is trying to control the board.

- There is some institutional inertia. The previous CEO had been here for 29 years and there were seriously embedded cultural issues that carried over to the board and how it did its business.

- You have to be exposed to new modes of thinking and you have to be open to them. You have to have buy-in from the administration and the board has to link arms and go into this together . . . and maybe even be a bit open to failing.

Like the personal trainer, a governance coach helps guide the board as it takes first steps, stumbles, and keeps going; the coach brings wisdom, expertise, experience, and outside perspective; and provides encouragement, feedback, and a means of accountability. (See Exhibit 7.6 for the services a board coach provides.)

Exhibit 7.6: Board Coach Services

Intake

- Assessment: board member surveys, interviews, institutional peer data, sophisticated analysis
- Direct observation of board and committee meetings
- Interviews with board members, CEO, and senior staff members

Recommend Path Forward

- A tailored process, responsive to hard data

During and After Meetings, Help with:

- Designing content and format of meetings
- Surfacing consensus and unspoken concerns among board and staff
- Naming dysfunctional behaviors and group dynamics issues
- Learning through grappling with real issues in real time
- Modeling; facilitating; relaying feedback; helping frame issues
- Real-time feedback at meetings
- Debriefing after meetings

The Future

- Board membership changes over time; coaches help transfer knowledge
- As boards practice and get better, the board's mindset changes
- Transference through habituation; governance as leadership becomes internalized and sustained
- Further assessment, as needed

Governance as leadership requires practice, experimentation, persistence, and sustained attention over time. Although governance retreats, workshops, or clinics with an outside expert offer a means to educate and engage the board about the principles of governance, a "one and done" mindset sends the wrong messages—that is, that all boards can get this right with one retreat and changing the board culture is simple. Without follow-up, a one-time "dosage" of governance as leadership can be transitory and insufficient. Why? Because human nature being what it is, the momentum and enthusiasm can evaporate quickly after board members leave the retreat; some even forget what they heard and did.

Coaching helps boards with substantive, symbolic, and cultural changes. It addresses board dynamics and issues of power because coaches can name the elephants in the room. Hiring a coach epitomizes, for an organization, a commitment to reflective practice, self-reflection, and accountability. Coaching mirrors what is required of the best boards—the capacity for sensemaking, finding and framing problems and opportunities, adaptation, and learning—not just implementing quick fixes to technical problems.

Ideally, as chief executives and board members become effective reflective practitioners who periodically stop to reflect on how governance and the organization are doing, and what they have learned and are learning, and as they build and nurture the governance-as-leadership culture, cultivate and orient newcomers, and build on excellence, the model will become engrained as "the way we do things around here." The governing body will be physically fit and healthy; it will continue to grow, adapt, and thrive along with the nonprofit it governs.

CHAPTER SEVEN HIGHLIGHTS

- **Sustaining governance as leadership requires the board to hold itself accountable for its collective performance.** Accountability requires measurement. There are a variety of ways for boards to come to understand their performance, including interviews; observations and feedback from an outsider; reflective practice, during which the board looks for evidence of trimodal governance in its past agendas, discusses the process of thinking trimodally, examines past decisions, and does some thinking forward; and self-assessment surveys.

- **There are numerous ways to graphically and vividly display results of board self-assessments.** This chapter provides samples of these methods, including how to highlight areas of most and least consensus, as well as differences by service on the executive committee compared to those who are not, years of board service, staff versus board members, and the like.

- **Board self-assessments alone do little to affect board performance.** What matters most is that the board takes the time to reflect on the findings and discuss surprising and troublesome results as well as scores that improved or declined over time and what to do moving forward.

- **Some boards find it helpful to touch base periodically with an outside consultant or work with a board coach to help sustain governance as leadership.** Until the governance-as-leadership practices become second nature to a board, and the CEO, board chair, and governance committee feel at ease with the new practices, it may help to have a coach.

EPILOGUE

The nonprofit sector does not get enough respect.
—Todd Cohen, editor and publisher of *Philanthropy Journal*

A Congressional Research Service report (Sherlock and Gravelle 2009) showed that, in 2009, there were 1.5 million registered nonprofits in the United States. Public charities (64 percent of the total) reported $1.4 trillion in revenues and $2.6 trillion in assets; private foundations (8 percent of the total) reported $181 billion in revenue and $621 billion in assets; and other nonprofits (29 percent of the 1.5 million) reported $386 billion in revenue and over $1 trillion in assets. From 1998 to 2005, nonprofits employed nearly thirteen million people (10 percent of the workforce); nonprofit employment overall grew 16.4 percent, compared to 6.2 percent for overall employment in the United States. Based on employment, the charitable sector is larger than the construction sector, larger than the finance, insurance, and real estate sectors combined, and it has nearly half as many employees as federal, state, and local government combined.

In 2010, the nonprofit sector accounted for 10.1 percent of our nation's private employment, making this workforce the third largest among U.S. industries, behind only retail and manufacturing (Salamon, Sokolowski, and Geller 2012). Three service fields—health care, education, and social assistance—account for the vast majority (84 percent) of U.S. nonprofit jobs (Salamon et al. 2012). Hospitals account for 37 percent of the nonprofit jobs, followed by health clinics and nursing homes with 20 percent, educational institutions (including private elementary and secondary schools, colleges, universities) with 15 percent, and social assistance with 13 percent (Salamon et al. 2012). Despite two recessions, nonprofit employment grew every year between 2000 and 2010, whereas for-profit employment contracted in some years and grew more rapidly in other years (Salamon et al. 2012).

Because of the range of nonprofit organizations—from small operations with annual budgets of under $25,000 to multimillion-dollar health complexes—there is no "one-size-fits-all" panacea or silver-bullet "best" way to govern. But no matter the size or complexity of the nonprofit, each faces challenges in at least six areas: financial, competition, effectiveness, technological, legitimacy, and human resources (Salamon 2002). Responses to these challenges have required that nonprofits successfully market to paying customers, pursue public funds and alternative revenue streams; create ever-stronger fundraising capacity; seek new alliances and partnerships; develop stronger infrastructures including technology; and, in many cases, become more sophisticated and effective with lobbying efforts in the political realm—all without losing sight of organizational mission and constituent relevance.

All of these responses require organizational adaptation and skillful leadership from the CEO, the staff, and the board. Just as the Securities and Exchange Commission and shareholder activism have driven changes in the private sector for CEO compensation, director independence, transparency, and disclosure, the public sector should expect its myriad stakeholders to demand still more of its executives and board members for the very reason that nonprofits hold their assets in the public trust—something that, once violated, can never be fully restored. If there ever was a time when board members could sit on the sidelines, those days are over; governance is no longer a spectator sport. Today, more than ever, consequential nonprofit governance requires engaged board members who truly partner with management—as fiduciaries, strategists, and sensemakers—to skillfully lead their organizations into a future that will most certainly continue to change and evolve—one where mediocrity is not sustainable, and only the fittest and those with the greatest integrity, will survive.

REFERENCES

Ackoff, R. 1989. "From Data to Wisdom." *Journal of Applied Systems Analysis* 16 (1): 3–9.

Alderfer, C. 2001. "The Invisible Director on Corporate Boards." *Harvard Business Review* 64 (6): 38–52.

Argyris, C. 1976. *Increasing Leadership Effectiveness*. New York: Wiley-Interscience.

Ariely, D. 2008. *Predictably Irrational: The Hidden Forces That Shape Our Decisions*. New York: HarperCollins.

Aronson, J., and E. Aronson. 2007. *Readings About the Social Animal*. New York: Worth.

Asch, S. E. 1955. "Opinions and Social Pressure." *Scientific American* 193 (5): 31–35.

Association of Governing Boards. 2011. "Making Metrics Matter: How to Use Indicators to Govern Effectively." *Trusteeship*, January-February 19 (1): 8–14.

Axelrod, N. R. 2007. *Culture of Inquiry: Healthy Debate in the Boardroom*. Washington, DC: BoardSource.

Bazerman, M. H., and D. Chugh. 2006. "Decisions Without Blinders." *Harvard Business Review* 84 (1): 88–97.

Bazerman, M. H., and D. Moore. 2009. *Judgment in Managerial Decision Making* (7th ed.). Hoboken, NJ: Wiley.

Berlin, I. 1953. *The Hedgehog and the Fox*. Chicago: Elephant.

Brooks, D. 2010. "The Humble Hound." *New York Times* Op-Ed, April 8. Retrieved from http://www.nytimes.com/2010/04/09/opinion/09brooks.html

Burton, R. A. 2008. *On Being Certain: Believing You Are Right Even When You're Not*. New York: St. Martin's Griffin.

Butler, L. M. 2007. *The Nonprofit Dashboard: A Tool for Tracking Progress*. Washington, DC: BoardSource.

Campbell, A., J. Whitehead, and S. Finkelstein. 2009. "Why Good Leaders Make Bad Decisions." *Harvard Business Review* 87 (2): 60–66.

Carlson, S. 2011. "Presidents Mull How to Work Most Effectively with Their Boards." *Chronicle of Higher Education* (January 9). Retrieved on January 10, 2011 from: http://chronicle.com/article/Presidents-Mull-How-to-Work/125904/.

Cascio, W. F. 2004. "Board Governance: A Social Systems Perspective." *Academy of Management Executive* 18 (1): 97–100.

Chabris, C., and D. Simons. 2010. *The Invisible Gorilla: And Other Ways Our Intuitions Deceive Us*. New York: Random House.

Chait, R. P. 2006. Sample Committee Assessment Questions (unpublished).

Chait, R. P., T. P. Holland, and B. E. Taylor. 1996. *Improving the Performance of Governing Boards*. Phoenix: The American Council on Education and The Oryx Press.

Chait, R. P., W. P. Ryan, and B. E. Taylor. 2005. *Governance as Leadership: Reframing the Work of Nonprofit Boards*. Hoboken, NJ: Wiley.

Chait, R. P., and C. A. Trower. (Unpublished, 2008). Board Member Trait and Preference Inventory.

Charan, R. 2001. "Conquering a Culture of Indecision." *Harvard Business Review* 79 (4): 75–82.

Charan, R. 2005. *Boards That Deliver: Advancing Corporate Governance from Compliance to Competitive Advantage*. San Francisco: Jossey-Bass.

Collins, J. 2001. *Good to Great: Why Some Companies Make the Leap . . . And Others Don't*. New York: HarperCollins.

Covey, S. R. 1989. *The Seven Habits of Highly Effective People: Restoring the Character Ethic*. New York: Simon & Schuster.

Crutchfield, L., and H. McLeod Grant. 2008. *Forces for Good: The Six Practices of High-Impact Boards*. San Francisco: Jossey-Bass.

Csikszentmihalyi, M. 2003. *Good Business: Leadership, Flow, and the Making of Meaning*. New York: Penguin.

DeGenring, S. 2005. "The Adaptive Leader: Risky Business? Staying Alive as a Leader in Times of Change." *The Adaptive Leader* (June). Retrieved on January 15, 2012 from http://www.interactionassociates.com/ideas/adaptive-leadership-risky-business.

Demb, A., and F.-F. Neubauer. 1992. *The Corporate Board: Confronting the Paradoxes*. New York and Oxford: Oxford University Press.

Eliot, T. S. 1934. *The Rock*. London: Faber and Faber.

Flavell, J. H. 1979. "Metacognition and Cognitive Monitoring: A New Area of Cognitive-Developmental Inquiry." *American Psychologist* 34 (10): 906–911.

Finkelstein, S. 2004. "The Seven Habits of Spectacularly Unsuccessful Executives." *Ivey Business Journal Online*, 1-1. Retrieved from http://search.proquest.com.ezp-prod1.hul.harvard.edu/docview/216178790?accountid=11311

Friedkin, N. E. 1999. "Choice Shift and Group Polarization." *American Sociological Review* 64 (6): 856–875.

Garvin, D. 2000. *Learning in Action: A Guide to Putting the Learning Organization to Work*. Cambridge, MA: Harvard Business School Press.

Geronimo Terkla, D. 2011. "What Performance Indicators Do Institutions and Their Boards Commonly Use?" *Trusteeship* (Jan-Feb) 19 (1): 12.

Goodwin, D. K. 2005. *Team of Rivals: The Political Genius of Abraham Lincoln*. New York: Simon & Schuster.

Groopman, J. 2007. *How Doctors Think*. New York: Houghton Mifflin.

Harvard Corporation Governance Review Committee. 2010, December 6. Report to the University Community. Available from http://www.harvard.edu/president/reports/101206_governance.pdf

Harvey, J. B. 1988. *The Abilene Paradox and Other Meditations on Management*. Lexington, MA: Lexington Books.

Heifetz, R. 1994. *Leadership Without Easy Answers*. Cambridge, MA: Belknap Press.

Heifetz, R., A. Grashow, and M. Linsky. 2009. *The Practice of Adaptive Leadership*. Cambridge, MA: Harvard Business School Press.

Independent. 2011. *A Newsletter of the Council of Independent Colleges* (Winter-Spring). Retrieved on February 6, 2012, from http://www.cic.org/News-and-Publications/Independent-Newsletter/Documents/winterspring2011.pdf

Janis, I. L. 1971. "Groupthink." *Psychology Today* 5 (6): 43–46, 74–76.

Janis, I. L. 1972. *Victims of Groupthink*. Boston: Houghton Mifflin.

Janis, I. L., and L. Mann. 1977. *Decision Making: A Psychological Analysis of Conflict, Choice, and Commitment*. Detroit: Free Press.

Kahneman, D., J. L. Knetsch, and R. H. Thaler. 1991. "Anomalies: The Endowment Effect, Loss Aversion, and Status Quo Bias." *The Journal of Economic Perspectives* 5 (1): 193–206.

Kahneman, D., and A. Tversky. 1979. "Prospect Theory: An Analysis of Decision Under Risk." *Econometrica* 47 (2): 263–291.

Kahneman, D., and A. Tversky. 1984. "Choices, Values, and Frames." *American Psychologist* 39 (4): 341–350.

Karau, S. J., and K. D. Williams. 1993. "Social Loafing: A Meta-Analytic Review and Theoretical Integration." *Journal of Personality and Social Psychology* 65 (4): 681–706.

Katzenbach, J. R., and D. K. Smith. 2006. *The Wisdom of Teams*. New York: Collins Business Essentials.

Klein, G., B. Moon, and R. R. Hoffman. 2006. "Making Sense of Sensemaking 1: Alternative Perspectives" *ISEE Intelligent Systems* (July/August). Retrieved on January 1, 2012 from http://xstar.ihmc.us/research/projects/EssaysOnHCC/Perspectives%20on%20Sensemaking.pdf

Knowledge @ Wharton. 2011. "Don't Mention It: How 'Undiscussables' Can Undermine an Organization" (December 20). Retrieved on December 21, 2011 from http://knowledge.wharton.upenn.edu/article.cfm?articleid=2921

Kotter, J. P. 1995. "Leading Change: Why Transformation Efforts Fail." *Harvard Business Review* 73 (20): 59–67.

Kotter, J. P. 1996. *Leading Change*. Cambridge, MA: Harvard Business School Press.

Kuran, T., and C. R. Sunstein. 1999. "Availability Cascades and Risk Regulation." *Stanford Law Review* 51 (4): 683–768.

Larson, J. R., Jr., C. Christensen, A. S. Abbott, and T. M. Franz. 1996. "Diagnosing Groups: Charting the Flow of Information in Medical Decision-Making Teams." *Journal of Personality and Social Psychology* 71 (2): 315–330.

Latané, B., K. Williams, and S. Harkins. 2006. "Many Hands Make Light the Work: The Causes and Consequences of Social Loafing." In *Small Groups: Key Readings*, edited by J. M. Levine and R. L. Moreland. New York: Psychology Press.

Lehrer, J. 2008. "The Next Decider." *Boston Globe*, October 5. Retrieved on October 8, 2008 from http://www.boston.com/bostonglobe/ideas/articles/2008/10/05/the_next_decider?mode=PF

Lehrer, J. 2009. *How We Decide*. New York: Houghton Mifflin Harcourt.

Lencioni, P. 2002. *The Five Dysfunctions of a Team*. San Francisco: Jossey-Bass.

Lerner, J. S., and P. E. Tetlock. 1999. "Accounting for the Effects of Accountability." *Psychological Bulletin* 125 (2): 255–275.

Lerner, J. S., and P. E. Tetlock. 2002. "Bridging Individual, Interpersonal, and Institutional Approaches to Judgment and Choice: The Impact of Accountability on Cognitive Bias." In *Emerging Perspectives in Judgment and Decision Making*, edited by S. Schneider and J. Shanteau. Cambridge, UK: Cambridge University Press.

Lewontin, R. 2000. *The Triple Helix: Gene, Organism, and Environment*. Cambridge, MA: Harvard University Press.

Light, M. 2004. *Executive Committee*. Washington, DC: BoardSource.

Linsky, M., and R. A. Heifetz. 2002. *Leadership on the Line: Staying Alive Through the Dangers of Leading*. Cambridge, MA: Harvard University Press.

Lorsch, J. W., and R. C. Clark. 2008. "Leading from the Boardroom." *Harvard Business Review* 86 (4): 105–111.

Mueller, R. K. 1989. *Board Compass*. Lexington, MA: Lexington Books.

Nadler, D. A., B. A. Behan, and M. B. Nadler. 2006. *Building Better Boards: A Blueprint for Effective Governance*. San Francisco: Jossey-Bass.

NASA. 1995. ASRS Report 295378, February. "Visual Approach to Wrong Runway." Retrieved from http://www.37000feet.com/report/295378/Visual-approach-to-wrong-runway

Parsons, T. 1951. *The Social System*. London: Routledge.

Paul, R., and L. Elder. 2008. *The Miniature Guide to Critical Thinking Concepts and Tools*. Dillon Beach, CA: Foundation for Critical Thinking Press.

Pfeffer, J. 1992. *Managing with Power: Politics and Influence in Organizations*. Cambridge, MA: Harvard Business School Press.

Pfeffer, J., and R. I. Sutton. 1999. "The Smart-Talk Trap." *Harvard Business Review* 77 (3): 134–142.

Pfeffer, J., and R. I. Sutton. 2006. *Hard Facts, Dangerous Half-Truths AND Total Nonsense: Profiting from Evidence-Based Management*. Cambridge, MA: Harvard Business School Press.

PRWeb. 2012. "U.S. Weight Loss Market Worth $60.9 Billion." Retrieved on February 29, 2012, from http://www.prweb.com/releases/2011/5/prweb8393658.htm

Roberto, M. 2005. *Why Great Leaders Don't Take Yes for an Answer*. Upper Saddle River, NJ: Wharton School Publishing.

Roberto, M. 2009. *Know What You Don't Know: How Great Leaders Prevent Problems Before They Happen*. Upper Saddle River, NJ: Pearson Education/Prentice Hall.

Robinson, J. H. 1921. *The Mind in the Making: The Relation of Intelligence to Social Reform*. New York and London: Harper & Brothers Publishers.

Salamon, L. M. 2002. "The Resilient Sector: The State of Nonprofit America." *Snapshots: Research Highlights from the Nonprofit Sector Research Fund.* The Aspen Institute, Sept/Oct.

Salamon, L. M., S. W. Sokolowski, and S. L. Geller. 2012. *Holding the Fort: Nonprofit Employment During a Decade of Turmoil.* Johns Hopkins University: Nonprofit Employment Bulletin No. 39 (January). Retrieved on March 30, 2012, from http://ccss.jhu.edu/publications-findings?did=369

Samuelson, W., and R. Zeckhauser. 1988. "Status Quo Bias in Decision Making." *Journal of Risk and Uncertainty* 1 (1): 7–59.

Schein, E. H. 1992. *Organizational Culture and Leadership* (2nd edition). San Francisco: Jossey-Bass.

Schein, E. H. 1993. "How Can Organizations Learn Faster? The Challenges of Entering the Green Room." *Sloan Management Review* 34 (2): 85–92.

Schön, D. 1983. *The Reflective Practitioner: How Professionals Think in Action.* New York: Basic Books.

Schulz, K. 2010. *Being Wrong: Adventures in the Margin of Error.* New York: HarperCollins.

Senge, P. M. 1990. *The Fifth Discipline: The Art & Practice of the Learning Organization.* New York: Doubleday.

Senn, L., and J. Hart. 2006. *Winning Teams—Winning Cultures.* Long Beach, CA: Leadership Press.

Sherlock, M. F., and J. G. Gravelle. 2009. *An Overview of the Nonprofit and Charitable Sector.* Congressional Research Service Report for Congress, 7-5700, R40919. Retrieved on March 30, 2012 from www.fas.org/sgp/crs/misc/R40919.pdf

Sonnenfeld, J. A. 2002. "What Makes Great Boards Great." *Harvard Business Review* 80 (9): 106–113.

Stasser, G., L. A. Taylor, and C. Hanna. 1989. "Information Sampling in Structured and Unstructured Discussions of Three- and Six-Person Groups." *Journal of Personality and Social Psychology* 57 (1): 67–78.

Stasser, G., and W. Titus. 1985. "Pooling of Unshared Information in Group Decision Making: Biased Information Sampling During Discussion." *Journal of Personality and Social Psychology* 48 (6): 1467–1478.

Stasser, G., and W. Titus. 2003. "Hidden Profiles: A Brief History." *Psychological Inquiry* 14 (3/4): 304–313.

Stasser, G., S. I. Vaughn, and D. D. Stewart. 2000. "Pooling Unshared Information: The Benefits of Knowing How Access to Information Is Distributed to Group Members." *Organizational Behavior & Human Decision Processes* 82 (1): 102–116.

Sunstein, C. R. 2000. "Group Dynamics." *Cardozo Studies in Law and Literature* 12(1): 129–139.

Sunstein, C. R. 2002. "The Law of Group Polarization." *The Journal of Political Philosophy* 10 (2): 175–195.

Sunstein, C. R. 2003. *Why Societies Need Dissent.* Cambridge, MA: Harvard University Press.

Tagg, J. 2012. "Why Does the Faculty Resist Change?" *Change* 44 (1): 6–15.

Tetlock, P. E. 2005. *Expert Political Judgment: How Good Is It? How Can We Know?* Princeton, NJ: Princeton University Press.

Tetlock, P. E., and Schoemaker, P.J.H. (in press). "Taboo Scenarios: How to Think About the Unthinkable." *California Management Review.*

Totten, M. K., and J. E. Orlikoff. 2007. "The CEO-Board Partnership." *Trustee Workbook*, Center for Healthcare Governance, July/August.

Trower, C. A. 2010. *Govern More, Manage Less* (2nd ed.). Washington, DC: BoardSource.

Tufte, E. 2006. "Airport Maps and Runway Incursions." Retrieved on May 24, 2012 from http://www.edwardtufte.com/bboard/q-and-a-fetch-msg?msg_id=0002NW&topic_id=1

Weick, K., K. M. Sutcliffe, and D. Obstfeld. 2005. "Organizing and the Process of Sensemaking." *Organization Science* 16 (4): 409–421.

Wolfe, J. M., Horowitz, T. S., and Kenner, N. M. 2005. "Rare Items Often Missed in Visual Searches." *Nature:* 435,439–440.

Woocher, L. 2008. "The Effects of Cognitive Biases on Early Warning and Response." Paper presented at the annual meeting of the ISA's 49th Annual Convention: Bridging Multiple Divides. San Francisco, March 26. Retrieved on December 30, 2011 from http://eeas.europa.eu/ifs/publications/articles/book3/book_vol3_chapter5_the_effects_of_cognitive_biases_on_early_warning_and_response_lw_en.pdf

Zeleny, M. 1987. "Management Support Systems: Towards Integrated Knowledge Management." *Human Systems Management* 7 (1): 59–70.

ACKNOWLEDGMENTS

I am the beneficiary of untold hours of reflection, guidance, and support from Dick Chait and Bill Ryan as we met over the past few years to talk about what we were learning in the course of our work with our board clients on improving governance and as we made sense of our individual experiences and sought each other's clinical advice.

I am grateful to Brendan Russell, Harvard University doctoral student extraordinaire, who interviewed the CEOs and board chairs for this book and provided insightful analysis of the data.

I am grateful to the leaders and board members of the following organizations featured in this book for allowing me the honor and privilege to work with them to enhance governance, and for the time of the CEOs and current (and in some cases past) board chairs for interviews, e-mail queries, and reading and approving the vignettes featured in the book.

Albright College

> Founded over 150 years ago, Albright College is a private liberal arts college associated with the United Methodist Church. Albright's mission is to inspire leadership and service in its students through a commitment to the liberal arts and sciences.

President: Lex MacMillan, since 2005

Board Chair: John Bailey, since 2007

American University of Beirut

> Educating about eight thousand students and offering over 120 academic programs, AUB is one of the premier universities in the Middle East. Founded in 1866, the university bases its operations on the American liberal arts model and aims to educate civically responsible leaders with integrity and the ability to think critically.

President: Peter Dorman, since 2008

Board Chair: Philip Khoury, since 2009

Baylor Health Care System

With over one hundred years of experience in the health care industry, Baylor Health Care System is a leader in providing affordable, quality medical care through a broad network of locations and doctors. BHCS is committed to innovative solutions based in research and to serving the northern Texas community at large.

President and CEO: Joel Allison, since 2000

Former Board Chair: Dick Brooks, 2000–2002

Boston Children's Chorus

The BCC brings children together from the diverse communities of Boston through the use of music. Started in 2003, the BCC provides opportunities for children to participate in musical practices and performances while learning skills in leadership and perseverance. The BCC has become a cultural learning experience for children in the Boston area and inspires social change through its work.

Executive Director: David Howse, since 2009

Board Chair: Tim Ferguson, since 2011

Cedar Crest College

As a private women's liberal arts college in Allentown, Pennsylvania, CCC is committed to educating the entire person and to preparing them to enter an interconnected, global market. Founded in 1867, the College has the mission of educating women leaders who aspire to greatness.

President: Carmen Ambar, since 2008

Board Chair: Sue Hudgins, since 2009

Centenary College

Located in Hackettstown, New Jersey, Centenary College is a four-year baccalaureate and master's level institution that prides itself on student-centered learning that prepares graduates for the demands of a global world. Founded in 1867, the College is an independent, private institution that offers students the opportunity to infuse community service and internships into their academic experiences.

President: Barbara Lewthwaite, since 2008

Copley Health Systems

As a critical access, not-for-profit hospital in Vermont, CHS provides medical care in a personalized manner without regard to the patient's financial status.

With twenty-four-hour emergency care and state-of-the-art facilities, CHS has been known for its patient satisfaction and ability to serve central and northern Vermont for over seventy-five years.

President: Melvin Patashnick, since 2007

Board Chair: Elizabeth Rouse, since 2010

Former Board Chair: Jan Roy, 2007–2010

Greenhill School

Located in Addison, Texas, Greenhill School is a coeducational, independent day school serving over 1,200 students. Since 1950, the school has offered kindergarten through the twelfth grade and aims to prepare students for college by focusing on academics, service, the arts, and athletics.

Head of School: Scott Griggs, since 2000

Board Chair: Karla Barber, since 2010

Jane Doe, Inc.

JDI provides sexual and domestic violence support and resources to over sixty member "hubs" in Massachusetts communities. As a nonprofit institution, JDI offers advocacy and counseling to victims of sexual and domestic violence as well as innovative social justice programs aimed at mitigating such violence.

Executive Director: Mary Lauby, since 2005

Board Chair: Mary Gianakis, since 2009

MGH Institute of Health Professionals

Based in Charlestown's historic Navy Yard, the Massachusetts General Hospital (MGH) Institute of Health Professionals is an independent, inter-professional graduate school founded in 1977. Specializing in communication sciences and disorders, medical imaging, nursing, and physical therapy, the Institute currently serves more than a thousand students on campus and online.

President: Janis Bellack, since 2007

Board Chair: George Thibault, since 2005

Parish Episcopal School

Started in 1972, Parish Episcopal School is a private, coeducational day school that prepares students for college. By combining service and worship with a rigorous commitment to academics, the School enrolls over 1,100 students in prekindergarten through the twelfth grade in the greater Dallas area.

Head of School: David Monaco, since 2009

Board Chair: Philip de Bruyn, since 2009

Ripon College

Ripon College is a private liberal arts college located in Ripon, Wisconsin, that offers four-year baccalaureate degrees. With over 150 years of experience, Ripon is a residential college that aims to prepare service-oriented, productive members of society.

Former President: David Joyce, 2003–2011

Board Chair: Robert Kirkland, since 2009

Southwest Vermont Medical Center

Serving more than fifty-five thousand people in southern Vermont and parts of New York and Massachusetts, SVMC is a not-for-profit health care provider that aims to improve the medical well-being of the communities it serves. With multiple locations and over one hundred years in health care experience, SVMC is committed to its core values of quality, empathy, safety, teamwork, and stewardship when caring for patients.

President: Tom Dee, since 2009

Board Chair: Mike Brady, since 2010

Former Board Chair: Richard Guerrero, 2008–2010

St. Paul's School

As a private, coeducational boarding school for students in grades nine through twelve, SPS serves a diverse community of over 530 students. Founded in 1856 and located in Concord, New Hampshire, SPS encourages its students to live morally guided lives and to serve as leaders who aspire to do work that helps the greater good.

Rector: Michael Hirschfeld, since 2011

Board Chair: Douglas Schloss, since 2006

United World College USA

Founded in 1982, UWC is a two-year residential school for students ages sixteen to nineteen from around the world. Located in Montezuma, New Mexico, UWC fosters diverse cultural understanding among its students and prepares them to lead in a global world.

President: Lisa Darling, since 2005

Board Chair: Tom Dickerson, since 2008

University of New Haven

As a private, not-for-profit university located in Connecticut and founded in 1920, UNH educates over six thousand students in over one hundred academic programs. UNH prides itself on giving students a personalized, demanding liberal arts education in combination with real-world experiential learning opportunities.

President: Steven Kaplan, since 2004

Board Chair: Sam Bergami, since 2006

• • •

Disclosure.   All of the above-named organizations elected to enlist the help of outside expertise and paid the author of this book for consulting services. They were selected by the author, not necessarily as exemplars and certainly not as failures, but rather as being representative of the broad range of organizations working on improving governance and at various stages in their ongoing quest to learn and improve. These organizations did not compensate the author to be featured in this book, and they are receiving nothing in return, other than a copy of the book.

THE AUTHOR

Cathy A. Trower, President of Trower & Trower, Inc., has studied nonprofit board governance for over a decade. She is author of the second edition of *Govern More, Manage Less* (BoardSource 2010) and co-author with R. Barbara Gitenstein of *What Board Members Need to Know about Faculty* (Association of Governing Boards of Colleges and Universities, 2013), and she has written several articles for AGB's *Trusteeship* magazine. In addition to her governance work, Trower has studied academic leadership, faculty work life, employment issues, policies, and practices including the experiences of early-, mid-, and late-career faculty through a generational lens, women in STEM disciplines, and underrepresented minorities. She has published an edited volume on faculty policies, numerous book chapters, articles, and case studies. Cathy's latest book about faculty work life and policies is called *Success on the Tenure-Track: Five Keys to Faculty Satisfaction* (Johns Hopkins University Press, 2012).

Dr. Trower joined the governing board of Wheaton College (MA) in 2012; she previously served on the board of a university and of a college. Trower has served as a consultant and coach to the boards and executives of nearly a hundred nonprofit organizations, and is a popular, energetic, and dynamic conference speaker. She has a bachelors and masters of business administration from the University of Iowa and a PhD in higher education administration from the University of Maryland, College Park.

BOARDSOURCE®

Building Effective Nonprofit Boards

BoardSource is dedicated to advancing the public good by building exceptional non-profit boards and inspiring board service.

BoardSource was established in 1988 by the Association of Governing Boards of Universities and Colleges (AGB) and Independent Sector (IS). Prior to this, in the early 1980s, the two organizations had conducted a survey and found that although 30 percent of respondents believed they were doing a good job of board education and training, the rest of the respondents reported little, if any, activity in strengthening governance. As a result, AGB and IS proposed the creation of a new organization whose mission would be to increase the effectiveness of nonprofit boards.

With a lead grant from the Kellogg Foundation and funding from five other donors, BoardSource opened its doors in 1988 as the National Center for Nonprofit Boards with a staff of three and an operating budget of $385,000. On January 1, 2002, BoardSource took on its new name and identity. These changes were the culmination of an extensive process of understanding how we were perceived, what our audiences wanted, and how we could best meet the needs of nonprofit organizations.

Today, BoardSource is the premier voice of nonprofit governance. Its highly acclaimed products, programs, and services mobilize boards so that organizations ful-fill their missions, achieve their goals, increase their impact, and extend their influence. BoardSource is a 501(c)(3) organization.

BoardSource provides

- Resources to nonprofit leaders through workshops, training, and an extensive website (www.boardsource.org)

- Governance consultants who work directly with nonprofit leaders to design specialized solutions to meet an organization's needs

- The world's largest, most comprehensive selection of material on nonprofit governance, including a large selection of books and CD-ROMS

- An annual conference that brings together approximately nine hundred governance experts, board members, and chief executives and senior staff from around the world

For more information, please visit our website at www.boardsource.org, e-mail us at mail@boardsource.org, or call us at 800-883-6262.

INDEX

Page references followed by *fig* indicate an illustrated figure; followed by *t* indicate a table; followed by *e* indicate an exhibit.